Musica getutscht (Basel, 1511) is the earliest printed treatise on musical instruments in the West. Written by a priest and chapel singer named Sebastian Virdung, it provides rudimentary instruction on playing three instruments: the clavichord, the lute, and the recorder. This early "do-it-yourself" manual of instruction not only tells us about music making in that era, it also illumines other aspects of society in the years just before the Reformation. Its author communicates in a popular style, choosing a mixture of media: a written text in the guise of an informal conversation, coupled with woodcut illustrations and visual aids. Beth Bullard's substantial introduction and annotations help explain the text of this important work and its place in intellectual history.

Musica getutscht

a treatise on musical
instruments (1511)
by Sebastian Virdung

CAMBRIDGE MUSICAL TEXTS AND MONOGRAPHS

General Editors: Howard Mayer Brown, Peter le Huray, John Stevens

The series Cambridge Musical Texts and Monographs has as its centers of interest the history of performance and the history of instruments. It includes annotated translations of important historical documents, authentic historical texts on music, and monographs on various aspects of historical performance.

Published

Ian Woodfield *The Early History of the Viol*

Rebecca Harris-Warrick (trans. and ed.) *Principles of the Harpsichord by Monsieur de Saint Lambert*

Robin Stowell *Violin Technique and Performance Practice in the Late Eighteenth and Early Nineteenth Centuries*

Vincent J. Panetta (trans. and ed.) *Treatise on Harpsichord Tuning by Jean Denis*

John Butt *Bach Interpretation*

Grant O'Brien *Ruckers: A Harpsichord and Virginal Building Tradition*

Nicholas Thistlethwaite *The Making of the Victorian Organ*

Christopher Page (trans and ed.) *Summa musice: a Thirteenth-Century Manual for Singers*

Ardal Powell (trans. and ed.) *The Virtuoso Flute-Player by Johann Georg Tromlitz*

Musica getutscht: a treatise on musical instruments (1511) by Sebastian Virdung

translated and edited by
BETH BULLARD

CAMBRIDGE
UNIVERSITY PRESS

Published by the Press Syndicate of the University of Cambridge
The Pitt Building, Trumpington Street, Cambridge CB2 1RP
40 West 20th Street, New York, NY 10011–4211, USA
10 Stamford Road, Oakleigh, Melbourne 3166, Australia

First published 1993

Printed in Great Britain at the University Press, Cambridge

A catalogue record for this book is available from the British Library

Library of Congress cataloguing in publication data

Bullard, Beth.
Musica getutscht: a treatise on musical instruments (1511) by
Sebastian Virdung / Beth Bullard.
      p.   cm. (Cambridge musical texts and monographs)
Includes translation of: Musica getutscht.
Includes bibliographical references and index.
ISBN 0 521 30830 5 (hardback)
1. Virdung, Sebastian, b. 1465? Musica getutscht. 2. Musical
instruments – Europe – Early works to 1800. 3. Tablature (Musical
notation) – Early works to 1800. I. Virdung, Sebastian, b. 1465?
Musica getutscht. English. 1993. II. Title.
MT5.5.V573B8 1993
784.19–dc20   92–19194 CIP MN

ISBN 0 521 30830 5 hardback

To Truman, Martin, and Dexter
To Anne Ruth Ediger Baehr
To Karl Baehr *in memoriam*

Contents

Preface

The scholarly and intellectual resources of many people and institutions helped to make possible this translation and study of Sebastian Virdung's *Musica getutscht*. I am indebted to librarians, especially Dr. John Roberts, as well as to keepers and curators of the myriad of rare books I consulted at libraries in France, Germany, Great Britain, Switzerland, and the United States. Also invaluable to me in this project were those who offered linguistic counsel, especially Amy Baehr, Hendrik Boswijk, the late Dr. Rudolf Hirsch of the University of Pennsylvania, and my colleagues at Dickinson College: Professors Beverley Eddy, Ingeline Nielsen, Dieter Rollfinke, and Robert Sider. I also acknowledge the input of David Robertson, former Director of the Trout Gallery at Dickinson College and specialist in German woodcuts of the Renaissance. To Howard Brown I extend thanks for his suggestions and for his challenges. I express my special gratitude to Professor Lawrence Bernstein of the University of Pennsylvania, not only for his advising of the dissertation that led to the present work, but also for his posing the question that sparked my study of Virdung's treatise in the first place.

I would also like to acknowledge the financial support awarded me by my undergraduate institution, Oberlin College, and by the American Association of University Women. Both the Oberlin College Graduate Fellowship and the AAUW Dissertation Fellowship enabled me to devote time and travels to completion of this study, which these organizations deemed worthy of fostering. In addition, I wish to thank Dickinson College, where I have served as a member of the faculty, for making available to me language enrichment opportunities as well as technical assistance for this project. For the latter I am especially indebted to Daniel Buchan, Agharese Ness, David Peckman, and Louise Verdekal. Finally I would like to thank my family – nuclear and extended – whose support has flavored every aspect of this work.

Abbreviations

Bibliographic abbreviations

Acta	*Acta Musicologica*
AfMw	*Archiv für Musikwissenschaft*
Dit	*Dit is een seer schoon Boecxken* . . . (Antwerp, [*ca.* 1528], 1554, 1568)
EM	*Early Music*
EMH	*Early Music History*
GS	Martin Gerbert, *Scriptores ecclesiastici de musica sacra potissimum* (3 vols., St. Blasien, 1784; repr. Hildesheim, 1963)
GSJ	*Galpin Society Journal*
JAMIS	*Journal of the American Musical Instrument Society*
JAMS	*Journal of the American Musicological Society*
JLSA	*Journal of the Lute Society of America*
Livre	*Livre plaisant et tres utile* . . . (Antwerp, 1529)
LSJ	*Lute Society Journal*
Md	*Musica disciplina*
MfM	*Monatshefte für Musikgeschichte*
Mus. get.	Sebastian Virdung, *Musica getutscht* (Basel, 1511)
Musurgia	Othmar Luscinius, *Musurgia seu praxis musicae* (Strassburg, 1536, 1542)
Mus. inst. deudsch	Martin Agricola, *Musica instrumentalis deudsch* (Wittenberg, 1529 etc.; rev. edn. 1545)
MGG	*Die Musik in Geschichte und Gegenwart*, ed. Friedrich Blume (14 vols. and suppl., Kassel and Basel, 1949–)
MQ	*The Musical Quarterly*
New Grove	*The New Grove Dictionary of Music and*

	Musicians, ed. Stanley Sadie (20 vols., London, 1980)
New Grove MI	*The New Grove Dictionary of Musical Instruments*, ed. Stanley Sadie (3 vols., London, 1984)
Notes	*Notes of the Music Library Association*
PäptM	Publikation älterer praktischer und theoretischer Musikwerke, ed. Robert Eitner (29 vols., Berlin and [later] Leipzig, 1873–1905; repr. New York, 1966)
Pat. Lat.	J. P. Migne, *Patrologiae cursus completus . . . series latina* (221 vols., Paris, 1841–66; repr. Turnhout, 1956–)
RCMI	Research Center for Musical Iconography (The City University of New York)
RdM	*Revue de Musicologie*
RIdIM	*Répertoire International d'Iconographie Musicale*
RISM	*Répertoire International des Sources Musicales*
Spiegel	Arnolt Schlick, *Spiegel der Orgelmacher und Organisten* (Mainz, 1511)
ZfMw	*Zeitschrift für Musikwissenschaft*

Pitch designations

C	Two octaves below "middle C" on a piano
c	One octave below "middle C" on a piano
c'	"Middle C" on a piano
c"	One octave above "middle C" on a piano
c'"	Two octaves above "middle C" on a piano

PART ONE

Translator's introduction

Compendium musicae practicae of *ca.* 1322) and Franchinus Gaffurius (his *Practica musicae* of 1496).[9] Virdung also brings familiarity with past and present musical trends from his experience as a practicing musician among other musicians. By imparting information from these sources in *Musica getutscht*, he acts as a music historian to his generation; as such, he illuminates the past for us as well. Some of his historical explanations of musical phenomena lend support to our modern views; others of his theories add new dimensions to our understanding; still others contrast with our interpretations. For example, Virdung's report that the clavichord and the harpsichord derived from the monochord and the psaltery, respectively (pp. 123 and 113 – sigs. E2–E2v, C3v–C4), matches our modern perception of the origins of these instruments. On the other hand, his hypothesis that white mensural notation evolved from black notation owing to the change from parchment to paper as polyphonic music became more popular (pp. 134–5 below – sigs. G2–G2v) enlarges the scope of our vision on this topic. But his linking Guido's invention of staff notation with a keyboard (pp. 128–30 below – sigs. Fv–F3) contrasts with our understanding that Guido's system referred primarily to vocal performance.

Virdung thus serves his readers as an agent of rapprochement between erudite culture and popular culture. Acting as a popularizer of the subject of musical instruments and instrumental music, Virdung brings his understanding of history and theory to illuminate and rationalize aspects of then contemporary practice. In the process, however, it will be seen that he is not averse to thrusting principles of present practice back into music history and theory. In any case, Sebastian Virdung's historical speculations and insights enrich our store of evidence on many fronts. This is true whether he speaks of particular events (such as the invention of lute tablature by Conrad Paumann [p. 156 below – sig. K3v]) or retraces earlier ways of thinking and acting in a musical context. And Virdung's views of history, of course, illumine the thought patterns and underlying assumptions of his own era as much as they may cast light on a more remote past.

In addition to his views on the past, Virdung's attitudes toward musical phenomena of his own day contribute as well to our knowledge of his era, both musically and culturally. The assumption that his readers would learn not just one but several musical

1 Why study *Musica getutscht*?

When Sebastian Virdung, a musician and priest from the city of Amberg, presented his draft for *Musica getutscht* to the Basel printer Michael Furter in 1510 or 1511, both were no doubt aware that they had something new to give the German-speaking world. For this little treatise is the first printed work in the West dealing exclusively with musical instruments.[1] Indeed, a remarkable portion of its contents consists of material that appeared in print for the first time. These include the following: illustrations of musical instruments in current use arranged by organological categories, German keyboard tablature, German lute tablature, recorder fingering charts, and instructions with diagrams on aspects of instrumental performance practice.[2] In addition, this is one of the earliest works on music in a vernacular tongue. (The short title by which it is known, combining the Latin *Musica* with the German *getutscht*, means "A treatise on music written in German.") By virtue of its anteriority in so many respects, therefore, *Musica getutscht* is assured a place among the important documents of music history. As such, it is worthy of study for its own sake. Moreover, since *Musica getutscht* acted as a major generative force in a proliferation of instrumental tutors during the sixteenth century, it demands consideration as well for its seminal role.

Musica getutscht, a book known from the sixteenth century for the many pictures and diagrams that enhance the text,[3] is designed to impart to its readers, by word and by illustration, some basic principles necessary for understanding and eventually playing certain of the instruments used for art music in German-speaking lands at the turn of the sixteenth century. Today, half a millennium later, this treatise can serve the same purpose.

Virdung's methodology in introducing instrumental music and performance from the period around 1510 consists of a twofold approach to the subject. First he provides an illustrated instrumentarium (see pp. 101–11 below – signatures B–C2v).[4] He does this so his readers will become more familiar not only with the individual instruments and their names, but also with the larger context within which instrumental music making takes place (p. 101 below – sig. B). To this end, Virdung lists and depicts the instruments in a rational and systematic way, that is, within three traditional categories – strings, winds, and percussion – and he places them within sub-categories based upon aspects of their construction and playing techniques. The author then makes a significant digression in this opening section of the book in order to indicate the kinds of instruments he deliberately omits from the list: first, the allegorical "instruments of Jerome" (pp. 111–18 below – sigs. C2v–D3);[5] secondly, ancient instruments that had been mentioned by writers from classical antiquity (pp. 118–19 below – sigs. D3–D3v); and thirdly, contemporary instruments that were being used for playful purposes or for other functions not worthy of the high art of Music,[6] for example, whistles, drums, and hunting horns (pp. 115, 119–20 below – sigs. D, D3v–D4). Virdung thus accepts for consideration in the treatise only recognizable instruments – those "that any peasant might know of and call by name" – that were actually in use within his cultural milieu at the time (in his words, *bei uns*) and "that serve sweet melody" (pp. 118, 119–20 – sigs. D3, D4).

As the second step in his twofold approach, Virdung chooses for instructional purposes three of the instruments in common use in his day, each a representative from a different sub-category in his classification of strings and winds. He introduces these three instruments in what he considers the best order of study: first, the clavichord (a stringed instrument with keys), secondly, the lute (a stringed instrument with frets), and thirdly, the recorder (a wind instrument with finger holes). It will be noted that Virdung selects as exemplars for his instructions three instruments of the indoor variety – the "bas" or soft ones, as opposed to the "haut" or loud ones more suitable for the outdoors.

Virdung's little treatise can tell us a good deal about music making with instruments in his era and cultural setting. For example, we gain insight into what did and did not constitute the basic instrumentarium for art music at that time and place; and from the illustrations we have some idea of how the instruments

might have looked (this with a warning, however – pp. 18–23). We also witness at second hand the follo related phenomena at the turn of the sixteenth ce coming into prominence of the amateur instrume burgeoning of instrumental music making and inst notation systems (tablatures), and a rise in instrumenta Virdung himself fosters this growth by means of an in method of instrumental instruction: self-help, using a book with diagrams and examples, instead of the usual r ship with a living teacher. Thus, the author, our "silent ma verbally leads us via the printed page through all the symb the two most important German instrumental notation syste the day, tablatures for keyboard and for lute; and he sim guides us through the fingerings of all the pitches on the t sizes of recorders. And, to complement these step-by-step des tions, we get clarifying diagrams as well. Interspersed among lessons, furthermore, Virdung includes a number of intrigu details about instruments and about performance practice. As a example of details regarding instruments, we may cite his state ment that larger clavichords at the time were usually triple strung had resonance strings, and even had pedals (p. 127 below – sig. F) As an example of details concerning performance practice, we may cite his advice as to how one should choose a fourth recorder for a piece in four parts, a problematic task since recorders in the early sixteenth century were constructed in consorts of three sizes: a bass in F, a tenor in c, and a "discant" in g (pp. 180–1 below – sig. 04).[8]

Over and above the "how-to-do-it" information imparted in th pages of *Musica getutscht*, modern readers of this treatise can s aspects of music history through the eyes of a man whose spanned the last third of the fifteenth century and the first dec of the sixteenth. Bringing to bear a university educatio Heidelberg as well as a practical background in his ro a professional singer in several prestigious chapels, Vi discusses contemporary instrumental music making with intellectual and historical context. From the academic rea quotes works by Boethius, Guido, Odo, and his older porary Johannes von Soest (see below, p. 111). Although not acknowledge them explicitly, he is also beholden to Jean de Muris (both his *Notitiae artis musicae* of 132 instruments and that mastering one would lead in turn to mastering several more (p. 121 below – sig. E), for example, says much about the esteem in which instrumental literacy was held at that time and place. And Virdung's eloquent testimony that then modern instruments had reached a peak of perfection undreamed of by even the musical paragons of antiquity (p. 118–19 below – sig. D3v) not only tells us about the perceived state of instrument building in 1511 but also expresses an important Renaissance view of the present relative to the past.[10]

Virdung's writings reflect some of the intellectual turbulence of the time, as controversies and conundrums – musical and non-musical – creep into his prose. Through his eyes we see theoretical concepts in flux, as ancient constructs appear in new guises and modern exigencies strain the confines of traditional explanations. Consider the semitones on a keyboard, for example: to Virdung they represent not merely *musica ficta*, as his contemporary Arnolt Schlick maintained, but a survival of the chromatic genus of the ancient Greeks (pp. 125–6 below – sigs. E4–E4v).[11] The semitones on a lute raise another question (p. 158 below – sig. K4v): how can they function as equal divisions of the tone, when half steps of equal size constitute an impossibility in terms of traditional Boethian theory? Even Virdung's choice of a musical example points to a contemporary controversy. In order to demonstrate the process of transcribing a piece for voices written in staff notation into tablatures for instruments, our author prints a polyphonic Lied of four parts (presumably his own composition) in mensural notation (pp. 145–6 below – sigs. H4v–I). The subject of its text, the Immaculate Conception of Mary, was a hotly debated theological issue in Basel and Strassburg[12] in 1511. By his inclusion of this text, Virdung identifies himself as an ally of the dedicatee of *Musica getutscht*, Wilhelm Honstein, Bishop of Strassburg.[13] For this man, to whom Virdung appeals in the dedication to *Musica getutscht* for support to publish his next work on music, favored formal adoption of this doctrine.[14]

In other subtle ways, *Musica getutscht* acts as a window on the decades immediately preceding the Reformation. Virdung's realism in studying only the viable artistic musical instruments actually in use in his day, for example, is consistent with his literal interpretation of the Biblical passages he cites in his introduction (pp. 97–9 below – sigs. A2v–A3v). By contrast, his medieval predecessors had favored allegorical interpretations of the musical instruments mentioned in the Psalms, following St. Augustine and other church fathers. In their eyes, for example, the ten strings on the psaltery symbolically represented the Ten Commandments – not physical means for musical expression. In fact, according to strict patristic tradition, none of the instruments listed in the Psalms was appropriate for actual use in praising God for Christian worship.[15] Virdung in his generation, however, takes the Biblical instruments and their playing realistically, not symbolically. In his introductory essay to *Musica getutscht*, therefore, he promotes performance on modern instruments as a Biblically sanctioned avenue toward salvation ("blessedness"), offering as the rationale for his writing and publishing this little book the idea that its use will increase the number of blessed people (p. 99 below – sig. A3v). So important is this point that Virdung reiterates it at his conclusion (p. 180 below – sig. O4), thus placing the entire treatise within the realm of religious duty.

Biblical authority, then, is the most prominent element in Virdung's defense of musical instruments and their actual use by non-specialists. In keeping with his goal of introducing instruments to a public composed of persons from diverse backgrounds and circumstances, he quotes Biblical passages that support his arguments, using the German language rather than Latin. By his use of the vernacular for these as well as liturgical texts (see his musical example, pp. 144–5 below – sig. H4–H4v), our author foreshadows Lutheran reforms, and he puts himself in the company of other German humanists of his day who placed high value on their mother tongue as a proper vehicle for bringing understanding of the literary monuments of antiquity (the Bible included) to a larger segment of society. On this, the "eve of the Reformation," furthermore, the use of his native language for praising God reflects a growing tendency at the time toward expressing religious piety. Verbal expressions of piety in the vernacular (including musical settings of texts of this kind, like Virdung's sacred Lied in *Musica getutscht*) could constitute acts of worship – by individuals or groups, apart from the church or within its walls; and they flourished in a context of great concern about attaining personal salvation.[16]

Virdung also plays the modernist when he elevates activity near to the level of contemplation (pp. 97–8 below – sig. A2v)[17] and chooses an empirical method of research over the more traditional scholastic one. As the beginning of the text and the woodcut portrait of Virdung (pp. 100–1 below – sigs. A4–A4v) make clear, the author has just returned from travels "in the field" (to borrow a phrase from the social sciences), from which he has brought actual examples of the musical instruments he was studying. To him, then, the major source for his treatise is to be the empirical evidence of the instruments themselves.

Virdung presents his material in the form of a dialogue between himself and a friend, Andreas Silvanus (see below, pp. 29, 97). The text of *Musica getutscht* imitates an actual conversation between two friends who are mutually seeking knowledge. Our author employs neither the catechismal exchange between master and pupil characteristic of a scholastic dialogue, nor the dialectic disputation characteristic of a classical dialogue, both of which properly would be conducted in Latin. Rather, the interlocutors in *Musica getutscht* share insights and the fruits of their individual researches, gently challenging each other on their differing assumptions and points of view.[18] Such informal dialogues became a common vehicle for similar heuristic vernacular treatises in the sixteenth century, as works by Arbeau[19] and Morley[20] attest.

Virdung is able to aim his treatise toward a wide spectrum of society. Writing in German and using a popular though educated style, Virdung provides material that would appeal to many types of people. He names these specifically in *Musica getutscht* – from Bishop Honstein (of high rank in the first and second estates), Andreas (the scholar),[21] and members of the clergy and the religious (pp. 98–9 below – sig. A3),[22] to educated adults in general – all of whom were literate in the vernacular, at least to some degree (taking into consideration the number of explanatory pictures that enhance the text).[23] Virdung does not eschew even the lowest level of the social hierarchy, for, as mentioned above, he even holds up as one of the standards for including a musical instrument in this book the societal condition that it be one which "any peasant might know of and call by name,"[24] the other being the musical requirement that it serve "sweet melody" (pp. 119–20 below – sig. D4). In language, style, scope, and perhaps price as well, *Musica getutscht* could have been within the reach even of wealthier members of the educated middle classes.[25]

In both his use of the vernacular and his limiting his focus to musical instruments in German areas, Virdung adds to the growing feeling of pan-German national identity of the time.[26] His use of the phrase *das volck* in Psalm 88 (p. 97 below – sig. A2v), furthermore, may also reflect rising ethnic consciousness in Germany at that time.

Virdung had an avowedly radical approach to education (see below, p. 30), which included self-teaching by means of visual aids: pictures, diagrams, and examples provided by a knowledgeable person for whoever desired to learn. He credits his development of this new pedagogy to his own frustration with the old ways of imparting knowledge[27] coupled with his compassion for the plight of modern youths (*iungen*) in these same circumstances (p. 122 below – sig Ev). In espousing new educational philosophies, Virdung was not alone. In the late fifteenth and early sixteenth centuries, educators in German lands were experimenting with new paths to learning.[28]

One fascinating look into the intellectual climate of the early sixteenth century comes from Virdung's long phrases explaining the Arabic numerals in his lute and recorder tablatures. He calls each symbol "the numeral that represents the number." Thus, he carefully separates the graphic symbol from the abstract concept. His unwieldy verbal formula, repeated in every case, reflects the fact that, at the beginning of the sixteenth century, Arabic numerals (really Hindu in origin, having been transmitted from India to the West via Arabs) were only just being adopted into practical use in northern Europe.[29] These numerals included the novel concept of zero, which Virdung takes pains to explain as well (p. 172 below – sigs. N2–N2v).[30]

Beyond its intrinsic value as a document of musical as well as intellectual and social history, *Musica getutscht* is worthy of study by virtue of the far-reaching influence it had as a generative force during the course of the sixteenth century. The contents of this treatise were widely disseminated throughout Europe during the next decades in five derivative works. First, a second edition (printing B), produced apparently in Augsburg, appeared before 1521. Secondly and thirdly, twin translations in Netherlandic[31] and French (anonymously prepared) came forth from Antwerp between *ca.* 1528 and 1568 (*Dit is een seer schoon Boecxken*[32] and *Livre plaisant et tres utile*).[33] Fourthly, a Latin reworking by Othmar Luscinius was published in Strassburg in 1536 and again posthumously in 1542 (*Musurgia seu praxis musicae*). And fifthly, a German redaction of much of Virdung's material by Martin Agricola saw four printings at Wittenberg between 1529 and 1542 (*Musica instrumentalis deudsch*),[34] with a revised expanded edition appearing in 1545.[35] (For more on these progeny of *Musica getutscht*, see Chapters 3 and 4 below). Thus, significant portions of Virdung's and Furter's pioneering venture lived on well into the sixteenth century.

Like many innovative endeavors, *Musica getutscht* has its flaws and inconsistencies. Within the text of his treatise, however, the author frequently expresses his own awareness of its shortcomings. Virdung explains any deficiencies as stemming from the necessity to be extremely brief, given the constraints of this introductory work. For *Musica getutscht* is but a tiny extract from his own *magnum opus* – a copiously illustrated and comprehensive treatise in German on the subject of Music, one that in 1511 was still in manuscript form. (He refers to it as "A German *Musica*" [*ein deutsche Musica*].) Virdung had sought to publish this work in 1510; he now hoped to receive the financial backing to have it printed as a sequel to *Musica getutscht* (p. 97 below – sig. A2). Unfortunately, "A German *Musica*" never made it to press, and the manuscript is lost. We know the larger work only from Virdung's descriptions of it in *Musica getutscht*; these descriptions convey Virdung's promises to remedy any omissions or truncations of important topics in the shorter work by including and developing them in the larger one.

Indeed, Virdung spends a significant portion of his little treatise pointing the reader beyond it to his next book. His frequent references in *Musica getutscht* to the forthcoming work were meant to serve a triple function. First, they help build potential sales for his promised publication (and presumably, therefore, they help motivate both the dedicatee and the printer to risk the capital necessary for funding the project); secondly, they keep the reader from expecting more information than can be imparted in the space allotted to the author (probably by the financially concerned printer); and thirdly, they deflect the reader from specific topics that would take too much space and too much effort on their own and Virdung's part for him to explain in a work aimed at so basic a level. Thus we find him constantly confining his material to a scope appropriate for so small a work – a work destined for a heterogeneous audience that would include neophytes in the fields of vocal as well as instrumental music. So doing, he makes many a tantalizing mention of a subject, only to touch upon it briefly or to let it drop immediately. Among those subjects he reserves for consideration in his next book, for example, are the following: making divisions (p. 166 below – sig. M2); tonguing on a recorder (p. 168 below – sig. M3v); improvising on a *cantus firmus* (p. 121 below – sig. D4v); placing frets on a lute (p. 158 below – sig. K4v); and learning alternative tablatures for the three instruments. In addition, Virdung is forced to dodge important topics that he deems too advanced for initial consideration in so brief a work. These include some of the more treacherous theoretical concerns (such as complexities of mensural notation) as well as some of the more idiomatic aspects of instrumental performance practice (especially the necessity of custom-tailoring polyphonic music when transferring it from staff notation to tablature, so that an entire piece can be satisfactorily realized on the lute or a keyboard instrument).

Virdung's careful delimiting of his subject begins with his very first phrase – the one on the title page – as follows: "*Musica* . . . with [instructions] for learning *how to transcribe* [emphasis mine] all song[36] from the notes into the tablatures of . . . the organ,[37] the lute, and the recorder . . ." Throughout the treatise Virdung reiterates these bounds within which he intends to stay. Thus, the organizing principle, the very *raison d'être* of *Musica getutscht*, from his organological classification system to his instrumental instructions, is *intabulation*. Intabulation is the process by which one takes a piece of music written in staff notation and converts it into symbols that direct a player's hands to the keys, frets, or finger holes of an instrument. To Virdung, learning how to intabulate constitutes the first step toward learning to play a musical instrument, especially for those unable to read mensural notation (pp. 120–1 below – sigs. D4–D4v). And Virdung assumes as a corollary to this central premise that intabulation is the very didactic method by which the first principles of instrumental performance are to be taught and learned (pp. 101–7, 121 – sigs. B–B4, E – etc.). Furthermore, to him, systems of intabulation form the basis for classifying instruments in differing sub-groups within the three main categories of string, wind, and percussion (pp. 101–7 below – sigs. B–B4). Thus, stringed instruments with keyboards have one kind of tablature, stringed instruments with frets have another, stringed instruments with a separate string for each note (not specifically discussed in *Musica getutscht*) have a third, while stringed instruments with no frets have no tablature and are, therefore, "unprofitable" instruments (p. 104 below – sig. B2), at least within the context of Virdung's little treatise. The same process of organization is true for the winds: each sub-group has a different kind of tablature. Bellows-blown instruments with keys (i.e., organs) have keyboard tablature, and winds with finger holes have another kind of tablature.

Most of the topics that Virdung knowingly omits from *Musica getutscht* and saves for treatment in his larger work, therefore, are those that he deems inapplicable to the main purpose of his little treatise. So Virdung simply takes the reader through all the symbols of three tablatures: one each for the clavichord (which serves all keyboard instruments), the lute (which would apply to viols as well), and the recorder (which would also work in principle for other wind instruments). This he accomplishes verbally as well as pictorially. As examples, Virdung gives his own intabulations for clavichord and for lute of his polyphonic Lied for four voices.[39] Using these intabulations as prototypes, the learner is to do the same with a composition of his or her own choosing. Unfortunately, Virdung provides no example of recorder music in tablature.[40] Nevertheless, as was the case for both the clavichord and the lute, Virdung invites the learner to set a composition into recorder tablature (p. 180 below – sig. O4).

No specimens of Virdung's recorder tablature survive, as far as is now known. It may be the case that he invented it in order to have a consistent method of instruction for all three instruments. Virdung's recorder tablature can be described as a fingering chart in abbreviated form. Each symbol indicates which fingers cover which holes of the pipe (p. 180 below – sig. O3v); thus each symbol stands for a different note on each of the three sizes of recorder. For example, the numeral 1 means that only the lowest hole is uncovered, giving the pitch that can be considered as G on the bass, d on the tenor, and a on the discant.[41]

With almost all his material related to the process of intabulation, therefore, Virdung makes relatively little mention of actually playing instruments. Playing them is, of course, the ultimate goal of the preliminary instructions that make up the

13

substance of *Musica getutscht*, but Virdung does not bring his readers to this point in the treatise. It will be noticed in this regard that the learner is invited not to play the first intabulation given as a musical example but to transcribe another composition from staff notation into tablature using Virdung's effort as model (p. 144 below – sig. H4). The next steps after learning the basic principles of intabulation from *Musica getutscht* would be first, to learn to make idiomatic instrumental intabulations, and second, to learn to play these intabulations. Virdung addresses neither of these stages in *Musica getutscht*.[42] According to his stated aims, these steps would fall outside the bounds of *Musica getutscht*; therefore he reserves them for consideration in his forthcoming book, "A German *Musica*" (but see p. 166 below – sig. M2). Thus, although *Musica getutscht* holds the honor of having so many firsts in print with respect to instrumental performance practice, nevertheless, by Virdung's own admission and according to his intent, this treatise cannot stand on its own as a manual of instruction for learning how to play Renaissance musical instruments. Actually learning to play from idiomatic instrumental tablatures, therefore, requires the use of *Musica getutscht* in conjunction with other coeval sources of information. Virdung had intended to provide just such a source, his "A German *Musica*"; that he was unable to have it published is our misfortune.

One of Virdung's decisions with respect to the simplification of his material for teaching has marred his reputation both in his day and in our own. Rather than choosing a musical example that would yield a piece of music suitable for performance on a single instrument (in this case, the clavichord or the lute), Virdung instead selected a Lied of four parts that was not likely to be satisfactorily converted *in toto* into playable versions for either of these instruments. In addition, for demonstration purposes in the treatise, Virdung elected to intabulate each voice part of the original Lied entirely separately ("following the notes exactly," p. 166 below – sig. M2), without regard for how each part would fit with the others to produce the entire musical texture on a given instrument. Therefore, although they have the appearance of polyphonic intabulations, his two examples of tablatures are playable on clavichord and lute only as separate single lines, like the vocal original, and not as a discrete polyphonic composition for one instrument. This is evident from certain vertical sonorities that would be physically impossible for the instruments to reproduce; had these musical examples been meant to be poly-phonically realized on one instrument, the player would be called upon to produce multiple pitches on a single string of the lute or clavichord. In one instance, for example, three separate notes would have to be produced simultaneously on one string of the lute.[43] It could be argued from a pedagogical standpoint that beginners should, indeed, play only one line of music at a time. It could be argued as well from a historical standpoint that this constituted an earlier performance practice.[44] However, because Virdung nowhere specifically stated that he intended the tabla-tures to be played in this manner, the author of *Musica getutscht* was summarily taken to task by Arnolt Schlick later in the year 1511.[45] Echoing Schlick, conventional wisdom in recent years has it that Virdung, along with his treatise, should be dismissed as completely unreliable.

The main impetus for this late-twentieth-century derogatory assessment of the treatise and its author stems in large part from an article by Edwin Ripin, "A Reevaluation of Virdung's *Musica getutscht*" (*JAMS*, 29 [1976], 189–223). After reporting important findings regarding bibliographic details and the publication history of this work (see Chapter 3, below), Ripin comes to several harsh and unwarranted conclusions. These conclusions are based on misunderstandings of several aspects of *Musica getutscht*, including Virdung's classification system, his stated aims in writing the little work, and the limits of his topic. Focusing on the intabulation examples alone and on Schlick's reaction to them, for example, Ripin concludes: "it seems clear that, at best, Virdung was not a practicing instrumentalist; that he had little knowledge of instruments other than clavichords; and, accordingly, that he was ill-equipped to attempt to give practical instructions to the beginning instrumentalist" (pp. 208–9). Yet, a careful reading of Virdung's introductions to the rules of intabulation (including the diagrams of which he is so proud [see p. 122 below – sig. Ev]) – which make up, after all, the main thrust of his material – shows him to have good command of the tablatures for all three of the instruments he presents.

No less unwarranted is Ripin's view that any departures from *Musica getutscht* in the derivative works constitute evidence that "Virdung's contemporaries did not take the actual content of

Musica getutscht very seriously, even if they obviously thought that the idea of an illustrated treatise dealing with the rudiments of music was a good one" (p. 208). Rather, the large amount of material the borrowers did retain argues strongly that they took Virdung's effort very seriously indeed (see Chapters 3 and 4, below). Each adaptor of *Musica getutscht*, after all, addressed a very different audience from that of the original treatise, and each bowed to the needs and expectations of a different geographic area as well as a different decade.[46] Nor is it true, as Ripin claims, that Luscinius in his work, *Musurgia*, takes Virdung's treatise a step further toward a "more useful work for the practical musician" because of his better "knowledge of both instruments and playing technique than it would appear Virdung possessed" (p. 223). Indeed, Luscinius's adaptation contains significantly fewer details about actual instrumental practice than *Musica getutscht*; for, to Luscinius, literary and historical aspects of the subject of musical instruments, especially those from classical antiquity, took precedence over teaching intabulation for modern German instruments.

Ripin attributes to Virdung, furthermore, a statement about instrumental performance that our author never made, with the accusation that although it "appears at first to be an insightful comment about a large group of instruments, on closer examination [it] again turns out to be uninformed and invalid" (p. 215). The sentence by Virdung in question reads as follows: "For, whatever you learn [to do] on the clavichord you [will] then have [as a foundation] for learning how to play well and easily the organ, the harpsichord (*clavizymell*),[47] the virginal, and all other keyboard instruments; next, whatever you learn about fingering and plucking on the lute you [will] have [as a foundation] for easily learning the harp, the psaltery, or the viol; finally, whatever you learn [to do] on the recorder you [will] have [as a foundation] for learning all the more easily later on all the other wind instruments with finger holes" (p. 121 below – sig. E). Virdung does not state that tablatures for the instruments are directly transferable, as Ripin claims he does. Looking at the entire passage from which this sentence is extracted makes it clear that to Virdung, instruments have their own individual tablatures – with overlaps, to be sure – but some of the basic principles of intabulation as well as some of the basic skills (e.g., "fingering and plucking on the lute") remain similar from instrument to instrument within the various categories and sub-categories. Not only is Virdung's point well taken, but he here articulates an important attitude of his day, namely, that a person literate in instrumental performance will ideally be able to play not just one but several instruments in each category.

Finally, Ripin misquotes Michael Praetorius, the seventeenth-century composer, theorist, and organologist, by taking his description of Virdung's work out of context and attributing to Praetorius a negative value judgment applied to the entire treatise, a judgment that he never made (see below, pp. 59–60). Clearly, Ripin's "Reevaluation" itself needs reevaluation.

As for Virdung's presentation of introductory intabulations as single lines of music rather than as polyphonic textures achievable on a single clavichord or lute, his decision seems less surprising when we remember that (1) his purpose in writing *Musica getutscht* was to teach only the first step to an understanding of musical instrumental performance, that is, the most basic principles of intabulation for a specific instrument, not yet how to prepare playable tablatures or how to play from them, and (2) as noted above, his choice of the specific musical example for intabulation probably had a primarily political rather than a purely musical motivation, owing to the subject of its text. In Virdung's defense, furthermore, it must be pointed out that not only were the same Lied and its two intabulations carefully copied out by hand on woodcuts for a second edition of *Musica getutscht* (printing B), but Virdung's original woodcuts, including these very musical examples, appeared a quarter-century later – in 1536, and again in 1542 – in *Musurgia* by Luscinius. Had the preparer of printing B or Luscinius considered the intabulations inappropriate, he could have omitted them or substituted others. Their inclusion, especially by Luscinius, an author and musician of very high international stature at the time, argues favorably for Virdung's decision to offer his samples of intabulation as simple, mechanical demonstrations of the most basic principles of the procedure rather than as polyphonic pieces suitable for performance by an individual player. For a player capable of rendering a polyphonic texture, even of two voices, would necessarily have had to attain a much more advanced level of technical ability than could be provided for within the scope of either *Musica getutscht* or

Musurgia. By his retention of Virdung's demonstration intabulations (along with the explanatory diagrams), then, Luscinius supports what anyone can find by studying the entire treatise, that Virdung's basic rules of intabulation are indeed reliable, as are his intabulations for keyboard and lute when considered as examples of single lines of music.[48]

Another decision regarding the contents of the treatise, although it delighted Virdung's contemporaries, invites criticism today. This decision concerns the illustrations of musical instruments. We do not know whether Virdung, his publisher, the cutter, or all three could claim responsibility for the contours and the quality of the woodcuts. Whoever their originator, the cuts present problems to readers in our era. The modern reader approaches these depictions from a perspective derived from five centuries of development in the history of illustrated books. And the pictures in *Musica getutscht* do not function as our contemporary visual consciousness tells us they rightly should. With few exceptions (the lute on p. 103 below – sig. B2 – for example), these pictures do not tell us enough of what we need to know in order to understand the instruments as the actual artifacts that their representations denote. Thus, most of the images in *Musica getutscht* cannot be translated into prototypes for us to replicate; even after thoroughly examining them, we cannot decipher significant aspects of many instruments as they appear on the pages of this little book.

Gerhard Stradner has characterized the difficulty of dealing with these illustrations as follows: "Unfortunately, these woodcuts are unreliable in many respects, especially concerning technical problems. [The woodcuts] are sometimes reversed [i.e., they form a mirror image of the depicted instrument], and they demand critical inspection in order to guard against false conclusions."[49] Stradner lists some of the conclusions that cannot be drawn from studying the pictures of the keyboard instruments in *Musica getutscht* (see sigs. B–Bv, p. 102 below): (1) we cannot tell if the lid of the clavichord is attached to the case by means of a cord or a rod; (2) we cannot say for sure whether the keyboards are inset or whether the keys extend out from the bodies of the stringed keyboard instruments; (3) we do not know why the *clavicimbalum* looks just like a backwards virginal; (4) we cannot know for certain whether the cross piece on the

18

clavicytherium represents a wrongly positioned jackrail or some kind of strut. Then too, obvious mistakes, like the incorrectly bent pegbox of the hurdy-gurdy (p. 102 below – sig. Bv),[50] inspire skepticism about the reliability of other drawings. Although Stradner here refers only to the keyed stringed instruments, his assessment would apply to representations of many other instruments in the treatise as well, since other instances of vagueness in depicting the instruments defy our attempts at understanding their construction. For example, is the hammered dulcimer (p. 104 below, sig. B2v) meant to be rectangular or trapezoidal in form? What is the shape of the bridge on the trumpet marine (p. 105 below – sig. B3), and how are the two strings attached? How does the sectioned bell (p. 110 below – sig. C2) make its sound? Where is the keyboard on the regal (p. 109 below – sig. Cv), and does this instrument really have three bellows? In many of these pictures the illustrator seems either to have misunderstood or to have consciously created ambiguity about features of importance to us. In addition, he has more often than not ignored perspective[51] and the relative sizes of instruments.[52]

Yet, as mentioned above, the pictures of musical instruments in *Musica getutscht*, inaccuracies and ambiguities notwithstanding, constituted the single feature of the treatise by which it was best known in the sixteenth century. As such, these images became models for all the subsequent treatises on the subject: They were copied *in toto* for printing B; they were reprinted very nearly in their entirety in *Musurgia* by Luscinius; most of the pictures of extant musical instruments were carefully copied and incorporated into *Musica instrumentalis deudsch* by Agricola; and several of the cuts were copied for the title page of the twin Netherlandic and French treatises, *Dit is een seer schoon Boecxken* and *Livre plaisant*. In addition, almost the whole lot of the pictures appears in a manuscript dating from before 1524,[53] and musical instruments with contours strikingly similar to those in Virdung's work can be found on border designs in prints from the 1520s and beyond.[54] With regard to the pictures of musical instruments, then, their frequent imitation, even to the extent of laboriously maintaining reversed keyboards and other avoidable inaccuracies,[55] indicates that to readers of the time, these illustrations were a resounding success. Virdung's woodcuts (insofar as they were his and not attributable primarily to either his printer or the cutter hired by the printer) obviously served their purpose well, by standards and expectations of the day.

The discrepancy between our modern assessment of these depictions as disappointingly crude and inaccurate and the positive judgment given them in the sixteenth century lies in the difference between two sets of expectations, separated over time, regarding the nature and role of illustrations within a text. In 1511, the use of the printing press for economic profit was little more than half a century old. To make ends meet, printers had to get their products out quickly and cheaply. Thus, proofreading of the text occurred during the process of printing,[56] and decorative and illustrative contributions to a book were in most cases kept as simple and practical as possible (depending upon both the market and the purpose for a particular book). The medium of the woodcut – with its clear lines, its potential for relatively fast execution, and its technical compatibility with printing from type – suited these requirements well.

Not surprisingly, the new process of printing retained characteristics of the earlier method of book reproduction – hand copying of manuscripts. In company with the text itself, manuscript illuminations had been copied from manuscript to manuscript, or from standardized models, with little direct reference to anything from life, except as individual artists put in subtle corrections from remembered experience as they saw fit.[57] This method of copying illustrations from other copies of illustrations rather than from the depicted object itself can be traced in herbals, for example.[58] In these books, the original drawings, even if "taken from life" at some point, gradually became so distorted in the process of copying as to render the images merely stylizations of their subjects. A manuscript tradition of long standing, as carried forth in the first half-century of the printing press, then, formed the context of visual and pictorial consciousness characteristic of the time, and this was the context within which the illustrations in *Musica getutscht* were created. Readers in 1511, like their medieval predecessors, therefore, expected a picture in a book to convey a concept, not an exact likeness; and they expected an illustration to please – by fostering some level of recognition, by enhancing the effectiveness of a text, by beautifying the book as an artifact – not to reflect accurately the structure of an object as if "drawn from life" according to our modern standards of "realism."[59]

The inverted commas surrounding the phrases "taken from life" and "drawn from life" and the word "realism," above, serve to call attention to the fact that, in earlier times as well as the present, what one perceives as realistic in an artistic representation is affected by familiar ways of depicting reality. Artistic standards and conventions regarding the relationship of a picture to the pictured vary greatly from culture to culture, from historical era to historical era, from medium to medium, and from genre to genre. Thus, in the early sixteenth century, for example, one standard of realism could obtain in painting or manuscript illumination, while another could be deemed appropriate for woodcuts used to illustrate treatises; furthermore, as in the case of woodcuts in German lands of the early sixteenth century, individual cuts destined for use as religious art that could be hung on a wall (especially those by masters like Dürer) often had one standard,[60] while cuts made for book illustrations could have another. These varying standards and conventions inform both the artist who executes an image and the person who "reads" it.[61] In the words of the philosopher Nelson Goodman, "Realism is relative, determined by the system of representation standard for a given culture or person at a given time. Newer or older or alien systems are accounted artificial or unskilled."[62] Goodman's latter point speaks directly to the issue of modern derogatory opinions on the woodcuts in *Musica getutscht.* For adoption of the accepted contemporary idea of realism in art – that one should draw "what one sees" instead of relying on conventional schemata – dates only from the Renaissance.[63] Moreover, in the field of printed book illustration (especially of treatises), this novelty caught on only in the 1530s and 40s, several decades after the appearance of Virdung's work. The radical trend toward producing woodcuts for books with a goal of reflecting scientific accuracy can once again be traced in herbals: in Otto Brunfels's *Herbarium vivae eicones* of 1530 and in Leonhard Fuchs's *De historia stirpium insignes* of 1542.[64]

How then, can we assess Virdung's woodcuts? As pointed out above, we know from the text of *Musica getutscht* (sigs. A2 and A4v – pp. 97 and 100 below) that Virdung created this treatise by extracting it from a much larger illustrated treatise, one that remained in manuscript form. It is possible that the drawings in

21

his manuscript served as models of some sort for the woodcuts in the smaller work that did go to press. The original designer of the woodcuts, then, could have been Virdung himself. Whoever this artist, even if he had sketched a likeness of an instrument from the thing itself, he still would have been influenced both by whatever aspects of the referent he wished to convey and by familiar ways of graphically encoding the object. Thus, he would naturally exaggerate certain features while suppressing others, consciously or unconsciously adopting some of the stylistic conventions of that time and place, appealing to the interests and expectations of his intended audience, and, of course, following his own inclinations based on the rationale for the depictions themselves. Indeed, given the popular nature of the treatise, it is not surprising that in this case a vernacular style of illustration was chosen to match the text.

It remains to consider Virdung's own purpose in providing illustrations of musical instruments in *Musica getutscht* and the relationship of this intention to the woodcuts produced in response to it. Virdung tells us his objective in picturing the indigenous instrumentarium of his day: "The [subject of] music has many divisions. These [instruments] are therefore pictured along with their names so that they will become known so much the better to each person who looks at the book" (p. 101 below – sig. B).[65] Thus, his aim in this section of his treatise was primarily to reinforce the association of a name with a recognizable object and vice versa, an association his reader already had in some form (since Virdung only considers instruments that "any peasant might know of and call by name"). His aim in the pictures was not to impart specific technical knowledge about the instruments other than to place them within appropriate morphological categories. In picturing them in the context of his classification system, our author saved himself innumerable words, words that might aid us today, but which in 1511 not only would have made the book too lengthy, but which could well have intimidated the sort of readers Virdung and his publisher had in mind. Further-more, because of this expressed aim in illustrating the instru-mentarium, to Virdung a depicted instrument need not represent a specific example of an item with that designation; rather, it served the author's purpose better to present a kind of generic conflation that would not limit the variations in actual examples to which the name might apply.[66] This, then, could account for at least some of the pictorial equivocations and ambiguities in detail listed above. For example, the hammered dulcimer could have either a rectangular or a trapezoidal shape; the keyboards of the clavichord, virginal, and clavicytherium could be either recessed or protruding; and a rod or a cord could have held open the lid of a keyboard instrument.

Musica getutscht lies well within the period during which book illustrations served primarily to edify (as then expected) rather than to inform (as taken for granted today).[67] Virdung's illustrations therefore reflect a central interest on his part in depicting not so much the instruments themselves as the categories into which they are to be grouped (for the reader's edification). Thus, the images did not have to represent objects with technical accuracy (for the reader's information), since anyone at the time could readily see what item was meant. Emmanuel Winternitz aptly summed up the situation when he described one of Virdung's illustrations as a "woodcut suggesting a clavichord."[68]

Our disappointment with the pictures in *Musica getutscht*, then, stems in large part from the gap of half a millennium between our eras, a gap which (1) cripples our ability to supply missing or ambiguous details (or, indeed, to correct errors) on the basis of first-hand experience with the actual instruments themselves, and (2) prejudices our attitude toward book illustrations so we unfairly expect pictures to express a level of technological reality characteristic of more modern times. Understanding of the historical context within which Virdung developed the woodcut illustrations for *Musica getutscht* (including the musical examples as well as the pictures), along with recognition of the author's own stated purposes for their existence, should deflect our anachronistic impatience with this aspect of the treatise and free us to study and appreciate *Musica getutscht* for what it is and what it does tell us, not for what we wish it were and what we expect it to impart.

In view of the importance of this treatise to the history of music, it is not surprising that *Musica getutscht* has generated a great deal of interest among music historians. These include Praetorius in the seventeenth century, who quotes Virdung extensively at several points in his *De Organographia*,[69] as well as Hawkins[70] and Burney[71] in the eighteenth century, both of whom make use of the Latin version by Luscinius. First-hand knowledge of this work has already been made available since the late nineteenth century through the publication of three facsimile editions and reprints of two of them.[72] Therefore, this treatise has frequently been quoted both verbally and pictorially in discussions of Renaissance music and musical instruments. Yet it is only in recent years that the text of *Musica getutscht* as a whole has been the subject of study and translation.[73] Scholars from the seventeenth century to the present day have tended to glean from the text only those passages relevant to their special interests. Such fragmented consideration of sections taken out of context, without regard to the work as a whole, has resulted in misunderstanding and misrepresentation of the treatise itself and of the aims of its author.[74] Then too, the archaic language in which it is written has obscured its author's message. It is hoped that the English translation provided here will form a basis for better understanding and further study of this seminal work.[75]

2   A biography of Sebastian Virdung

The name Sebastian Virdung would, no doubt, have remained within the darkest shadows of recorded history had he not produced the little work on the musical instruments of his era, *Musica getutscht*. With information gleaned from surviving documents (listed and translated below, pp. 34–46),[1] we can piece together a fragmentary biography and a not altogether flattering picture of the man. Very little is known about the early and final years of his life. A birth date no later than 1465 can be postulated on the basis of his appointment in April 1489 to a position reserved for clergymen past the age of twenty-four (document no. 3).[2] Presumably his birth took place in Amberg (then capital of the Upper Palatinate) because most of the extant documents relating to his activities style him "Sebastian from Amberg." This, however, is by no means certain, especially since his father, Wenzel Virdung, achieved the status of a burgher there only in 1475 (doc. no. 23), when Sebastian would have to have been at least ten years old. Although our author retained the surname Virdung, his father had acquired the name Grop in 1468, when Emperor Frederick III presented to him a coat of arms with that name – the last male members of the family that had previously carried the name having died (doc. no. 22).

Virdung matriculated at the University of Heidelberg in 1483 at about the age of eighteen (doc. no. 1). Three years later, in 1486, he purchased textbooks on jurisprudence from Peter Drach, a printer in Speyer. Drach sent the bill for them to Virdung's father, who at the time was innkeeper at The Wild Man (*zum Wilden Man*) in Nuremberg (doc. no. 2), having purchased citizenship as a burgher in that city the same year (doc. no. 24). From Drach we learn that as early as 1486 Virdung was carrying on his studies concurrently with duties as a singer at the court of the Elector of the Palatinate, Count Philip, at Heidelberg.[3] His relationship with this court lasted about twenty years, until sometime between 1504 and 1507.[4] No record tells of Virdung's having earned any degrees at the University of Heidelberg, but by 1489 he had become a priest. In that year the Elector named him for the first of two ecclesiastical benefices connected with the Palatinate (and Heidelberg as its capital) that Virdung was to hold, a post as *pastor* at Lengenfeld near Neumarkt in the Upper Palatinate, in the diocese of Eichstätt (docs. nos. 3, 5, and 6 [also 8]). He received a second benefice, at Stahleck (Stalburg Castle, near Bacharach, in the diocese of Trier) in July of 1500 (docs. nos. 7 and 8). These appointments suggest that Virdung's status with his patron was not impaired by an allegation of slander lodged against him in 1490 by one of his colleagues at court. The ensuing quarrel was serious enough for Count Philip to request official arbitration by the civil authorities of Heidelberg (doc. no. 4), but information on the outcome does not survive.

Two letters from Virdung at Heidelberg – one in 1503 (doc. no. 9) and the other in early 1504 (doc. no. 11) – to the Elector's son, Prince Ludwig (then in France at the royal court of Louis XII in Lyons),[5] indicate that Sebastian acted as chaplain as well as singer at Heidelberg at that time. In these letters Virdung speaks on behalf of other members of the chapel,[6] and he demonstrates a lively interest in studying theoretical works by modern authors (specifically the *Practica musicae* of Franchinus Gaffurius) and in obtaining music by the giant of the previous generation of composers, Johannes Ockeghem. We know neither the date of Virdung's departure from Heidelberg nor the reason for it. The warm response of Prince Ludwig to Virdung's first letter, happily extant (doc. no. 10), speaks well of our author's relationship with his employer at the Heidelberg court. Virdung's second letter would also indicate that he enjoyed the favor of his patron (doc. no. 11). However, political turbulence over the succession in Bavaria and the subsequent defeat of the Palatinate by King Maximilian[7] and his allies in 1504 may have necessitated cuts in personnel at court,[8] and his name does not figure among those at Heidelberg proper after that year. Virdung's name does appear in a payment record of the Cathedral of Constance for 1 September 1506 as "Sebastian, singer from Heidelberg' (doc. no. 12), and his resignation from the position at Stahleck was not noted until 12 March 1507 (doc. no. 16), when his successor was named. By

9 January 1507 Virdung had been hired as one of nine succentors at the Cathedral of Constance (doc. no. 13). The document recording this transaction refers to his having been released from responsibilities as altist for the Württemberg court at Stuttgart prior to this appointment. Records are lacking, but he had evidently been employed there by 1506 (if not earlier) as part of the musical establishment of Duke Ulrich. This young ruler (b. 1487) had profited from the war of 1504, gaining territory that had formerly belonged to the Palatinate; he may have gained singers as well. The reason for Virdung's departure from Stuttgart in 1506 and his subsequent employment at Constance are unknown.

As succentor at the Cathedral of Constance during the course of the year 1507, Virdung had more and more tasks heaped upon him. In addition to singing, these included (as of 22 January) composing and teaching counterpoint to the choirboys (doc. no. 14),[9] recruiting for the chapel (doc. no. 15), seeing to the care of some of the choirboys (as of 30 July) (doc. no. 17), and, finally, seeing to the care and instruction of all the choirboys (as of 24 September) (doc. no. 18). Under the circumstances, it comes as little surprise that on 14 January 1508 – only one year after having been hired – he was dismissed from his position. He seems to have put child care at the very end of his list of priorities, for the cathedral chapter named as the grounds for terminating his employment that he had been undependable and neglectful of his duties with the boys (doc. no. 19). Virdung officially left Constance on 18 January 1508 after promising in writing that he would take nothing from the cathedral – "no choirboy or other singer, no book or anything else belonging to the choir" (doc. no. 20). Evidence that Virdung himself did not carry full blame for his failure there comes from records of events immediately following his dismissal. On 15 January 1508, Virdung's predecessor as teacher of the choirboys, Hans von Rheinfelden (who likewise had proved unsuccessful in that capacity, but whose performance had not provoked his sacking) was asked to resume this occupation. He did so under protest, lodging a written complaint about intolerable working conditions connected with the position. While most of these were subsequently ameliorated by the chapter, nevertheless another caretaker for the boys was appointed on 5 June, the third change in less than a year.[10]

Further strains on Virdung during his tenure at Constance may have stemmed from the presence of dignitaries and their personnel from all over the empire for the Imperial Diet held there from 29 April to 26 July 1507. King Maximilian and his retinue thus stayed in Constance for most of the period between 27 April and 9 August of 1507.[11] Maximilian's singers accompanied him at this time.[12] These included the court composer Heinrich Isaac,[13] and also Ludwig Senfl.[14] It could well be that Virdung found it difficult to concentrate on his humble tasks in the face of such distractions.

The last known archival reference to Virdung mentions his payment to a man in Eichstätt of a sum of money he owed to the cathedral at Constance (1 May 1508) (doc. no. 21). Three printed works from the ensuing years, however, provide a few further details about his life and his character. These are his own *Musica getutscht* of 1511, the preface to *Tabulaturen Etlicher lobgesang und lidlein uff die orgeln und lauten* (in the form of a letter dated 30 November 1511) that Arnolt Schlick published in 1512 (doc. no. 22), and the dedication of *Musurgia seu praxis musicae* by Othmar Luscinius, printed in 1536 (doc. no. 23).

Glimpses of Virdung's situation in 1511 appear throughout *Musica getutscht*. At the time of writing this work he was also completing a manuscript of his copiously illustrated treatise in German verse on the comprehensive subject of Music, which he called "A German *Musica*." This he had shown to potential benefactors at the Imperial Diet at Augsburg in 1510 (held between March and May of that year). One of these, Wilhelm Honstein (b. 1475), Bishop of Strassburg (1506–41), had evinced sufficient interest in the project for Virdung to dedicate to him the short, truncated interim work based upon this manuscript, *Musica getutscht*. (The honor did not prompt Honstein to lend the financial support necessary for Virdung to achieve his frequently stated aim of publishing the larger work, however.) The simple designation "Priest from Amberg" on the title page of *Musica getutscht* suggests that Virdung was not employed with any musical establishment in 1511. Although his use of the phrase "his gracious lord" when referring to the Bishop of Strassburg (on the title page and subsequently in the dedication) might indicate some form of service on the part of Virdung to this prominent man, in all likelihood it reflected merely an aspiration. This language at the time expressed politeness; it was used as a formula characteristic of written communications from one of lower status to a person of high rank.

Virdung's little treatise is cast in the form of a dialogue between Sebastian (the author himself) and "a good friend named Andreas Silvanus." Their relationship is one of colleagues, not master and disciple as has sometimes been assumed. The tone of the dedication, in which Virdung first names him, makes clear that Silvanus is a real person.[15] Virdung probably meant Andreas Waldner ("Silvanus" being a Latinization of the German "Waldner"), a man who, like himself, had come to the University of Heidelberg (albeit two years later than Virdung), and who may also have taken part in the musical activities at the Heidelberg court.[16] For didactic purposes, however, Virdung not only invented the actual conversation (although interactions of this sort may well have been common in this age of intellectual curiosity and sharing of knowledge) but he fictionalized his interlocutor to some extent as well. This can be seen from the fact that while Virdung identified Silvanus as a musician (*musicus*) just prior to the dialogue proper (sig. A3v),[17] nevertheless Andreas, the person in the treatise, acts totally ignorant of musical matters, both theoretical and practical.[18] Thus serving as a foil to Sebastian, Andreas with his lack of knowledge provides Virdung with the opportunity to set forth his material.

While it is difficult to separate fact from fiction regarding Andreas, nothing indicates that Sebastian, the character in *Musica getutscht*, differs in any way from Sebastian Virdung in life. For instance, in the treatise Sebastian names as his *meister* the recently deceased Johannes von Soest (Johannes de Susato). This man had in fact held the position of Sängermeister at the Heidelberg court during much of Virdung's tenure there (see n. 60, p. 231 below). Before leaving in 1495 to become a medical doctor in other cities, Soest wrote several literary works in German verse and a musical treatise (apparently in Latin), "Musica subalterna" ("Music in its alternative aspects"), which is no longer extant. The manuscript by Soest that Sebastian described and to which he was beholden in *Musica getutscht* for the "Instruments of Jerome" (sig. C2v, p. 111 below) may have been a copy of this lost work. We do not know if by the term *meister* Virdung meant a formal pedagogical relationship between himself and the older man.

As further evidence of identity between the author and the main character of *Musica getutscht* we may cite Sebastian's passionately held views on proper musical education of youths (*iungen*) (sig. Ev, p. 122 below). Virdung had recently been involved in this profession with the choirboys at Constance. Indeed, his release from duties there may have resulted in part from his unorthodox opinions on this subject, as expressed in *Musica getutscht*. For in this treatise, Sebastian promises that (especially in his larger, forthcoming work) he will accelerate the teaching of music to students by means of innovative short-cuts to accepted pedagogical practice (hence, perhaps, the charge that he neglected his duties); he proposes to do this through simplified written instructions with accompanying diagrams and illustrations for further clarification. Then too, in the dialogue, Sebastian alludes to his having recently wandered for quite some time while engaged in research for the larger work that he hoped to publish in the near future (sig. A4v, p. 100 below). These travels could account for a hiatus in documentation for the period between Virdung's dismissal at Constance in early 1508 and his presence at Augsburg in the spring of 1510. He would then have had a full year between the latter date and the summer of 1511 to extract *Musica getutscht* from this more comprehensive project.

Virdung's dating of the dedication of *Musica getutscht* at Basel on 15 July 1511[19] probably places him in that city at that time. Moreover, owing to the close coordination between text and illustrations, we may assume some participation by the author in the publication process of this, his *parvum opus*. We may even conjecture that he prepared this extract from his larger work while in Basel, in consultation with the printer, Michael Furter,[20] as well as the presumed artist, Urs Graf.[21]

In addition to providing these few bits of biographical information, *Musica getutscht* tells us something about the character of its author as well. Although in this vernacular work Virdung sought to popularize aspects of the subject of music for a wide audience, he nevertheless attended to the ethical element of his rhetorical approach by making his erudition subtly but not intimidatingly manifest. At one point, however (on sig. E4v, pp. 126–7 below), Virdung attempted to gain academic credibility by slurring his former colleague at the Heidelberg court, the blind organist and author Arnolt Schlick. Provocation for Virdung's vitriolic attack stemmed ostensibly from a statement in Schlick's *Spiegel der Orgelmacher und Organisten*, published earlier in 1511.[22] Since this statement would appear to have hardly warranted so angry a response, Virdung's underlying motivation for his outburst may have been jealousy of Schlick: jealousy that this organist still enjoyed the patronage of the Elector, and jealousy that Schlick had obtained an Imperial privilege from the Emperor Maximilian to protect the author's rights to the *Spiegel* and to his subsequent publication as well. This controversy in print between Virdung and Schlick derived from the fact that in his treatise on the organ (sig. b3c), Schlick had mentioned that playing transpositions involving black keys on the organ constituted *musica ficta*. Virdung, citing Boethius as his authority, reacted in *Musica getutscht* to Schlick's contention by insisting that this phenomenon should instead be considered the chromatic genus. Rather than pointing out their difference on this point in a gentlemanly fashion, however, Virdung not only jeered sarcastically at the epithet applied to Schlick on the title page of the latter's organ treatise, "illustrious and learned master," but, using a pun on the title, cruelly alluded to Schlick's blindness as well: "[The author] should be pardoned, however, because he overlooked [Boethius]. Either his eyes are to blame, or the mirror has become dim. It would be better if it were polished clean by organists and organ builders" (sig. F, p. 127 below).

Schlick's response (doc. no. 22), dated 30 November 1511,[23] appeared as part of the introductory matter of his *Tabulaturen Etlicher lobgesang und lidlein uff die orgeln und lauten* (published in 1512). In it he castigated Virdung not only for this tasteless breach of common courtesy to a handicapped person, but for two other failings as well. First, he exposed Virdung's lack of expertise in the very subject for which he posed as a guide, instrumental music. As proof of this Schlick cited the many mistakes and awkward passages in the tablatures printed in *Musica getutscht*.[24] Second, he pointed out Virdung's ingratitude in response to Schlick's helpfulness to him in the past. Schlick reported here that, in addition to other occasions, he had spoken highly of Virdung to members of the nobility and others attending the Imperial Diet of Worms (*zu wormbs uff dem grossen reichstag*, sig. π3v). Although many scholars assume that Schlick here referred to the politically significant (therefore *grossen*) diet (*reichstag*) that took place in

31

that city in 1495,[25] it is far more likely that he meant the more recent one that Emperor Maximilian had convened there in 1509,[26] the year after Virdung had been relieved of his position at Constance. At that time he would have needed such assistance from Schlick, whereas in 1495 Virdung had enjoyed employment at the Heidelberg court and at Lengenfeld.

Thus, a picture emerges of an apparently unemployed singer/ priest traveling from Reichstag to Reichstag in search of a patron. Because of the involuntary nature of his departure from Constance, Virdung had to depend upon the recommendation of at least one of his colleagues at a previous place of employment, the Heidelberg court. When this proved fruitless, Virdung took advantage of the climate of the time by devoting himself – most probably between 1509 and 1510 – to the preparation of an illustrated work in the vernacular that might appeal to members of the nobility: those desirous of gaining fashionable musical knowledge and skills without encumbrance of the need for fluency in Latin, those wishing to own attractive books for their libraries, and (most significantly for him) those who might offer him a position. In *Musica getutscht*, the abbreviated work he did publish for a wider audience on a subject outside his professional expertise, while attempting to show his own credentials, Virdung took a cheap shot at the very person who had tried to help him in his effort to find employment, Arnolt Schlick.

Our final clue to the span of Virdung's life comes from *Musurgia seu praxis musicae* by Othmar Luscinius (see pp. 61ff. below). The author, a well-known humanist scholar of the time, came from Strassburg, Basel's sister city on the Rhine. Luscinius based part of this Latin treatise upon Virdung's *Musica getutscht*, even incorporating the very same woodcuts used in the 1511 print. He tells us in the dedication (sigs. a2–a2v) (doc. no. 23) that he had prepared this redaction at the request of the dedicatee, Andreas Calvo. Calvo was a bookseller and publisher in Milan who wished to bring Virdung's little work to interested transalpine readers, those for whom the German language acted as a formidable barrier. Luscinius states that Calvo had proposed this project to him an undisclosed number of years before publication of *Musurgia* by Johann Schott at Strassburg in 1536. Internal evidence proves that Luscinius had completed the manuscript for *Musurgia* by 1518: on sig. n2v he refers to Maximilian as "our

Emperor," even though Maximilian had died in January 1519.[27] Further evidence may be read in a book order sent in the year 1517 by Calvo's brother and fellow book dealer, Francesco Calvo, to the Basel printer Johann Froben. The order, for twenty-five copies of "a book printed in Strassburg with illustrations of musical instruments"[28] probably indicates that Luscinius had already prepared his Latin version of *Musica getutscht* at that time and that publication was expected in the near future.[29] That this did not come to pass until nineteen years later must have been due to the great quantity of weightier subject matter, including Biblical and classical scholarship as well as politically-charged religious writings unleashed by the challenges of Luther and others, that required dissemination in Strassburg shortly after 1517. For this city felt the impact of the Reformation as early as 1518.

Luscinius tells us in the dedication to *Musurgia* that Virdung was "prematurely taken away from the living" before he could place "the finishing hand" on his project (sig. a2v). Whereas Edwin Ripin assumed that this meant that Virdung had died while *Musica getutscht* was in the process of publication, thereby preventing him from correcting the mistakes in that volume,[30] it is hardly likely that Schlick would have taken a dead man so thoroughly to task the way he did in November of 1511, after *Musica getutscht* had already appeared. Indeed, at the time of writing, Schlick refers to him as very much alive (see doc. no. 22). Rather, the statement by Luscinius must refer to the fact that Virdung died before he could publish his *magnum opus*, the work from which *Musica getutscht* represented but a brief extract. Thus, Virdung's death falls somewhere between 1512 and 1536 (the publication date of *Musurgia*), more probably between 1512 and some time prior to the completion of *Musurgia* in about 1516 or 1517. The 1513 printing in Mainz by Peter Schöffer (the younger) of four songs by Virdung does not necessarily indicate that he was alive in that year.[31] Nor does the appearance of a second edition of *Musica getutscht* some time before 1521 (when Ferdinand Columbus purchased a copy)[32] imply that Virdung was present then in Augsburg,[33] the presumed place of publication. Until further documents come to light we must leave Virdung at Basel in the summer of 1511. He had left for posterity a different sort of work from the one he had intended. At the time, Virdung was apparently still unemployed and still seeking a benefactor for the realization of his ambition to publish his comprehensive treatise "A German *Musica.*"

Documents relating to the life of Sebastian Virdung[34]

(1)   23 December 1483. Record of matriculation at the University of Heidelberg: "Sebastian from Amberg of the Regensburg diocese" (*Sebastimanus* [*sic*] *de Amberga Ratispon. dyoc.*).[35]

(2)   [After October] 1486. An entry in an account book of the printer Peter Drach of Speyer showing that he had sent five textbooks on the subject of jurisprudence (and would send two more) to "Sebastian Virdung from Nuremberg, the singer of my lord, the Count Elector of the Palatinate" (*dem senger mijnss hern pfalczgrauen Sebastianus Virdungen von Nornberg*), for which Virdung's father, the innkeeper of The Wild Man (*der wirt zum Wilden Man*) in Nuremberg, would pay him 12 florins.[36]

(3)   9 April 1489. A listing in the *Registrum presentacionum ducis Philipi* (*Inceptum a. 1477*) that the Elector of the Palatinate, Count Philip, had presented Virdung to the Bishop of the Eichstätt diocese (Wilhelm von Reichenau) as recipient of an ecclesiastical benefice: Virdung was to be made *pastor* at Legenfeld (in the Upper Palatinate), under the jurisdiction of Helfenburg castle.[37] Philip recommended that the position be awarded to "our beloved faithful Sebastian from Amberg, priest from the Regensburg diocese, [who is now] of age" (*discretum fidelum nostrum dilectum Sebastianum Virdung de Amberga clericum Ratispon. dioc.*).[38]

(4)   3 March 1490.[39] A notice that Count Philip had asked the civil authorities of Heidelberg to mediate a quarrel "between our chaplain at our Heidelberg castle, Herr Jorg,[40] and Bastian from Amberg, our singer" (*Zwuschen unsernn caplan zu Heidelberg uff unser burg Hern Jorgen und Bastian von Amberg unsern senger*).[41]

(5) and (6) *ca.* 1495.

(5)   A description of the benefices of the Palatinate listing the Lengenfeld position as held by "Sebastian from Amberg, Wenzel Grop's son" (*Sebastian von Amberg, Wentzel Groppen sone*).[42] (See documents relating to Virdung's father, p. 46 below). His salary was 100 gulden yearly minus 40 gulden per year due to absences.

(6)   A register of these benefices, identifying Sebastian Grop,

verus pastor, as present holder of the post at Legenfeld (*Ist itzunt hern Sebastian Grop verus pastor*).[43]

(7) 30 July 1500. A listing in Count Philip's *Registrum* that he had presented Virdung "to the altar of St. Peter in the citadel of Stahleck [Stalburg castle] near Steeg in the diocese of Trier" (*ad altare s. Petri in arce staleck prope Stege Treuir. dioc.*).[44]

(8) 31 July 1500.[45] Text of the contract written and signed by Virdung regarding his duties as a newly installed cleric at the castle of Stalburg, a post associated with the Heidelberg court:

How Herr Sebastian Virdung, Chaplain, registered himself for the Stalburg chaplaincy:

I, Sebastian Virdung from Amberg, priest of the Diocese of Eichstätt, do [hereby] acknowledge in my own handwriting that, since the most renowned noble prince and lord, Lord Philip, Count Palatine of the Rhine, Duke of Bavaria, Chief Cupbearer and Elector of the Holy Roman Empire, etc., my most gracious lord, has granted me St. Peter's altar in Stalburg Castle (in the diocese of Trier, under the jurisdiction of his grace's chapel at Heidelberg), in which a person celebrating the divine service is given an income with which he [Count Philip] has provided me, I have vowed and promised with [my] word of honor in lieu of an oath, to serve his princely grace and his gracious heirs faithfully, obediently, and piously in the chapel, at court, or wherever I am assigned at his princely grace's expense, [to serve] as a singer with the skill in music and [polyphonic] song (*gesang*) that God has granted me, and to execute my duties, and to arrange to read Mass on holy days, and to read Mass whenever God urges me. In addition, I shall and will not [go] from Heidelberg nor from the places to which I am assigned without permission or counsel from his princely grace, [unless] it be for one night or three or four unintentionally. [If I do leave,] then the board or food and clothing that I have had up to that time will be cut off. Or, should I become sick, the same will not be supplied. I shall and will [serve] the altar at Stalburg by reading Mass and having it read according to the instructions fully provided, so as not to degrade the worship service. And if I deceitfully do not hold to this [contract], or [if] without permission [I leave] Heidelberg or places to which I am assigned for over a month, or if I already have permission and overstay my leave without special new permission, [or if I engage in] any improper activity or otherwise [give] legitimate cause, then immediately, without any recourse, the said benefice of his princely grace shall revert to being empty and vacant, so that his princely grace may grant it and therewith present it to whomever or to whichever persons his princely grace desires, without my or anyone's unpleasantness. And if at any time present or future it should come to pass that I have resigned and given up the benefice voluntarily and freely, then I shall and will not recover, reaccept, or regain [the said position]; nor will I have myself absolved [from this contract]. Rather, I will hold fast and firmly to all these points, being his princely grace's faithful and beloved [servant], preserving his grace, carrying on piously and most faithfully, as well as keeping forever concealed whatever of his princely grace's words and secrets I might know or discover; all of this [I will do] loyally and without guile, and as further assurance [of my vow] I have hereby set my seal.

Dated on Friday after St. James the Holy Apostle's Day [31 July], AD 1500.[46]

(9) 12 October 1503.[47] A letter from Virdung to the Elector Count Philip's son, Prince Ludwig (who at Philip's death in 1508 became Count Ludwig V), during the latter's sojourn to the French court of Louis XII, then at Lyons:[48] *P184*

To the most illustrious noble prince and mighty lord, Ludwig, Count Palatine of the Rhine, Duke of Bavaria; to my gracious beloved lord, [delivered] into his princely grace's own hand:

I, along with Herr Hans Kargel,[49] Herr Jacob [Salzer],[50] and our colleagues, [we who] above all else are in [your] humble service, [are] always ready with complete humility to be bidden by your princely grace. Since your princely grace has thought to send us greetings by the agency of Meister Hans Hassfurt,[51] who has diligently done that (in which we rejoice and take consolation, each and every one of us, especially that your princely grace thought of us with favor), because of this we too most obligingly and humbly ask and pray that your grace will return in health and happiness.

Item: Gracious lord, Meister Hans Hassfurt brought a [book about] music with him that was given to him in Lyons. It is named and entitled with the name and title that your princely grace will find in the appended note. There is also another [book about] music made in France, the name of which is also there. I most humbly pray your princely grace, in order to honor your grace and lord's father [Count Philip] and the principality as well, to commission Herr Nicolas, your grace's chaplain,[52] to bring these [books] to me, or to all of us in the chapel, or better still to your lord and father's library, so that they can be read or seen by us. In your princely grace's honor, I wish you to call us to remembrance [who are at Heidelberg], where I would pray continually every day for your princely grace's long life, so that I may humbly serve you. Dated on Thursday after St. Dionysius's [Day], in 1503.

From your princely grace's humble chaplain,
Sebastian Virdung, singer[53]

The appended note reads as follows:[54]

Practica musice utriüsque cantus
excellentis franchini goffori
laudensis. quatüor libris
modulatissima.

(*The practice of music and both kinds of song* (i.e. chant and polyphonic
   music)
by the excellent Franchinus Gaffurius
from Lodi. Four books
most beautifully arranged.)

titülus primi capituli:
De introdüctorio ad müsicam exercitacionem necessario
caput primum sic incipit:
Et si hanc armoniam scienciam. titulus 2ⁱ capituli:
De sillabicis sonorum nominibus et earum distantijs.
caput 2m sic Incipit:
Septem tantum essenciales cordas.

(The title of the first chapter:
"Concerning an introduction necessary to the practice of music."
The first chapter begins as follows:
"And as this science of harmony . . . " The title of the second chapter:
"Regarding the syllable names of the notes and their intervals."
The second chapter begins as follows:
"As few as seven basic strings . . . ")[55]

The second [book on the subject of] music is not printed. Tinctoris or
Ockeghem wrote it, and it begins just like the [Grammar] by Donatus:
Partes prolacionis quae sunt ("The kinds of proportions that exist . . . ")[56]

(10)   7 November 1503.[57] In the extant reply to Virdung's
request, Prince Ludwig explains that neither book is available in
France:

Ludwig, etc. to [his] devoted and beloved excellent [members of the
chapel, Virdung, Salzer, and Karg]:
   We have understood your faithful and well intentioned written
suggestion, [which we have] accepted with thanks and pleasure. Your
request will not be forgotten. We have too many times longed to be there
at court for a day or two with [you in] your work with the chapel singers
and also with Meister Arnolt [Schlick] in [his work at] the organ,
together with our lord and father's trumpet players [i.e. the wind band?].
For, although we once judged the king's [i.e., Louis XII's] singers [to be]

37

extremely good, it seems to us nevertheless that the organs and wind instruments (*piffen*) that serve them are not as lovely and agreeable as these [at Heidelberg]. We do not know, however, whether we are correct [in this assessment] or not. The note that your Herr Bastian sent us we have shown to one of the royal singers [here], the good German man born at Neumarkt. He says that these books are not to be found in France but in Brabant, to which [place] we will not be traveling. Otherwise, we would gladly provide and sent them to you as you desire. [We ask for] nothing more than that from time to time [you] think of us while quaffing and toasting, and [that you] greet for us all those who ask about us with good will. Dated at Lyons, on Tuesday after All Saints' Day, 1503.

To the devoted, our beloved, excellent Herr Sebastian Virdung (*Vijrdong*), Herr Jacob Salzer, and Herr Hans Karg, singers, etc. together and separately.[58]

(11)   5 January 1504.[59] A letter from Virdung to Prince Ludwig in Lyons requesting that specific pieces of music by Ockeghem be sent to the chapel at Heidelberg:

To the most illustrious noble prince and mighty lord, Ludwig, the first-born and Count Palatine of the Rhine, Duke of Bavaria, my gracious beloved lord, into his princely grace's own hands.

Most illustrious noble prince, gracious lord. My humble services are always in obliging readiness to your princely grace. Gracius lord, [regarding] the polyphonic music (*gesang*) which your princely grace has sent us with Haberkorn[60] – a short four-voice motet in which each [voice] is a canon *a 2*[61] at the fifth and (also showing great skill) an excellent Mass for four [voices] to unite in singing, in which there are canons that are masterfully and skillfully done or worked out – I have presented all of these to my gracious lord, and [I have] sung them with my associates in his princely grace's place of residence. His princely grace was especially astonished that your princely grace occupies yourself with such matters. I have also often reread the letter that your princely grace sent to me, in which there is nothing on earth that is other than good, and I thought that on that account it could only come to please your princely grace's father, without disadvantage to your princely grace. [So,] to his astonishment I have shown his grace the letter, which his grace has thoroughly examined several times inside and out, [from] the seal [with your] name to all the details; but I did not want to conclude much [from this], for he examined it thoroughly on your grace's behalf.

Item: Gracious lord, a master of all composers was named Johannes Ockeghem, and as far as I know he is a prior at Tours, where St. Martin is buried or [where this saint] became a bishop.[62] He composed a motet of six voices. Each of the voices is a canon *a 6*, so that altogether [there are] 36 voices.[63] He also set a prolation Mass: it consists of two voices, each of which is a canon at the unison, at the third, at the fourth, at the fifth, at the sixth, at the seventh, [and] at the octave.[64] We have these two works here with us, as well as a Mass *cuiusvis toni*,[65] but all these works are written with mistakes; and I think that if your grace could arrange for the singer from Neumarkt to procure correct [copies] so that your princely grace can send them to my gracious lord [Count Philip], your grace will thereby especially please his princely grace. For there is no other joy or amusement better than making merry and singing behind the stove[66] in a heated room. And, inasmuch as it concerns [both] utility and pleasure to me, I express to your princely grace [my] immeasurable thanks, and the same from my associates as well; for we desire nothing else than to serve in all humility at your princely grace's bidding. And we commit ourselves totally to your princely grace, as we shall have committed your princely grace constantly in our prayers in all loving kindness.

Dated on Friday after New Year's Day, 1504.

Your princely grace's humble chaplain,

Sebastian Virdung, singer[67]

(12)   1 September 1506. Record of payment to *cantor Sebastianus de Haidelberg* by the cathedral chapter at Constance.[68]

(13)   9 January 1507. Record that *Sebastianus altista* joined the cathedral singers at Constance at succentor, having been released from duties as singer at the Württemberg court at Stuttgart.[69]

(14)   22 January 1507. Record that the duties of *Sebastianus Virdung altista* included "composing and teaching counterpoint to the choirboys" (*componieren oder die knaben contrapunct leren*).[70]

(15)   Early 1507. Documentation that Virdung journeyed to recruit some singers and choirboys for the cathedral establishment at Constance.[71]

(16)   12 March 1507. Record that Virdung had resigned his post as chaplain at Staleck.[72]

(17)   30 July 1507. Record that some of the choirboys at the Constance Cathedral were placed under Virdung's care.[73]

(18)   24 September 1507. Record that all choirboys at the cathedral were Virdung's responsibility. He was "in charge of board, instruction, and discipline" (*in tisch, ler und zucht zehalten*), and was to teach the boys singing.[74]

(19)   14 January 1508. Record of Virdung's dismissal from Constance on the grounds that he was "erratic and negligent [in his duties] with the boys" (*er irrig und mit den knaben unflyssig sye*).[75]

(20)   18 January 1508. Record that Virdung received a written dismissal from his position at Constance, that he was forgiven a debt of 10 florins, and that he had promised to take nothing with him from the cathedral – "no choirboy or other singer, no book or anything else belonging to the choir" (*weder knaben, ander senger, bücher oder anders zur sengery gehörend*).[76]

(21)   1 May 1508. Reference to Virdung's having paid to a man in Eichstätt the sum of 15 florins he owed to the cathedral chapter at Constance.[77]

(22)   30 November 1511. Arnolt Schlick's response to the request of his son, Arnolt Schlick the younger, that the renowned musician bring the fruits of his expertise with organ, lute, and song to all music lovers by publishing some intabulations. Both the son's request and the father's response were printed as a preface to the elder Schlick's *Tabulaturen Etlicher lobgesang und lidlein uff die orgeln und lauten* (Mainz: Peter Schöffer [the younger], 1512). The words of the father follow (see n. 23, p. 206 below):

[Sig. π2v] Dear son, I am most willingly obligated to share with you [my] paternal faithfulness and all that God has granted me in reason. But you wish from me, a poor blind man, too many great and almost impossible things, [things] which are accomplished with difficulty [even] by a fully-sighted person, especially since the corporeal eyes – together with the intellect – would have to be greatly taxed while occupied *in bringing to light what in this world has never before been heard of or seen.* [I refer] in particular [to] the *Tablature for organ and lute of some songs of praise and [some] short Lieder – with two [voices] to play and pluck and one voice to sing* [i.e., his *Tabulaturen Etlicher lobgesang und lidlein . . .*] – [which is] set in type and published by means of printing, [a process] which [applied to German lute and keyboard tablature] has never been seen, heard of, or understood before this time. For Father Sebastian Virdung, priest from Amberg *who boasts of sharp vision and high artistry* attempted this at Basel and [managed to produce] no more than one little song. *And [he did] not even [do this] by means of the true art of printing, but [he] merely had it cut completely in wood.*[78] *Even where it was done incorrectly, that cannot be blamed on the printers, for it could have been printed no other way than as it was written [by Sebastian].*

I report as follows on this print: [it is] so inartistic, so unrefined, so impossible and so corrupt that by me and others it is scorned, derided, berated, deprecated, exposed [for what it is], and its faults acknowledged – especially those that have been pointed out to me. In his little song that he intabulated for lute, and which is no more than thirty tempora in length, a review of sixteen of these [discloses] mistakes: impossible fingerings [sig. π3] are posited and taught; the sweet sound is unheeded [and] ignored; and [the intabulation is] written quite contrary to the nature of the sound made by the strings. Dear son, take care to examine the fourth, sixth, seventh, eighth, 10th, 11th, 15th, 18th, 19th, 20th, 22nd, 23rd, 26th, 27th, 28th, and the 29th [tempora]. I have been told the same by everyone: they are totally unrefined, inartistic, and corrupt. At times in one of these [measures], a number and a letter are set twice on a single course – as, for instance, o. 4. o. in the fourth tempus [in which three separate notes of the chord have to come from the same course!]. Now, from this you and anyone else can observe that he pretends to teach others [a subject] about which he himself is untutored and ignorant. [He shows this] by such [examples that are] impossible to finger and [which], upon hearing, do not satisfy the ears of knowledge-able people.

The same is true of all the above-mentioned tempora: they are defective, faulty, inartistic, impossible to finger, dissonant, discordant. And, for so short a little song by one who elevates himself above other artists and [who] passes himself off as a maestro making something special, [this song] is a mere patchwork, *for which reason he should not at all be ashamed to go back to school and learn [how to do it properly]*. He has done [it] too crudely, too hastily, too foolishly and carelessly, also too childishly and unskillfully.

I beg you by your good name to take this to heart and not to become so shameless in your purpose as to pretend to teach others something that you [yourself] have not yet learned, nor to believe [too much] in your intention or to trust too much your reason alone. Despise no one and you will remain undespised.

Furthermore, in the little song that the aforementioned Father Bastian has intabulated for the organ, notice especially the tenth, twelfth, and eighteenth tempora. What is true of [his] writing out of the [symbols] for the neck of the lute applies likewise to [his writing out of the symbols for] the keyboard of the organ. You too will find it as I [have had it] reported [to me]: as completely unmasterfully and crudely written out. *And with his [kind of] teaching and printing, it harms our times rather than serving them.* And since his inartistic, unrefined work [has] actually [been] published and is available [for all to consult], so that anyone with a little under-standing of music and the art of instruments can see this for himself, I will not delay you any longer. But where you, [or] Father Bastian, or anyone else might have doubts about what has been pointed out above and [what you or others] might not understand, upon request I will gladly show you and teach you about what I have said. [I will do this] in spite of Father Bastian's derisive slander and [his] print, especially wherein he reverses the title of my little book on the organ and most shamefully misinterprets it [i.e., *Mus. get.*, sig. E4v], which I nevertheless [am] not]altering] in [his] way; on the contrary, I have [sig. π3v] agreed to print a second [edition with] the same [title]. And also, when he thinks that had I known what the chromatic genus was, I would not have called it *musica ficta*, dear son, believe me, if Herr Bastian meant the Greek word *chromaticus* the way Tortellius and other Greeks knowledgeably interpreted it, then he is much better practiced than I [in Greek] and has used it daily. But if he means it as the musicians (*die musici*) [use it], and especially the [most] learned and expert of our authors – Johannes de Muris, Johannes de Felle, Johannes von Soest, Franchinus Gaffurius, etc. – these [authors] call it *musica ficta*, and they write a special chapter about *musica ficta*. But they were not as learned, especially in interpreting the Greek language, as Herr Bastian. So, as I see it, the difference between *musica ficta* and the chromatic genus is the same as [the difference] between the Rhine and the Main rivers in the essence of their waters when they come together at Mainz.

I must display a touch of anger about this matter not in order to smear anybody, but rather to bring the truth to light and also so that the rudeness [of Sebastian Virdung] will be taken into account, which his reputation does not excuse. For I did not deserve this insult on Herr Bastian's account – [*witness*] *that time at the great Diet in Worms*[79] *and at other places where I was helpful and of service to Herr Bastian, where his reputation and good name were applied to him* [*by me*] *in the presence of princes, lords, and other people of lesser rank* – and I should deservedly have been better rewarded for it.

But that having been neglected, I [will] take into consideration your admonition not to seek revenge – because, in addition, it is woman-like – and [I] will follow [your advice] and further carry out your wishes. And if things are as you hear [them] from me, why then do you tempt me by laying upon me this heavy burden? For if indeed I were willing with reason to produce such a thing, I would nevertheless always question [whether] the printer sometimes set a white note for a black one, a breve for a semibreve, a fusa for a semifusa, an *a* for a *b*, [whether] at times he omitted [a character] or extracted [one and] incorrectly inserted [another] and then had it printed. As a result of these errors, you and I would be derided and perhaps condemned without our being at fault. But, taking leave of this matter and complying with the plea and lofty exhortation from you, my beloved son, I will (inasmuch as it is possible for me) undertake to make settings and intabulations for the organ and lute of some polyphonic pieces (*gesang*) and little songs that are easy to sing, [presenting] these as a beginning and as a demonstration. And so that you can review them and prepare them for printing, I herewith have entrusted [them] to you. [Sig. π4] Wherever you find a glaring error, make it intelligible; and – along with those who asked you to procure such of me to publish it as [something] worthy, serviceable, and useful – let it be printed after [the corrections have been made] and not before. And now that I know this will be diligently carried out – to be pleasurable and beneficial to the whole world and helpful to God – I will subsequently notate and intabulate another work for several more instruments and with more rigorous exercises. Also, in addition to this [work] that I have begotten, [I will] tell more clearly than in this [present] publication why, where, how, and in what points Herr Bastian in his new *English Musica*[80] has made a flawed, inartistic, unrefined, impossible, and corrupt work – [one] in which he also slanders and offends me without identification, without validity, without any grounds whatsoever, [and] he excused it, defended it, and published it. And I ask you and all those who receive this – my first experiment – not to look at it unfairly, but rather to regard it with happy eyes and a generous temperament, to give it heed, to scrutinize and examine it thoroughly. And where something has been written, set in type, and printed inexpertly, without refinement, or corruptly by me, or [where something] has been overlooked by the typesetters, printers, and proof-readers, [I ask you] to correct and emend it in a brotherly manner and not with jealous vengeance. And give priority to my warm-heartedness toward you, my son, rather than to the thing [itself] that is newly made, thereby considering it leniently and defending it. With that may I be set free from your request. Be commended to God, who will long preserve your life in honor. Dated on St. Andrew the Apostle's Day, 1511.[81]

There follows on sig. π4v a poem by Schlick written as if this book were speaking to the reader:

Musicians, singers, organists,
Lutenists as well,
You who are lovers of true art:
Come, I beg of you the favor
To look at me and learn [from me] with diligence.
Scholars and gray[-haired] masters too,
Where I have erred, make corrections,
And be not so quick to jealously deride [me]
As Bastian Virdung has done.
His own work gives him his reward, [the treatise]
That he made so difficult [from which] to learn.
[For] anyone may see and note for himself
Whether he can finger on the lute

L. c. 4. kk., as [Bastian] thought.
And one finds many similar cases
Where he missed the mark
In his music, which he himself fancies
Is fashioned with art and style.
And, as I understand it,
Michael Furter had it printed at Basel.
Here begins my first piece: "Salve."[82]

(23)   1536. Othmar Luscinius's dedication in *Musurgia seu praxis musicae* (Strassburg: Johann Schott, 1536; repr. 1542);

[Sig. a2] To the noble Lord Andreas Calvo of Milan, [from] Othmar Luscinius: Greetings.

Greatest honor is most justly owed to you from all people, O noble Andreas, because of your highest learning and [because of] your other distinguished virtues. Above all, your diligence, by which you have delivered ancient written records (*monumenta librorum*) from destruction by having them printed, wins for you great commendation and immense favor among scholars, and with rich seed you sow a new growth of talent in the world. For, just as (in my opinion) it is of no less merit to have performed brilliant deeds than to have written about the deeds with a fertile pen – so that you might find not a few (if one of these were to be chosen) who would prefer to be a Homer than [to be] an Achilles – so [likewise] I should have thought that those who, like Jupiter, "produce offspring from the head" when they embellish literature with some fresh production [i.e., scholar writers] have no less regard for the welfare of the entire commonwealth of letters than those who then receive a child of this sort into their bosom and nourish it [i.e., scholar publishers]. At length they thrust it forth into the light of day, printed from their own resources or at their own expense in a large number of copies [lit., "in a thousand copies"], and in so great a proliferation of books, they do this precisely so that it might not be a case of "blind wealth," as they say. And therefore I do not know who is most responsible [for the fact] that we have a great many silent masters [i.e., printed books] at home (as it is said in the proverb) with whom we may associate both day and night for the sake of enlivening our intellectual abilities: the authors themselves who have produced these [books] for us, or those by whose resources they have been kept intact up to the present day. Therefore, since, under your leadership, various and sundry distinguished books – like the dauntless warriors from the wooden horse – have repeatedly come forth from the shop of Johann Schott, the extraordinarily skillful printer, [sig. a2v] you graciously encouraged me in earlier days to translate the little book about musical instruments by Sebastian Virdung from German to Latin so that it could also be read by foreign scholars of music. Yet [it was] on this condition: that I should be free from that faithfulness to the original which is required of most translators, and that permission be granted to me (provided I might expect as much from the reader) to differ considerably from the author. Now, to encourage me to do it more freely, you put forward the example of many who had labored to renew the books of others, not without renown. This [is] what you thought would be worth my work in the case of this little book, to which, as may be deduced from unmistakable signs, the finishing hand simply did not extend [i.e., the completed or intended product was not achieved], since Sebastian was prematurely taken away from the living. You said, therefore, that it was quite unlikely that I would ever be blamed if anywhere I should depart with good reason from Sebastian's meaning; on the contrary, [you said] I would even gain considerable thanks from scholars for doing this. For you thought it was unlikely that anyone would embrace this work (whatever it is) more eagerly because it was translated with the greatest care than because it seemed useful in some respect at least. Although at first I thought that it would be contrary to my sense of duty to build an edifice at my own inclination on another's land, and, in the second place, that the time which I had determined to devote to more serious studies I should lose in gathering up these lighter twigs, nevertheless, I was at length overcome by the desire to please you, O best of men, and [to please] all scholars of music as well. And indeed, at the very outset of this work of mine (in order to respond to your wishes), the plumb line of Sebastian quite ingeniously coincided with the lines of my own building. But when I repeatedly sought digressions, one after another, to blend together the practical and the pleasant, somehow or other what began as a wine jar (*amphora*) has now at length turned out as a water pot (*urceus*). [Sig. a3] Henceforth I will delay the gentle reader no more on this account. And it does not make much difference under whose name these dialogues are read – however much fashioned by our own wit – whether that of Sebastian and Andreas, since the beginning of the little book fits them, or that of Othmar and Bartholomew Stoffler. For he is my fellow countryman, a man not a little skilled in letters and in the subject of music. Indeed, trusting in that same fellowship with him [as between Sebastian and Andreas], we have conversed most happily in stolen hours, [touching upon] many things about music – which [things] I shall never be ashamed to have written about, and which will not, I am confident, burden the reader (unless by chance he should be extremely fastidious). Therefore I have warned [you], lest I seem to have substituted a corrupted text [lit., "a bastard child"] for Sebastian's [own], making public his name for that which he himself had not written at all. May you be in good health, most excellent man. At Strassburg, AD 1536.[83]

45

Besides these documents we know of several relating to Sebastian Virdung's father. Peter Drach's 1486 identification of the elder Virdung as innkeeper at the Wild Man in Nuremberg has been noted above (doc. no. 2). In addition we have the following:

(24)   21 August 1469. A reference in the records of Emperor Frederick III that he had presented *Wernczlein Vierdung* with two coats of arms, one with the name *Grop*, all male members of the family with this name having died.[84]

(25)   2 August 1475. Record that the elder Virdung/Grop obtained burgher status in Amberg.[85]

(26)   1486. Record that *Wenntzlaw Vierdung von Amberg* became a burgher of Nuremberg.[86]

3   The publication history of
Musica getutscht

Musica getutscht survives in two separate editions, the original of 1511 (source of all facsimile editions to date) and a copy brought out sometime before 1521. Following Edwin Ripin's designations, scholars generally refer to the former as "printing A" and the latter as "printing B."[1] As noted above in Chapter 2, although neither edition indicates printer or date of publication, the author's dedication (sig. A2v) gives Basel as the original place of publication and 15 July as the date that Sebastian Virdung presented this part of the copy to his printer.[2] Internal evidence (the type font, initials, and ornamental borders) as well as external evidence (Schlick's identification in his *Tabulaturen Etlicher lobgesang*)[3] point to Michael Furter as the man responsible for bringing the first edition of this work to the public.[4] Since the passage in which Schlick named Furter was dated 30 November 1511, the publication date of *Musica getutscht* can be placed in that year between 15 July, when Virdung presented his dedication to Furter, and sometime before the following fall. An estimated date of middle or late summer would thus allow time for the blind organist to have gained access to *Musica getutscht*, to have had it read to him, and to have prepared a response by the end of November.

The format of *Musica getutscht* requires comment, as it has been described variously as quarto,[5] octavo,[6] and even duodecimo.[7] Made up of sheets of paper folded twice, with signatures in groups of four, and bound so that the width is greater than the height of the book and so that the watermarks appear in the top margin (albeit cut in two and trimmed from binding), Virdung's treatise is unquestionably in oblong quarto format.[8] Its dimensions, however, are somewhat small. The source of ambiguity in this regard stems from the fact that among present-day publishers, terminology used in describing format – how the book is put together in gatherings of folded sheets of paper – can refer as well to the size of a book, irrespective of the way each sheet of paper is folded. The true bibliographic format of this treatise, however, is quarto. It was so described by the sixteenth-century bibliographer Ferdinand Columbus,[9] as well as by Michael Praetorius in the seventeenth century,[10] and – for the sake of historical and bibliographic accuracy – so should it be today.

Rivaling the importance of the typeset text of *Musica getutscht* are the many woodcut illustrations that advance Virdung's exposition of his material on musical instruments. Throughout the treatise, our author amplifies his verbal instructions with explanatory pictures, diagrams, charts, and musical examples. Most scholars have assumed all the woodcuts to be by the eminent sixteenth-century Swiss artist Urs Graf,[11] on the basis of the single illustration in the print signed by him – the lutenist on sig. I2v (p. 149 below). But the crudeness of most of the remaining cuts has caused others to doubt this assumption. Edwin Ripin, for example, argued that Graf made only the one cut that bears his monogram.[12] Tilman Seebass, on the other hand, offered the opinion that Graf was responsible for those that demonstrate superior artistic quality, having left to assistants those illustrations and diagrams that could merely be copied from whatever models Virdung or Furter provided.[13] Representing the other side of the controversy – namely, that Graf did all the woodcuts himself – is Dr. Frank Hieronymus, former Curator of Rare Books at the Universitätsbibliothek at Basel. His point of view is based upon familiarity with Graf's larger output in books of the time as well as knowledge of the situation regarding illustration of all books emanating from printing establishments in Basel in 1511.[14] Hieronymus reminds us that Graf was hired to carry out Virdung's and Furter's pictorial intentions quickly and cheaply, not to produce artistic masterpieces. Graf, like other illustrators of books at that time and place, was entirely capable of "hack work." That he successfully accomplished his task is attested to by the faithfulness with which these illustrations were copied in subsequent editions and adaptations of *Musica getutscht.*

The second edition of *Musica getutscht*, printing B, represents a fairly faithful imitation of the first: it is in the same small oblong quarto format, with the same number of pages in the straightforward collation A–O4, having basically the same distribution of text on each page, and incorporating woodcuts so similar to the originals in size and content that they were in all likelihood traced from the printed page onto paper and then reversed on the wood-block in order to replicate the model closely. Differences between the two printings are easily discernible, however, showing that another printer brought out this copy of the work by Virdung, Furter, and Graf. In the first place, the type font used for printing B is not the same as that for printing A. Then too, the new type-setter used his own spellings rather than slavishly following the prototype; therefore the spacings of words are somewhat at variance from those of the original. In addition, he changed several terms. These reflect a local usage that differed from that of Virdung and his compositors. For example, the compositor of printing B substituted *afftermontag* for the original *zinstag* ("Tuesday") (sig. A2v), *heb an* for *fang an* ("begin") (sig. E3v), *aylff* for *aynlaff* (*ainlaff* in printing A2)[15] ("eleven") (sig. M2), and *oft* for *dick* ("often") (sig. N3). He also corrected a few mistakes,[16] added some of his own,[17] and copied others.[18]

A more immediately apparent difference can be seen in the new, more elaborate title page. Unlike the first edition, which had the lengthy title enclosed within a frame made up of five separate reusable border pieces, printing B features an artistic woodcut compartment around a truncated title (omitting reference to the dedicatee), an enclosure that was specially designed and executed for this print.[19] The artist fashioned the handsome compartment out of most of the original illustrations of individual instruments that Virdung had included within his categories of acceptable musical instruments. (Omission of the keyboard instruments from the new border is most likely to have stemmed from their large size and, therefore, their poorer adaptability to graceful design.) The elegance and artistry of this title page contrast with the haphazard quality of the title page of printing A.[20] The inferior design of the earlier title page may be attributed to its combination of obviously uncoordinated ornamental borders, with the bottom two placed sideways instead of right-side-up, although this informal style of embellishment was standard for publications in Basel at the time of the original printing.[21] In addition, the use of red ink for three lines of text on the title page of B (a feature which required double printing on one side of the first sheet) enhances the decorative effect of this part of printing B as compared with that of A.

In other respects, however, printing B shows inferiority when compared with the original. The most obvious sign of corruption can be seen in the serious mistake in imposition on the first sheet of the second edition. Instead of beginning the text proper on signature A4v (leading to its continuation on the next page – i.e., on sig. B), the typesetter of printing B started the treatise on sig. A2, the leaf following the title page. Having omitted the arms of the dedicatee on sig. Av, the printer may have intended to leave out the dedication as well. However, the typesetter inserted both the dedication and the introduction, as well as the portrait of the author and his partner in dialogue, *between* the beginning of the text on sig. A2 and its continuation in sig. B. Thus, although the special decorative title page provides evidence of care in preparing this edition, the blunder in imposition points to hastiness of production and carelessness on the part of the person who placed the typeset pages into the formes (see the diagram on p. 51). The error in sequence of material of edition B may be easily understood from a comparison of the first nine signatures of the two prints given below:

PRINTING A	signature	PRINTING B
Title page	A	Title page
Arms of the dedicatee	Av	Blank
Dedication	A2	Beginning of text
Introduction	A2v	Woodcut portrait
Introduction, continued	A3	Dedication
Introduction, concluded	A3v	Introduction
Woodcut portrait	A4	Introduction, continued
Beginning of text	A4v	Introduction, concluded
Continuation of text	B	Continuation of text

Thus, on the first sheet (prior to folding), only the title pages of the two editions correspond. In an attempt to relate the now widely separated sections of the treatise proper, the typesetter of the second edition added a heading at the start of sig. B: *Sebastianus spricht.* He then forgot the name of the other character in the dialogue (or, if he was a second typesetter, he did not know

A comparison of signature A in the two editions of *Musica getutscht*

Printing A — outer forme

A3	A4v
Introduction Continued *(inverted)*	Beginning of Text *(inverted)*
Introduction	Title
A2v	A

Printing B — outer forme

A3	A4v
Dedication *(inverted)*	Introduction Concluded *(inverted)*
Woodcut	Title
A2v	A

outer forme

Printing A — inner forme

A4	A3v
Woodcut *(inverted)*	Introduction Concluded *(inverted)*
Arms	Dedication
Av	A2

Printing B — inner forme

A4	A3v
Introduction Continued *(inverted)*	Introduction *(inverted)*
[Blank]	Beginning of Text
Av	A2

inner forme

Printing A   Printing B

the name) and wrote *Alexander fragt,* instead of identifying him simply as *A*, as in the original.

In other respects as well, the printer of B cut corners to save time and money. This can be seen in the illustrations, which, being obviously more quickly done than the originals, may have cost relatively less to produce. Most of the illustrations in printing B, for example, have simpler lines, showing less attention to detail and less precision on the parts of tracer and cutter[22] than was demonstrated by the artist (or artists) who executed the woodcuts in printing A. This is dramatically evident in the copy of the lutenist found on sig. I2v. The tracer/cutter (who acknowledged his source by copying the monogram of Urs Graf – this in addition to identifying himself as well with the initials CH)[23] stylized most of the lines used for shading. He thereby obscured features of the figure, his clothing, and his setting. Unable or unwilling to reproduce quickly the elaborate border pieces forming a three-sided frame around the cut, furthermore, CH substituted a stark border consisting of a simple double line.[24] Other examples of laxity can be cited as well: in one instance, the cutter failed to invert several letters in a diagram (sig. K3); thus they appear upside down. In another, a woodcut was placed upside down in the forme (sig. C4v).

Internal evidence of watermarks, orthography, and the linguistic substitutions mentioned above (p. 49) point to Augsburg as the place of publication for printing B.[25] The use of a double outline around the copied woodcut of the lutenist on signature I2v (instead of decorative border pieces framing the original cut – the style characteristic of Basel publications) presents further evidence of an Augsburg provenance.[26] Since the type font used in this second printing of *Musica getutscht* matches that employed by Johann Schönsperger the younger,[27] who was active as a printer in Augsburg between 1510 and 1523,[28] it is now generally assumed that he was responsible for this second edition.[29]

The date of printing B is more difficult to ascertain. We know that the edition of *Musica getutscht* that Ferdinand Columbus purchased at Nuremberg in December of 1521 must have been a copy of the second printing, because of a detailed entry in one of his catalogues of books in which he carefully outlined the mistaken imposition.[30] *Musica getutscht* printing B had to have been published, therefore, sometime between 1511 and 1521.[31]

One further bibliographic detail requires comment. Extant copies of the first edition show two typesettings of the second half of the book. This difference was noted upon comparison of the two exemplars in the British Library, in which signatures I through O departed from each other in orthography and exact placement of text.[32] Thus, we need to distinguish between printings A1 and A2 of the first edition. A watermark different from the ones that appear consistently in A1 (this one carried only by the differently set sheets) corroborates this distinction and indicates that A2 appeared later than A1.[33] A hitherto unnoticed fact, however, is that one side of one sheet in the differently set half of the book has the first typesetting throughout. In all copies of A1 and A2, the inner formes of sheet N (that is, sigs. Nv, N2, N3v, and N4) have the same typesetting (albeit in variant states),[34] while the outer formes (sigs. N, N2v, N3, and N4v) differ.[35] Since A2 is demonstrably later than A1, and since the woodcuts for both are the same, it is highly unlikely that Furter used two presses at the same time to speed the process of manufacture. Some economic factor or problem in production must have induced Furter to reduce the size of the run after the full number of signatures A through H had been printed. The extra sheets were then stored until conditions improved and the project could be completed. It may well be that the supply of paper had dwindled temporarily, a not uncommon occurrence, since the raw materials – good linen rags – were often in short supply.[36] Alternatively, Furter may for some reason have lost confidence in the profitability of his venture. Since paper represented the single highest-cost item of production, he may have decided to cut down his initial risk, choosing to store the incomplete portions of *Musica getutscht* until the market became more promising. In any event, one of the press operators apparently forgot this decision and printed the original number of one side of sheet N. These extras were then kept, along with the remaining sheets carrying signatures A through H, until the rest of the book could be reset and put to press.

Of the fifteen extant copies of *Musica getutscht*, seven are of printing A1, two are of A2, and six are of printing B:

PRINTING A1

Basel, Öffentliche Bibliothek der Universität, k k II 27 (incomplete copy, sigs. I and K only)

Berlin, Staatsbibliothek Preussischer Kulturbesitz, Musikabteilung, Mendelssohn-Archiv, Mus. ant. theor. V 30 (complete copy)

Boston, Public Library, M. 149a.71 (complete copy, the illustrations hand-colored in tints contemporary with *Musica getutscht*)

Edinburgh, Reid Music Library, C 186 (incomplete copy, lacking leaves O2, O3, and O4)

London, The British Library, M.K. 8. c. 9 (complete copy)

Munich, Bayerische Staatsbibliothek, Musiksammlung, 4° Mus. Th. 1616 (complete copy)

Nuremberg, Bibliothek des Germanischen National-Museums, 8° M 80 (incomplete copy, lacking signatures A through B and leaves C1, C2, and K4)

PRINTING A2

London, The British Library, Hirsch I. 594 (incomplete copy, lacking leaves B2 and D3)

Wolfenbüttel, Herzog-August-Bibliothek, Musikabteilung, 43 Musica Helmst. (complete copy)

PRINTING B

Den Haag, Gemeentemuseum, 4 D 26 (complete copy)

Innsbruck, Universitätsbibliothek. 175.E.23 (complete copy)

Karlsruhe, Badische Landesbibliothek, 42 A 1804 RH (complete copy)

Vienna, Gesellschaft der Musikfreunde, 847/135 (incomplete copy, lacking sig. A and leaves O1 and O4)

Vienna, Österreichische Nationalbibliothek, S.A. 71 F. 68 (complete copy)

Wolfenbüttel, Herzog-August-Bibliothek, Musikabteilung, 4 Musica (complete copy)

Some measure of the popularity enjoyed by *Musica getutscht* can be gauged by the dissemination of its contents (as a whole and in part) throughout much of continental Europe in the half century or so following its appearance at Basel in 1511. The second edition meant that a great enough demand existed in the years prior to 1521 for Schönsperger in Augsburg to copy the work as a whole, including the many woodcut illustrations and diagrams. Yet, interest in this little treatise extended beyond the boundaries of German-speaking countries. We have seen that the Spaniard Ferdinand Columbus acquired a copy of the second edition on a trip to Nuremberg in 1521. He did this despite the weakness of his

German-language ability, as his translation of the title into Latin attests: *Musica theutonica sebastiani virdvarg* [*sic*] *de omni cantu & notulis intabulaturarum traducta horum quattuor* [*sic*] *instrumentorum vz. organi luttine sive laud & fistule* . . . [37] We have also seen that two Milanese bookseller/publishers, Francesco and Andreas Calvo, sought to provide access to the contents of *Musica getutscht* for their learned clientele in Italy and other non-German-speaking areas by having this treatise translated into Latin (see pp. 32–3 above). For this they engaged the musical and linguistic expertise of Othmar Luscinius. The resultant work, *Musurgia seu praxis musicae*, though completed *ca.* 1517, was published in 1536.[38]

In addition to having inspired an adaptation into the international scholarly language of Latin some five or six years after its publication, Virdung's *Musica getutscht* was also modified and translated into two other regional European vernaculars, Netherlandic and French. Neither of these works carries identification of the translator or acknowledgment of the original source. We know the French treatise from a unique copy still in the library of Ferdinand Columbus.[39] Its title is as follows: *Livre plaisant et tres utile pour apprendre a fair & ordonner toutes tabulatures hors le discant, dont & par lesquelles lon peult facilement et legierement aprendre a jouer sur les Manicordion, Luc, et Flutes* (*A Pleasant Book, and very useful for learning how to make and prepare all tablatures from the discant* [i.e., mensural notation], *whereby and by means of which one can easily and quickly learn to play the clavichord, lute, and recorders*). Publication of this volume by Willem Vorsterman (active *ca.* 1504–43) took place at Antwerp on 12 October 1529, and Columbus bought his copy, he tells us, in Brussels in 1531. We have access to the Netherlandic work in two exemplars of separate printings also from Antwerp – this time by Jan van Ghelen the younger (active *ca.* 1544–83) – one brought out in 1554 and the other in 1568. This work bears the title *Dit is een seer schoon Boecxken, om te leeren maken alderhande tabulatueren wten Discante. Daer duer men lichtelijck mach leeren spelen opt Clavecordium luyte ende Fluyte* (*This is a Very Beautiful Book for learning how to make all kinds of tablatures from discant* [i.e., mensural notation], *by which one can easily learn to play the clavichord, lute, and recorder*) (see plates 1 and 2, pp. 82–3 below).[40]

The texts of the *Livre plaisant* (hereafter abbreviated as *Livre*) and *Dit is een seer schoon Boecxken* (referred to in this study as *Dit*), correspond so extensively that one of them is obviously a translation of the other. The earlier date of the extant French copy would suggest that it formed the basis of the Netherlandic version. To date most scholars have made this assumption.[41] Linguistic evidence, however, unequivocally shows the French to be a translation of the Netherlandic. Comparison of the two reveals that the translator (or translators) of *Dit* followed the language of *Musica getutscht* quite strictly, whereas the person who made the French version followed the Netherlandic adaptation.[42] The adaptor of Virdung's *opus* into Netherlandic often chose cognates, and some of these proved to be inappropriate equivalents. A particularly striking example of the use of an incorrect cognate occurs in the passage describing the monochord as so named because of its single string (*Mus. get.*, sig. E2v; *Dit*, sig. A2v). The original German reads *sait* for "string"; the Netherlandic renders it as *side*, meaning "side," rather than the correct *snar*. The French translation has *cotez*, or "side" (*Livre*, sig. A2). Thus, the sentence has become meaningless in both Netherlandic and French: "The monochord is so named because of its single side." In other cases the French translator tried to make sense of a passage obscured by too literal a rendering of the German into Netherlandic, with varying degrees of success (see below, e.g., p. 87). In addition, throughout the treatise the French translator often provided two words or phrases in *Livre* for one in *Dit*. This can be seen, for example, in the titles. In the French version, the concept of *schoon* was extended from "pleasant" to "very useful" as well. Not content with the Netherlandic infinitive "to make," the adaptor added "and prepare" to the title in French. Again, the concept "easily learn" became in the French "easily and quickly learn." The most obvious evidence that *Livre* derived from *Dit* and not the reverse, however, comes from the fact that whoever prepared the latter lifted the Latin terminology and phrases verbatim from *Musica getutscht*, whereas the person responsible for *Livre* translated all the Latin into French. Then too, the clinching detail would have to be the inclusion in both *Livre* and *Dit* of a musical work of Netherlandish provenance with a Netherlandic text, "Een vrolijk wesen" – a work that does not appear in the German version – for the demonstrations of intabulation.[43] The French translation of the text of this song in *Livre* does not fit with the music.[44]

Thus it is clear that an edition of *Dit* must have existed at the very latest from the year 1529 (the publication date of its French descendant), more probably sometime before that date. Since Vorsterman printed twin versions of other works in Netherlandic and French, some within the very same year,[45] he may have done *Dit* and *Livre* together as well. But since the text of *Livre* indicates no contact on the part of the translator with either *Musica getutscht* itself or the person who had earlier adapted Virdung's work into Netherlandic, we can assume that some time must have elapsed between printings of these two books, perhaps even a year or so. Therefore, a plausible date to conjecture for *Dit* would be *ca.* 1528. It is most likely, then, that when Ferdinand Columbus bought his copy of *Livre* at Brussels in 1531 – ten years after he had purchased a copy of the parent treatise – he had a choice of French or Netherlandic. Although it is possible that Vorsterman brought out both,[46] he may have collaborated on these works with Jan van Ghelen the elder (active from 1519 to 1533), as they had in *ca.* 1527.[47] Jan van Ghelen the younger then continued to print later editions of *Dit* as the supply ran out but demand remained.

Wide dissemination of portions of *Musica getutscht* during the sixteenth century, then, was achieved through an abbreviated and modified translation into Netherlandic, which was subsequently converted into French, and through an independent though related treatise in Latin. The first of the twin vernacular works (*Dit*) appeared initially sometime between 1511 (the date of *Musica getutscht*(and sometime prior to 12 October 1529 (the date of the only extant French exemplar). *Dit*, and perhaps *Livre* as well, went through an unknown number of further editions, of which we know two: the 1554 and 1568 printings of *Dit*. The Latin work, *Musurgia*, although not published until 1536, had been requested and completed at an earlier date, by *ca.* 1517. Since both of these two reworkings of *Musica getutscht* (i.e., *Dit* and *Musurgia*) represent offspring of Virdung, Furter, and Graf's effort rather than that of Schönsperger and his shop[48] – indeed, *Musurgia* even has the very woodcuts used in the original printing of Virdung's work – we may postulate that the second edition (printing B) dates from later in the period between 1511 and 1521, probably *post* 1517. With Furter – and, in all likelihood, Virdung as well – dead by 1517, Schönsperger could have felt free to publish the fruit of their labors. It must be acknowledged in this regard, however, that the concept of ownership of rights to a given publication was in its infancy in 1511. At that time very few works had protective privileges, Arnolt Schlick's case (see above, p. 31) being decidedly anomalous. Lacking an Imperial privilege, therefore, *Musica getutscht* could have been pirated with impunity at any time after its initial appearance.[49] For in the first century after invention of the printing press, the traditional view characteristic of the manuscript age continued to hold sway – that is, that proliferation by copying was the norm. The economic and moral problems connected with this approach when applied to mechanically reproduced books were only beginning to be seriously addressed at the time Virdung, Furter, and Graf produced *Musica getutscht*.[50]

Besides the two reworkings of *Musica getutscht* discussed above, one further sixteenth-century publication depended heavily upon Virdung's treatise. This was *Musica instrumentalis deudsch* by Martin Agricola. The author's preface dates from St. Bartholomew's Day (24 August) 1528, but the printer, George Rhau of Wittenberg (1488–1548) – to whom Agricola dedicated this book – published four editions, in 1529, 1530, 1532, and 1542.[51] Agricola brought out an enlarged and completely revised version in 1545, also published by and dedicated to Rhau,[52] in which Agricola continued his unacknowledged indebtedness to Virdung. It was, however, the initial version of *Musica instrumentalis deudsch* that derived so extensively from *Musica getutscht*. Although his organization of the material differed from that of the prototype, in his approach to the subject as well as in his choice of content (see below, pp. 72–8), Agricola followed the lead of Virdung. Indeed, so successful were Virdung and his illustrator's woodcuts that Agricola and Rhau had them copied quite faithfully, obvious mistakes and all.

Thus the pioneering venture of an obscure singer/priest and an adventurous printer in the early sixteenth century sent ripples throughout Western Europe during the next half century. This was due, no doubt, to Virdung and Furter's responsiveness to the tenor of the times. However, we must give some credit as well to the advantaged position of Basel, the city from which this little yet influential work emanated. Basel's standing as a center of trade routes spreading to the north, east, south, and west of Europe is reflected in the path of *Musica getutscht* as it went through duplication, imitation, translation, and adaptation. Spokes from a giant wheel of commerce radiated from this European capital. Basel linked Milan (place of business for Francesco and Andreas Calvo, the booksellers who requested Luscinius's translation of *Musica getutscht*) with Strassburg (city of Othmar Luscinius and Johann Schott, the author and printer of *Musurgia*); Basel sent forth its products and influence eastward to Augsburg (site of production of *Musica getutscht*, printing B) and northward to Magdeburg and Wittenberg (where both editions of *Musica instrumentalis deudsch* had their birth); it broadcast its wealth of intellectual and material goods northwest along the Rhine toward Antwerp (where Vorsterman and van Ghelen converted *Musica getutscht* into books suitable for their French- and Netherlandic-speaking customers).

After this process of dissemination had dissipated in the latter half of the sixteenth century, however, copies of the little volume and its offspring lay dormant in libraries, the attractive pictures probably saving them from total oblivion as their contents became obsolete.

We meet *Musica getutscht* next in 1619, when Michael Praetorius (1571–1621) cites it as the only source he could find regarding ancient instruments.[53] He does not give it much credence in this regard, however, for two reasons. First, the book is not old enough to offer reliable information about Biblical instruments. Second, the drawings of these instruments (i.e., the instruments of Jerome) do not give the information necessary to comprehend either their characteristics or their method of use. In his words:

It would be most desirable to know today exactly what kinds of musical instruments and ecclesiastical instruments there were at the time of David and Solomon, as well as before their time and afterwards – how each was formed, tuned, and made, according to its own type – and to be able to have them in use at present. Unfortunately, however, such [knowledge] has come down to us in no antique sources; therefore, the ancient music of instruments has remained so little known – even completely unknown – to us. In some libraries one finds a book [that was] printed in quarto at Basel in 1511 AD. In it are illustrated some ancient as well as some modern instruments. But this work is not all that old; and, in addition, the use and nature of the illustrated [ancient] instruments cannot specifically be learned from it.[54]

Praetorius hereby echoes the very objections voiced by Virdung to including these instruments within his consideration: that he has neither heard nor seen them, and that he has no idea how or for what purpose they were used (sig. D3, p. 118 below). Like Virdung before him, however, Praetorius does include these fantastic artifacts in his treatise, explaining that

Since I was unable to obtain any [other] account or information about them – how these instruments that are unknown to us at present were formed and used – I have thought it necessary to quote here word for word the descriptions [of these instruments] from this book.[55]

Praetorius then quotes from *Musica getutscht* (though updating the language and paraphrasing somewhat) about the instruments of Jerome.[56] He also includes Virdung's assessment of the musical instruments of his day, along with the earlier author's opinion of "foolish instruments."[57] Earlier in the treatise, Praetorius had quoted Virdung on another ancient instrument, the monochord, as well as its descendant, the clavichord.[58]

Virdung's treatise and its progeny again lay in obscurity until, at the end of the eighteenth century, Charles Burney and John Hawkins mentioned Luscinius's *Musurgia* in their histories of music. Burney devoted a paragraph to describing the contents of the first book of the treatise, the one on musical instruments, from the 1542 edition.[59] Hawkins, on the other hand, presented a lengthy synopsis of this same part of the 1536 edition. He dedicated five of his large pages of text to this subject, including copies of all of the illustrations of the instruments that Virdung had considered in use in his day in his land – all, that is, except for bells. Hawkins also chose to reproduce neither the Jerome instruments nor the hammer and anvil, nor any of the diagrams from the self-instruction sections of the treatise.[60]

In the nineteenth century, some scholars addressed aspects of the subject matter of *Musica getutscht*, but it was not until 1882, when Robert Eitner published the first facsimile edition, that the entire treatise became available for more general scholarly consultation.[61] Study of the derivative works has been facilitated by recent facsimiles of all but one of them – *Musurgia*.[62] Taken together, these works provide valuable literary and visual clues to understanding both musical instruments and instrumental performance practices as they evolved in the first half of the sixteenth century.

4   The offspring of *Musica getutscht*

We have seen that within the first two decades after its publication, *Musica getutscht* generated two adaptations into other languages (*Musurgia* and *Dit*) and a direct translation of the second of these into yet another language (*Livre*). We have also seen that Virdung's treatise lived on as well in a German work by Martin Agricola: *Musica instrumentalis deudsch*. The authors of these four derivative works selected some of the elements contained in *Musica getutscht* and presented these in contexts that differed from the original.

"Musurgia seu praxis musicae" by Othmar Luscinius

Othmar Luscinius – noted scholar, musician, and theologian – produced the earliest offspring of *Musica getutscht* in his Latin treatise, *Musurgia seu praxis musicae*. The manuscript (not extant) that generated the 1536 print dates from *ca.* 1517.[1] Of the two sections that comprise this work, only the first is beholden to the contents of Virdung's published effort. The second part contains two "commentaries": one on the principles of mensural notation and the other on rules for composing polyphonic music. Both of these were subjects that Virdung had saved for his larger, unpublished (and now lost) "A German *Musica.*" Although the work came about as the result of a request by the Milanese publisher and bookseller, Andreas Calvo, that Luscinius translate Virdung's treatise for the benefit of those unversed in the German language,[2] *Musurgia* has an almost entirely new text – one that the author based only loosely on the prototype. Luscinius himself characterizes the relationship between what had been originally called for and the completed product when he states in his preface to *Musurgia* that "what began as a wine jar (*amphora*) has now at length turned out as a water pot (*urceus*)."[3] In another

61

metaphor, Luscinius compares his use of *Musica getutscht* to a carpenter's use of a plumbline.[4] He explains, furthermore, that he undertook this task on one condition: "that I be free from that faithfulness to the original which is required of most translators, and that permission be granted to me . . . to differ considerably from the author."[5] Luscinius cites as a rationale for departing from Virdung's text the fact that he wished to provide "digressions . . . to blend together the practical and the pleasant."[6]

The elements of *Musica getutscht* that Luscinius retained as a foundation for his own treatise include the following: (1) the original didactic method, namely, a simulated conversation between the same two friends, Sebastian Virdung and Andreas Silvanus (although Luscinius states that as he wrote, he had in mind a dialogue between himself and his good friend Bartholomew Stoffler);[7] (2) the very same woodcut illustrations that had appeared in the 1511 print, minus several that apparently did not directly serve his purpose;[8] (3) the conviction that it was desirable for people to become acquainted with contemporary German musical instruments, both by means of pictures and through an understanding of their classification into categories; and (4) essentially the same classification system as the one delineated by Virdung (but see below, pp. 68–70), with the instruments presented in almost the same order.

To these borrowings, Luscinius added his own material ("digressions"), reflecting his own interests and biases as well as the tastes and preferences of his projected international audience. For example, his text begins with thoughts on the nature of music, classical theories regarding the origins of music, and a discussion of the benefits of music – subjects expected by the erudite to be included in a treatise about music. As a German, furthermore, he could not resist slipping in a defense of the intellectual and moral virtues of his people to counteract strong negative prejudices in this regard on the part of many Italians.[9] In all his added passages, Luscinius liberally peppers his prose with classical allusions (and some Christian ones as well). Thus, the discussions of musical instruments in *Musurgia* include classical references, with homage paid to the instrument of antiquity most like the modern one in question. While still emphasizing contemporary musical instruments – and German ones at that (most with their vernacular names retained in the captions rather than Latinized) – Luscinius and his partner in dialogue nevertheless also recount stories illustrating practices of the ancients. In this way Luscinius displays the results of his training in Latin and Greek. For example, in the opening discussion on the category of wind instruments (sigs. c2v–c3), Andreas (alias Bartholomew Stoffler) – still in his role as the more erudite of the two interlocutors – describes how the wind players (*tibicines*) of Rome, in protest against prohibition of their eating in the temple of Jove (in which they were employed for public worship services), left the city. Their presence in this capacity being sorely missed, they were brought back only after they had been made too drunk to protest. Upon their return, the consuls revoked the prohibition and successfully begged them to resume their roles in the worship services. This digression came about in response to the observation by Sebastian (alias Luscinius) that the organ, an instrument made up of many pipes and sounded by wind, was in their own day deemed almost the only one suitable for the worship of God. That the ancients had used wind instruments for the same purpose added to the feeling of intellectual rebirth characteristic of the times. Luscinius, like other humanists of his day, could find modern activities flatteringly comparable to those of the ancients, whose heights of wisdom and culture he admired. His classical allusions, then, arise naturally out of their perceived relevance to the contemporary situation.[10]

In another gesture toward the interests and sensibilities of his mainly non-German audience, Luscinius does not engage in lengthy explanations of the many practical diagrams for teaching the specifically German tablatures that he included in *Musurgia* along with the other illustrations from *Musica getutscht*. When he does discuss modern practice, as in reference to his own instrument, the organ, Luscinius – true to his Renaissance world view – praises the greatest organist of his day, Paul Hofhaimer, and compares the influence on the world of this famous musician with that of figures from antiquity. He also selects for commendation several famous disciples of the renowned master (sigs. c3–c4).

In these departures from *Musica getutscht* and in his use of a complex and erudite style of Latin, Luscinius reveals himself as a member of the younger generation of German humanists active in the first half of the sixteenth century.[11] This younger group placed greater emphasis on classical studies *per se* than had their predecessors. They regarded the ancient Greek and Latin sources as valuable in and of themselves, rather than as disciplines complementary to the main task of grappling with Christian theology. In this, Erasmus served as luminary and model to his contemporaries, for he had high (if controversial) standing and an international reputation among scholars throughout Europe. He and his intellectual colleagues (of whom Luscinius was one) – though often at odds among themselves on many issues – agreed in exalting classical learning above anything in a living vernacular tongue. Thus, they emphasized expert knowledge of Greek and Latin, with an elegant and stylistic classical Latin as the proper vehicle for expressing their own literary creations. Forming an educated elite, these men dedicated themselves to unearthing hidden or obscured intellectual treasures from antiquity (including Christian as well as classical antiquity). Luscinius himself was highly regarded, both in his native land and in Italy, for his erudition and, more specifically, for his contributions in the fields of Greek studies and theology as well as music. Indeed, in terms of the wide scholarly interests of this renowned man, his reworking of Virdung's treatise in the first part of *Musurgia* represented merely a "twig" (his own word – sig. a2v; see above, p. 45), a diversion from his more weighty pursuits. Thus, *Musica getutscht* – rooted as it was in the present and the practical – represents a fruit of the earlier generation of German humanistic endeavors (via Johannes von Soest and Virdung at Heidelberg in the last decades of the fifteenth century and the opening one of the sixteenth). By contrast, *Musurgia seu praxis musicae* – bending as it did to the past and the "pleasant" as well as serving the present and the practical – stands as a "twig" from the branches of learning cultivated by the generation of German humanists that reached maturity in the second decade of the sixteenth century.

The life of Othmar Luscinius (*ca.* 1478–1537) overlapped with that of Sebastian Virdung at two known points: at Heidelberg, and at Augsburg. In 1494, Luscinius (or Nachtgall, his name in German), a native of Strassburg, matriculated at Heidelberg University. He passed the examination for the baccalaureate in 1496. During these two years, then, he could have had contact with Virdung, for the latter was associated at the time with the musical establishment at the court of the Elector Palatine in the same city – although he had duties elsewhere as well (see above, pp. 25–6).

Luscinius, however, seems never to have participated as a musician at the court, and no evidence survives indicating that Virdung, in his turn, had anything to do with the university after his studies ended there in the 1480s. Fourteen years after the younger man's graduation from Heidelberg, the lives of Luscinius and Virdung again intersected, raising once more the possibility that they knew each other. After having pursued further studies at other universities (Louvain, Padua, and Vienna), and after travels to the Near East, Luscinius paused for several months at Augsburg in 1510, at the time of the Reichstag. As noted above (p. 28), Virdung had also been in this city for the same occasion. Having recently studied music at Vienna,[12] Luscinius may have met Virdung[13] along with other musicians who had gathered at Augsburg. He could, therefore, have seen the manuscript of "A German *Musica*," which Virdung was then showing to possible patrons in hopes of having it published. That in his preface to *Musurgia* Luscinius nowhere mentions any such connection with Virdung – either at Heidelberg or at Augsburg – however, argues against their personal association at either or both of these times.

Whereas after 1511 Virdung disappears from our view, from this point the career of Luscinius leads him to be numbered among the intellectual luminaries of his generation. Already highly educated, Luscinius devoted the years between 1511 and 1514 to the study of Greek and theology at Paris, the great north European center of humanistic studies. He must have worked on his musical skills as well, for in 1515, the year after he returned from Paris to his native city, he became organist at the Church of St. Thomas in Strassburg.[14] Later that year, to satisfy the requirement of the church that musicians serving there be able to function as clerics as well, Luscinius was ordained a priest.[15] While at Strassburg, Luscinius engaged in intellectual activities in keeping with his humanistic background and interests. Thus, he held membership in the *sodalitas litteraria* of the city (in company with literary figures of the stature of Sebastian Brant and Jacob Wimpfeling), and he also taught Greek, for which ability he was highly esteemed by his fellow German humanists, few of whom at that time had mastered this key to the treasures of antiquity. Luscinius acted as editor and translator of Greek texts for the Strassburg printer Johann Schott (1477–1548), whose shop was located at St. Thomas Platz (by Luscinius's place of employment), and who later published both editions of *Musurgia*.[16] Except for a leave of absence in 1518–19 to earn a degree as Doctor of Canon Law from the University of Padua, Luscinius retained his post as organist until 1520, at which time the chapter abolished his position for political reasons. The next year he found employment at St. Stephen's church. However, owing to the Reformation growing ever stronger in his native city – a state of affairs in which he could not flourish, given his religious convictions – Luscinius left Strassburg for Augsburg in 1523.

The period of less than a decade that Luscinius spent in Strassburg (1515–23) was the time of his greatest scholarly productivity, especially in the fields of classical studies.[17] His two works on music stem from these years as well: *Musica institutiones* (published in that city, with the dedication dated 1515), which he based on the lectures he had given at Vienna a decade earlier; and *Musurgia seu praxis musicae* (completed by him *ca.* 1517). During his Augsburg period, on the other hand, Luscinius turned to theology – as teacher, preacher, and spokesman against the Lutheran heresy – performing these roles in person as well as in print.

Although in Augsburg Luscinius enjoyed the friendship and support of influential friends, including the patronage of the Fugger family, zealots of the Reformation caused him professional hardship. By 1527 the religious atmosphere in Augsburg had become as hostile to his orthodox views as had been the case at Strassburg several years previously; and in 1528, having been banned from preaching in the city, he left Augsburg. Luscinius was welcome in Freiburg im Breisgau, where he became a preacher at the cathedral. However, in 1531 Luscinius chose to live apart from the religious strife around him, and he became a permanent guest of the Carthusian monastery near Freiburg for the rest of his life. At his death in 1537 – a year after he had finally seen his *Musurgia* put to press – Othmar Luscinius was interred at the monastery, according to his wishes.

When Luscinius accepted the challenge by Andreas Calvo that he translate *Musica getutscht* into Latin for the non-German-speaking public, he was by no means engaging in an unusual or, as some would have it,[18] regressive undertaking. Even before the advent of printing in the middle of the fifteenth century, important vernacular works in the major European languages – works in a variety of genres on many different subjects – had been converted into Latin for the purpose of insuring international circulation among learned people.[19] Nor did the freedom taken by Luscinius in recasting some of the essence of the original treatise into his own work constitute unwarranted liberty on his part. For the attitude at that time toward translation of then current works differed from the attitude toward translating treasures from antiquity. The latter orientation forms the foundation of what we mean today by the term "translation." Whereas we expect in every case a faithful rendering of text from one language to another, in the sixteenth century, to translate something current could also mean to adapt and to interpret.[20] Then too, the various tongues had personalities of their own that affected the text. Just as different typefaces belonged with different languages, so languages themselves had individual styles and appropriate ways of proceeding. It was inevitable, then, that for Luscinius, the Latin language itself would color the content of *Musurgia*, at least to some extent. For Latin at the time inspired argument by evidence from antiquity using classical modes of thought conveyed in Ciceronian syntax. Even though Luscinius did retain the casual dialogue form of *Musica getutscht*, then, the conversation had to be expressed in a more elevated style than the vernacular one engaged in by the original interlocutors, a more erudite style valued by Luscinius's intended audience – those who would have had far more formal education than was needed for *Musica getutscht*. Thus, although the medium of dialogue, the same woodcuts (including the musical examples), and the same rationale served as a foundation for Luscinius's own material, he unfolded it in a manner proper to the recently revitalized artificial language of the educated elite in which he wrote.

Besides the essentially new text emphasizing musical instruments and music making in the experience of the ancients as well as in contemporary society, Luscinius greatly expanded Virdung's material by including in *Musurgia* a second "book" or section. This latter half of the treatise covers the rudiments of music in two "commentaries": the first gives fundamentals of mensural notation (sigs. i2–m2v), and the second takes up principles of composition (sigs. m3–o2v). This part of the treatise, though entirely new, does follow very closely what Virdung said in *Musica getutscht* that he had included in his larger "A German *Musica.*" This raises the interesting speculation that Luscinius might actually have seen the manuscript of Virdung's larger treatise at the Diet of Augsburg in 1510, when the latter was attempting to interest a patron in supporting publication of this comprehensive work. Two facts argue against this possibility, however. First (although admittedly an argument from silence), Luscinius nowhere made any reference to his first-hand knowledge of this treatise. Second (a more telling consideration), in his very brief Latin treatise of several years before, *Musica institutiones* (1515), Luscinius had promised a second work incorporating this material (sigs. cv–c2). Since, as Luscinius tells us in the prefatory material to *Musurgia,* the idea of converting *Musica getutscht* into the language suitable for an educated Italian audience came not from Luscinius himself but from Andreas Calvo, and since we know that Calvo's request apparently came after *musica institutiones* (in *ca.* 1517), then it is unlikely that Luscinius would have been influenced in a primary way by Virdung's larger treatise at the time of writing *Musica institutiones* (1515), even if he had seen Virdung's *magnum opus* in 1510. The subjects on which both authors wrote, after all, were basic to the discipline of music and therefore common property of all schooled musicians. On the other hand, one of the attractions to Luscinius of taking Calvo's suggestion that he Latinize *Musica getutscht* may have been the opportunity of publishing his own projected (and indeed publicly promised) work as a second part to the recasting of Virdung's treatise; and this plan may have come to Luscinius because he had already seen these very topics treated in a context that had included musical instruments – i.e., in Virdung's larger work. Conversely, Luscinius may have known of the contents of Virdung's *magnum opus* only as we do today, through clues left in *Musica getutscht.* Until further evidence sheds new light on the interaction between these two men regarding their related treatises, it seems most likely that Luscinius simply combined two projects of his own in *Musurgia,* the first a reworking of Virdung's *Musica getutscht,* and the second a separate treatise which he had had independently in mind at least as early as the two years before he actually committed *Musurgia* to manuscript.

It has been noted above that although Luscinius retained several basic elements from *Musica getutscht* he nevertheless freely adapted Virdung's material for his own purposes. This also holds true with regard to the instrumental categories to some extent, for Luscinius made several subtle improvements in the classification system. Although he presents the same three categories in the same order as Virdung (strings, winds, and percussion instruments), within these divisions Luscinius distinguishes among the instruments by using slightly different bases of comparison. Unlike Virdung, who divided stringed instruments into categories based on that aspect of their structure that could be notated in tablature (i.e., keys, or frets, or multiple strings),[21] Luscinius separates stringed instruments into: (1) those that are capable of sounding more than one line of music (i.e., keyboard instruments [including the hurdy-gurdy], plucked fretted instruments, and plucked ones having a single string for each pitch [harp, psaltery, and hammered dulcimer]); and (2) those that normally realize but one line of music (i.e., all bowed stringed instruments). Of the latter type, rather than following Virdung in rejecting the trumpet marine and rebec as "unprofitable instruments," Luscinius dismisses only the hammered dulcimer. He does this because of the clashing sonorities created when the strings continue to ring long after they have been struck (sig. c2).[22]

Among the wind instruments, Luscinius claims primacy for the organ, a value judgment not present in *Musica getutscht*. He holds to this claim because, in his view, this instrument "almost alone" is suitable for the praise of God: it requires no pauses for breath, and no other instrument has such a variety of sounds (encompassing the timbres of almost all other instruments). Furthermore, all manner of music can be played upon it, to especially good effect by the educated hands and feet of the great master, Paul Hofhaimer, and by those who followed in his distinguished tracks. As for the other wind instruments, those that can be sounded with human air, Luscinius (after briefly echoing an ancient distaste for the change of facial expression required to inflate one of these) then proceeds to distinguish between those that change pitch by means of finger holes and those that change pitch with the mouth (i.e., brass instruments). In the former category, Luscinius, unlike Virdung, separates instruments that have a thumb hole from those that do not. He lauds those that do, especially the recorder (because of the size and evenness of its range). As for wind instruments of the latter kind – brass instruments, about which Virdung

sl. de type
o depositones

said he would write only in the larger treatise – Luscinius adds an interesting comment. He admires the ability of *tubae ductiles*[23] to make multiple tones from one single tone; thus one of these instruments sounds almost polyphonic, owing to the chordal patterns obtainable because of the accoustic properties (sig. d3). Luscinius must mean here the tones derived from the overtone series.[24]

Regarding percussion instruments, Luscinius, like Virdung before him, distinguishes between those capable of rendering the primordial proportions into sonorities and those that emit only noise. Of the latter, Luscinius amplifies his predecessor's special disdain for drums. His rationale for rejecting these instruments, however, has less to do with the fact that the noise disturbs the peace of innocent people (*Mus. get.*, sig. D, p. 115 below) than it does with the evidence (ancient and modern) that these particular sounds incite men to baseness, cruelty, and all the inhuman attributes associated with waging war (*Musurgia*, sigs. d4–e).

Luscinius reprints the pictures of the Jerome instruments for curiosity's sake alone. Less open than Virdung to the possibility that more research will enable him to understand them in a sense other than allegorical, he dismisses them as evidently having been devised neither for utility nor for delight (sig. cv).

Luscinius follows Virdung in dividing his material into two discrete sections: one devoted primarily to listing, depicting, and categorizing the instruments, and the second dedicated to making known three kinds of tablatures – German keyboard tablature, German lute tablature, and recorder tablature. While the section in *Musurgia* analogous to the first part of *Musica getutscht* was greatly expanded by Luscinius's digressions, the section of the derivative treatise corresponding to the second half of *Musica getutscht* has been greatly simplified. One supposes that the market in Italy for technical instructions on how to use these foreign notations was not as great as the market for pictures of recognizable instruments along with a learned, though light, discourse about them. Not surprisingly, Luscinius gives the most practical instructions for the tablature of his own instrument, the organ. For the notational symbols, he substitutes those used by his hero, Paul Hofhaimer, for those given by Virdung. In this version of German keyboard tablature (sig. fv), the gamut begins with capi-

70

tal letters for the first four pitches (F G A B [= B♭]), then shifts to lower-case letters for the next octave (h [= B♮] c d e f g a b [= b♭]), followed by lower-case letters with lines above them for the next octave (h̄ [= b♮] c̄ d̄ ē f̄ ḡ ā b̄ [= b♭']). However, Luscinius chose to change neither the original diagram of a keyboard nor the musical example to conform to this different system. Nor does he explain the discrepancy. This incongruity, along with his greatly abbreviated instructions on lute and recorder tablature (the latter reduced to diagrams alone, with virtually no explanation whatsoever), shows that he meant *Musurgia* to be less of an actual practical guide to tablature and intabulation than *Musica getutscht*.

In two other significant areas Luscinius either parts company with Virdung or adds to our understanding of an issue. In the first place, without referring to the controversy between Virdung and Schlick regarding the proper perspective on the black keys (do they represent the chromatic genus of the ancient Greeks in modern practice [Virdung], or are they *musica ficta* [Schlick]?), Luscinius places himself in the camp of Schlick, his fellow organist. He does this when he explains the semitones as having resulted from the need to transpose music to other pitch levels (sigs. fv–f2). In the second place, on the subject of mensuration of music in tablature, Luscinius avoids dealing with the problems inherent in perfect mensuration not by simply ruling it out in his discussion, as Virdung had done, but by rationalizing this decision, stating that since instrumental music in *tempus perfectum* is so rare, he will only discuss intabulation in *tempus imperfectum* (sig. f2v).

Luscinius did not attempt to translate all the names of the musical instruments. Many of them had already carried Latin appellations in Virdung's original print of 1511 (e.g., almost all of the keyboard instruments – string and wind), and for those that did not, anachronistic terminology would have caused confusion. Of those few instances in which Luscinius did choose a Latin alternative for its identification, only one is instructive. Corroborating the evidence of the picture itself (*Mus. get.*, sig. B2, p. 103 below), Luscinius called Virdung's *quintern* "lutina." Thus, we know that by the term *quintern* a small lute was meant.

Unfortunately for us as modern observers of historical musical instruments, an exchange of captions in *Musurgia* for two of the keyboard instruments compounds an enigma already present in *Musica getutscht*. In the derivative work, either Luscinius or the compositor has labeled Virdung's *claviciterium* as *clavicimbalum* and vice versa (sigs. b3v–b4). These very instruments have been the subject of much controversy and conjecture among organologists owing to their proximity to Virdung's description of an instrument referred to by the author only as the demonstrative pronoun *das* (*Mus. get.*, sig. Bv; see below, p. 102 and n. 36). Perhaps the presence of three terms beginning with *clavi-* (the other being *clavicordium*) confounded the typesetter of *Musurgia*.

It was twenty-five years after *Musica getutscht* appeared in print that the Latin adaptation by Luscinius of some of its contents saw the light of day for the first time. The new treatise had been designed from its inception (some nineteen years before publication) to appeal to a more international and intellectual audience than the one served by the original work. Yet *Musurgia* testifies to the enduring popularity of Virdung's original effort. Indeed, so successful was Luscinius's tardy modernization of the parent treatise, that in 1542 – five years after the death of the author – the same printer (Johann Schott) produced a second printing of *Musurgia*.

"Musica instrumentalis deudsch" by Martin Agricola

If *Musica getutscht* can be seen as a product of the earlier generation of German humanists, and *Musurgia* as stemming from the next surge of popular yet intellectual endeavors in the following decades, then *Musica instrumentalis deudsch* represents an outgrowth of a subsequent trend (this one in the second quarter of the sixteenth century) connected with education of the youth according to principles espoused by disciples of Martin Luther. Martin Agricola brought out this second offspring of *Musica getutscht* in the German language, like its parent. He dated the dedication of *Musica instrumentalis deudsch* as follows: "Magdeburg, on Bartholomew's Day, 1528" (i.e., 24 August [sig. A4]). George Rhau (or Rhaw) – to whom this volume was dedicated – printed the treatise in 1529. Although Agricola nowhere acknowledged his debt to the innovative treatise that Virdung had produced in 1511, even a cursory glance shows his work to be beholden to its predecessor in significant ways. Besides the common language, the most obvious borrowing involves the illustrations, for Agricola merely had most of the woodcuts in *Musica getutscht* copied for incorporation into his own work. Then too, the instruments he discusses are grouped into the same categories given seventeen years previously by Virdung. The title, of course, is too similar to be the result of a coincidence.

In other respects, however, *Musica instrumentalis deudsch* resembles what we know of Virdung's lost larger work, "A German *Musica*," more than it does *Musica getutscht*. For one thing, Agricola and Virdung both intended that their treatises be used to lighten the burden of boys in their rigorous studies of music at school as well as to give pleasure to amateurs,[25] whereas *Musica getutscht*, the small extract from Virdung's major treatise, was aimed mainly at the latter group. Because of the intended audiences of "A German *Musica*" and *Musica instrumentalis deudsch*, both authors composed their texts in German verse, a time-honored method of insuring that the information be better understood and retained longer in the memory of all readers (see *Mus. inst. deudsch*, sig. A2v). In this regard, Agricola made an improvement upon the efforts of Virdung. In contrast to the large and comprehensive treatise that Virdung had attempted unsuccessfully to publish, Agricola divided his didactic material into a series of three tiny, easily portable, octavo-sized textbooks, of which this manual of instruction for instrumental music is but one part.[26] Taken together, these three books incorporate the material that Virdung said he would cover in his one larger book (*Mus. get., passim*). Agricola, however, chose to put only one of them, *Musica instrumentalis deudsch*, in verse.

No evidence links the lives of Sebastian Virdung and Martin Agricola. Born in 1486, when Virdung was already a young man, Agricola (né Sore) came from a peasant family. According to his own testimony, he taught himself music. He did not frequent the musical circles and establishments with which Virdung was associated, and it is most likely that Virdung had died before Agricola became active as a teacher and choirmaster in Magdeburg – from 1519 to his death in 1556. Thus, the influence of the older man on the younger one had to have come from the product that Virdung left for posterity, his popular little book, *Musica getutscht*.

As we have seen, so successful were the illustrations for *Musica getutscht* that Agricola had them copied almost exactly from the earlier treatise.[27] Following common contemporary practice when "borrowing" pictorial material from earlier publications, the cutter did not bother to reverse the woodcuts so that they would appear as in the original; rather, he simply drew what he saw onto the new blocks. Thus, the illustrations in *Musica instrumentalis deudsch* show the musical instruments in mirror image from those in *Musica getutscht.* That is, with two exceptions: for Agricola's treatise, the cutter did take care to reverse the harp,[28] and, significantly, the keyboards – but no other aspects – of all keyboard instruments. He did this apparently not recognizing that in the original print, the cutter (most probably Urs Graf) had failed to reverse the original drawings from which he had derived *his* woodcuts, and produced, therefore, keyboards that are mirror images of what they should be. Ironically, if the illustrator of Agricola's treatise had not been so conscientious in reversing what to him had to be the characteristic of these instruments most worthy of accuracy (because of the trouble he took), he could have improved the pictures of the keyboard instruments; instead, he unwittingly renewed the old error. There is one exception to his practice of copying all the keyboard instruments and reversing the keyboard of each: the illustrator of *Musica instrumentalis deudsch* put the keyboard from Virdung's clavicimbalum on both the clavicimbalum and the virginal, whereas in the original print the two were different. Then, he or the compositor reversed the captions for these two instruments when these woodcuts were transferred to the new print (*Mus. inst. deudsch,* sigs. D3–D3v), thus adding to our confusion surrounding these enigmatically similar instruments (see below, p. 102 and n. 36). Another example of transposed captions occurs in connection with the brass instruments: Virdung's *clareta* is Agricola's *Türmer horn* and vice versa (*Mus. inst. deudsch,* sig. B8v; *Mus. get.,* sigs. B4v–C). Whereas in this case Virdung was correct,[29] in the former case, our understanding of the terms *virginal* and *clavicimbalum* in 1511 give us insufficient basis to judge which treatise presented the more accurate depiction of these instruments. The possibility exists, furthermore, that some terminology was in a state of flux at the time.[30]

In the instances cited above, Agricola's incorporation of the woodcuts from *Musica getutscht* into his own work has caused or compounded confusion on our part. In other cases, on the other hand, the illustrations in *Musica instrumentalis deudsch* have clarified our understanding of certain instruments. This can be seen in the pictures of the four recorders[31] (*Mus. inst. deudsch*, sig. A8v; *Mus. get.*, sig. B3v), in which the depiction of the thumb hole is better executed in the derivative work. Other examples of greater accuracy in Agricola's treatise can be cited. For one thing, he placed the bagpipe properly within the sub-group of wind instruments having finger holes rather than showing it in company with the brass instruments (*Mus. inst. deudsch*, sig. B3v; *Mus. get.*, sig. B4v).[32] Then too, whereas Virdung's picture of a single member of the viol family has an improbable nine strings (sig. B2), Agricola's many viols have entirely credible numbers of strings: the two types of viol shown by Agricola have four (sig. F6v) and three (sigs. G3v–G4) strings respectively, and – although he does not illustrate it – he discusses a larger type of viol with five strings, the bass having six (sigs. F4v–F6). Of particular interest to us today is the retention by Agricola of the lute- or guitar-type bridge for these bowed instruments. Although some scholars consider this a mistake in *Musica getutscht*,[33] enough iconographic evidence exists (apart from its presence in Agricola's treatise) to accept this feature as plausible for at least some of the bowed stringed instruments of the time in northern European lands.[34]

Some pictures in *Musica instrumentalis deudsch*, on the other hand, show changes in the original concept, and they do so at the expense of accuracy. For example, Agricola's illustrator depicts the lute with only nine strings instead of the more common number of eleven as shown in *Musica getutscht* (*Mus. inst. deudsch*, sig. E; *Mus. get.*, sig. B2). For still others, it is difficult for us today to assess the differences. For example, did the *quintern* (*lutina* to Luscinius) have ten strings as it did in *Musica getutscht* or six as in *Musica instrumentalis deudsch*?

Though the woodcuts in *Musica getutscht* formed the basis for teaching about practical aspects of instrumental performance in *Musica instrumentalis deudsch*, Agricola added both to the instrumentarium and to the instructions provided by Virdung. We can see in the first place that Agricola depicted two new instruments not shown in *Musica getutscht*: the "keyed fiddle" (*Schlüssel fidel*, sig. D4) and the xylophone (*Strofidel*, Sig. H3v).[35] Secondly,

Agricola included tablature symbols in the pictures of instruments having a separate sounding agent for each note, namely, the xylophone, as well as the harp (sig. G6) and the psaltery (sig. G6v). More importantly, Agricola augmented the possibilities for learning many wind instruments by including fingering charts for transverse flutes (*Schweitzer Pfeiffen*), which had six holes (sigs. B5v–B6v), and for the four-holed recorder (?) (*Klein Flötlin mit vier löchern*) (sig. B7v).[36] And he extended the possibilities for developing expertise on stringed instruments as well by providing tablatures (in reality, charts of pitches) for four kinds of bowed stringed instruments: fretted viols of five or six strings, the same with four strings, the same with three strings, and rebecs (also with three strings but unfretted). Furthermore, the charts as well as the pictures show these instruments in several sizes.[37] In addition to the consorts of two shawms (*Schalmey* and *Bombardt*), of two lutes (lute and *quintern*), or four recorders (in three sizes), and of four crumhorns shown by Virdung, Agricola also depicted consorts of the following: transverse flutes (sig. B5), two kinds of fretted viols (sigs. F6v, G3v–G4), and rebecs (sigs. G7v–G8). Thus, Agricola gave more specific evidence of the consort principle at work in the first quarter of the sixteenth century than had Virdung – namely, that at least by 1528, most of the wind instruments with finger holes, as well as almost all of the bowed stringed instruments (excluding the trumpet marine), came in three sizes. In this regard it is important to recognize that although these instruments are often pictured in groups of four (in keeping with the sixteenth-century predilection for polyphony in four voices), in reality they were only made in three sizes.[38] This can be seen in that the accompanying fingering charts and tablatures for all the consorts apply to three sizes only. The three actual sizes (discant, tenor, and bass) were used for four polyphonic voices: discant, alto, tenor, and bass. As Virdung had explained at the end of *Musica getutscht* (sig. O4, pp. 180–1 below), the choice of a tenor- or discant-size recorder for a middle part in a piece of music written for four voices depended upon the ambitus of the composed part in question. We have here, then, a vestige in instrumental practice of the three-voice texture that had prevailed in previous decades. Even Agricola's greatly revised new edition of *Musica instrumentalis deudsch*, which he published in 1545, shows these instruments and their tablatures in only three sizes.

A second glance at *Musica instrumentalis deudsch* shows that Agricola altered the order in which Virdung presented the instruments. In Agricola's manual of instruction, wind instruments (rather than keyboard instruments) come first, with the prototype (as in *Musica getutscht*) being the recorder. (It is interesting that in the twentieth century the recorder regained this status as a favorite instrument for beginners – and amateurs – especially in Germany.) Thus, the neophyte need not confront first the technicalities of tablature; rather, a novice instrumentalist can play from a single line of mensural notation. Agricola then turns his attention to the most imposing wind instrument, the organ, from which the discussion turns naturally to keyboard tablature – thus prompting a display of all keyboard instruments – and thence to tablatures for plucked and bowed stringed instruments of many sorts.[39] Percussion instruments come last; he depicts only those that demonstrate the proportions, can convey a melody, or both. Therefore we find no illustrations of drums.

As far as the tablatures are concerned, Agricola offers none for wind instruments, and his keyboard and lute tablatures differ from those given by Virdung. Agricola chides those who propose tablatures for wind instruments, dismissing these attempts as "chickenscratch" (*kökelwreck* = *kökelwerk* [sig. A7v]), an apt description indeed of Virdung's shorthand (see *Mus. get.*, sig. O3v, p. 180 below). Agricola's notational symbols for keyboard instruments depart from Virdung's only slightly, both systems being variants stemming from the same basic principles. However, Agricola totally rejects the German lute tablature of his day (as presented by Virdung and others), characterizing it as a case in which the blind inventor has made sighted persons blind (sig. D5v). For, in this system, the symbols – though made up of letters of the alphabet – bear no relation to the letter names of the pitches. He therefore advocates an entirely new tablature, with the letters of the actual notes (from staff notation) standing for the pitches – as in German keyboard tablature (sigs. Ev–E2v). He does reluctantly include a diagram of the old tablature for lute and viol, labeling it "very useful to know" (sig. E4v). In view of these differences, it is not surprising that most of Virdung's diagrams connected with tablature do not appear in *Musica instrumentalis deudsch*; nor do his musical examples.

In addition to the new fingering charts and tablatures, Agricola brings in much more practical information about playing the various instruments than Virdung had attempted in his ground-breaking work. Whether for its mention of vibrato for transverse flutes (*zitterndem odem*; sig. B4), its comments on an easier way to tune the lute (by octaves rather than by fourths and a third; sig. F2v), or the myriad other hints at performance practice, Agricola's *Musica instrumentalis deudsch* imparts – in quality as well as quantity – more knowledge of use to a budding instrumentalist than either *Musica getutscht* or *Musurgia*.

"Dit is een seer schoon Boecxken" and "Livre plaisant et tres utile"[40]

The third offspring of *Musical getutscht* is the Netherlandic translation of the second half of its contents, *Dit is een seer schoon Boecxken* (here abbreviated as *Dit*). As demonstrated above, this treatise dates from some time before 12 October 1529, the day that Willem Vorsterman, a printer in the flourishing city of Antwerp, completed production of the French translation of *Dit*, a work carrying the title *Livre plaisant et tres utile* (here abbreviated as *Livre*). Because the text of *Livre* is a literal rendering of *Dit*, it will not be considered here separately, except where it departs significantly from *Dit* or when it sheds light on the Netherlandic version. No exemplar of the original printing of *Dit* (*ca.* 1528) survives, however; for this reason, we must base our knowledge of this treatise upon two later typesettings, both from the shop of Vorsterman's younger colleague in the trade, Jan van Ghelen the younger. Van Ghelen (son of one of Vorsterman's contemporaries, Jan van Ghelen the elder) produced one of these extant printings of *Dit* some twenty-six years later, in 1554, and the other in 1568, at least forty years after its initial appearance. We do not know the persons responsible for bringing out the original edition of this Netherlandic version of *Musica getutscht* – either the printer or the translator(s). We can only conjecture that the man behind production of the earliest edition of *Dit* might have been either the same one who printed the only copy of *Livre* that survives, Willem Vorsterman, or Vorsterman's contemporary, Jan van Ghelen the elder, father of the printer of the two extant editions of *Dit*.

In considering the relationship between progeny and parent,

then, *Dit* must represent the primary basis of comparison of this twin pair, since it has the closest ties with the original. *Livre*, being twice removed from *Musica getutscht*, offers more possibilities for error. Its position as the oldest of the two versions available to us, however, means that it can illuminate corruptions that might have crept into the subsequent printings of *Dit* that do survive.

The anonymous person or (more likely) persons[41] who adapted and translated *Musica getutscht* into Netherlandic for publication at Antwerp, *ca.* 1528, began this translation with material from Virdung's little book found immediately prior to the actual lessons on making tablatures for the three instruments (i.e., at the end of sig. D4v, p. 121 below). Thus, the adaptor/translator omitted all that Virdung had presented in the first four signatures of his work (sigs. A–D) – that is, approximately 30 percent of his text. Contrary to what Luscinius and Agricola did in their derivative works, then, the preparer of *Dit* chose to present neither a pictorial instrumentarium nor a formal discussion of the classification of musical instruments. Eschewing any acknowledgment of indebtedness to Virdung, furthermore, he also rejected all material that related to *Musica getutscht* as an artifact in itself, such as the names of the interlocutors, all references to the larger treatise from which it was extracted, etc. He did, however, retain the didactic dialogue form, although he changed the relationship of the interlocutors from one of close friends to one of teacher and pupil. This has effected an important shift of emphasis from the mutuality of adult colleagues to the inequality of master and disciple.

The main outlines of the instructions on tablature and intabulation for clavichord, lute, and recorder that make up the contents of *Dit* follow those in *Musica getutscht* quite closely. However, some of this material has been changed or modified, some has been omitted, and some has been amplified.

The most notable change in content in *Dit* is the substitution of what we now call "French lute tablature" for the German lute tablature taught by Virdung. Up to now it has been thought that *Livre* contained the earliest example of French lute tablature of six lines. However, since we now know that an edition of *Dit* preceded *Livre*, and that some time must have elapsed between preparation of the former and the latter, *Dit* (with a probable date of *ca.* 1528) must be given pride of place in this regard. For both treatises share the same woodcut musical examples. The original edition of *Dit* may even have preceded what has been thought to be the earliest printed French lute tablature – this one composed of five rather than six lines – in a publication from July 1528 by Pierre Attaignant in Paris: *Tres breve et familiere introduction pour entendre & apprendre par soy mesmes a jouer toutes chansons reduictes en la tablature du Lutz, avec la maniere daccorder le dict Lutz.*[42] If so, we might be more justified in calling this notation "Netherlandish lute tablature," as Hans Gerle did only four years after publication of *Livre.*[43]

A second substantive modification has been noted above (p. 56): the substitution for Virdung's own musical example of a song by a native of Antwerp, Jacques Barbireau. This song, "Een vrolijck wesen," had great popularity at the time in the Low Countries and in German lands.[44] A wise choice, this one, since the three-part setting of this secular song is far better suited to keyboard intabulation – especially for beginners – than was the four-part composition by Virdung. Moreover, the musician employed to adapt *Musica getutscht* to the Netherlandic-speaking audience put only the lower two parts of this piece into lute tablature. He placed the top line of the song at the end of the section on the recorder, presumably intending that this melody complete the instrumental rendering of "Een vrolijk wesen" in the form of a duet for lute and recorder.[45] This recorder melody survived only in *Livre* on the very back leaf (sig. K3); in the quarter century or so between the original printing of *Dit* and the 1554 edition of this work, the recorder part evidently disappeared.[46] Since this music was simply a reprinting of the superius part in mensural notation, subsequent printers of *Dit* may have seen little point in including it at this point in the treatise, as it could be found earlier in the print.

In contrast to the instrumental intabulations by Virdung of his song in *Musica getutscht*, furthermore, the keyboard and lute intabulations of "Een vrolijck wesen" in *Dit* (and, of course, *Livre*) depart to some extent from the version given in mensural notation. These simple alterations and embellishments of the music reflect styles of performance that were idiomatic for keyboard and lute. Virdung had skirted this important issue in two ways: (1) by showing only a mechanical, literal transcription from one medium of notation to the other and (2) by promising to demonstrate in his forthcoming work ("A German *Musica*") the stylistic nuances involved in more artistic intabulation. (See sig. M2, p. 166 below: "In the other book I will also give you a better way, that of breaking up some of the pitches so that the music does not proceed so very simply.") The transcriber of the song in *Dit*, on the other hand, decorated the intabulations from the beginning in a way appropriate to each instrument's characteristic style and technique. This can be seen especially in the superius of the clavichord setting and the top part (i.e., the tenor of the song) in the lute setting.[47] (Presumably a recorder player would have improvised ornaments to the superius of the music in mensural notation.)

The author of *Dit* incorporated relevant woodcuts from the second, instructional part of *Musica getutscht*.[48] The title page (see Plates 1 & 2, pp. 82–3) served as an appropriate place for a copy of the pleasing and artistic picture of a lutenist by Urs Graf. Here the seated instrumentalist is flanked on both sides by column-like diagrams of recorders with the numerical symbols for the finger holes indicated upon them, woodcuts first seen in *Musica getutscht* in the section on playing the recorder (sigs. Nv and N2v). Above the lutenist is a clavichord. The woodcutter for this illustration conflated elements from two keyboard instruments in Virdung's work: the clavichord found on sig. B, and the clavicimbalum found on sig. Bv. The outside case and keyboard more nearly resemble the latter, while the inside aspects (i.e., equal-length strings, curving tangents, and tuning pins on the right side) derive from the former. Thus, the three instruments featured in *Dit* appear prominently on the title page, where they effectively advertise the content of this attractive little book.

Besides these modifications of the original material, the author of *Dit* has omitted some of the information included in the part of *Musica getutscht* that he did translate. Missing in *Dit*, for example, is any definition of the chromatic genus or any reference to the enharmonic one, although the teacher does at least mention the former during the dialogue (*Dit*, sig. A4).[49] Regarding the clavichord, the teacher states that the largest size of these instruments has thirty-eight keys and a range of four octaves (*Dit*, sig. B3), this despite the fact that Virdung had described some clavichords having an expanded range owing to the presence of more keys than that as well as pedals in some cases (*Mus. get.*,

Plate 1 Title page of *Livre* (1529)

ℭ Liure plaifant et tref=
utile pour apprendre a faire ꝗ ordonner toutes tabu=
latures hors le difcant / dont ꝗ par lefquelles
fon peuft facilement et legierement apren=
dre a iouer fur les Manicordion / Luc/
et flutes.

Plate 2 Title page of *Dit* (1568)

sig. F). Nor does the teacher speak of multiple strings in choirs or of resonance strings on the clavichord, as had Sebastian (*Mus. get.*, sig. F). Concerning the recorder, the author of *Dit* left out any allusion to the use of the tongue as well as any hints as to the choice of a discant- or tenor-size instrument for the middle voices of a four-voice polyphonic piece of music. He did, however, retain Virdung's recorder tablature.

One apparent omission probably occurred in one of the later typesettings of *Dit.* When the pupil asks of what material clavichord strings are made (sig. A3), his teacher responds that they are made of iron (*stalen*) (sig. A3v). The original German had "brass" (for the lower notes) and "iron" (for the upper notes) (sigs. F–Fv).[50] Since the French translation of this passage has "wires of iron or of copper" (*fil dachier ou de cuyure*) (sig. A2v), it appears that the compositor of a later typesetting of *Dit* inadvertently left out the second metal, and that the French translator had rendered the Netherlandic word for "brass" (*mod.* = *geel koper*) as "copper."

The author of *Dit* also added some new information to that given in the parent treatise. For example, in his list of keyboard instruments (in company with the clavichord, the organ, the clavicembalo, and the virginal [sig. A2]), he names one not mentioned by Virdung: the *herpecordium* (French: *herpicordion*). This may be the mysterious *arpichordo* referred to by other authors and possibly alluded to elsewhere in *Musica getutscht* by Virdung himself, first without a name and possibly later called *harpfentive* (sig. I4v; see below, n. 140, p. 152). In the section on the clavichord, the author of *Dit* also interpolates a new passage on the perfect and imperfect consonances (sigs. Bv–B2). Furthermore, in the chapter on the lute, he gives an alternative way to tune the instrument – by unisons and octaves from the highest string, which has been set "as high as it is possible to set it" (sigs. F4–F4v). He also explains a notational symbol not dealt with by Virdung: a dot under a letter of lute tablature indicating that one is to strike the string from below (*Dit*, sig. H2v). In addition, the author of *Dit* specifies something that Virdung did not dwell on, namely, that "whenever you find two or three letters, one above the other, that signifies that those strings must be fingered together and played [together] where the letters are situated" (*Dit*, sig. H2v).[51] Given the impossibility of Virdung's examples to be played in this manner, it is not surprising that he mentions this subject but once in *Musica getutscht* (sig. K2, p. 154 below).

The translator and adaptor of *Dit* also inserted details that amplify or explain some of the information in *Musica getutscht*. For example, regarding clavichord strings, he states that the wires should be of "the smallest [gauge] that one can obtain or is possible to find' (sig. A3v).[52] As for the clavichord itself, our Netherlandish author describes it as "an instrument on which one learns in order to play the organ in churches" (sig. Av),[53] a suggestion that clarifies Virdung's references to clavichord tablature as "organ tablature." The definition of a fret is set forth more clearly in *Dit*: "each fret [consists] or two little [gut] strings next to each other" (sig. F4v).[54] This is also true of the explanation of the *punctus divisionis*: "It is not sung or added. Rather, the notes between [which] or by which it stands are separated. It also ought to be in front of the note that is separated" (sig. D3).[55] The discussion of rhythmic values in *Dit* – unlike the parallel passage in *Musica getutscht* – distinguishes between black and white longas and breves (*Dit*, sigs. C2v–C3v), even though in the case of both treatises, imperfect time alone was used for teaching intabulation, and smaller note values than these were considered as solely duple in duration.

Interpretation of one difficult sentence in *Musica getutscht* has been greatly aided by referring to *Dit*. This concerns the reason that the lute has gut rather than wire strings (*Mus. get.*, sig. I4v). The Netherlandic has (sigs. F3–F3v): "But those [strings] that are made of other guts or substances will not sound as the sheep guts do on the lute when one presses on them with bare fingers. But these strings that are made of other guts or substances sound good on other instruments on which they are underlaid (*onderleyt*; Fr.: *ordonnez dessoubz* [i.e., 'arranged underneath,' sig. E4v]) with iron or wood."[56] This passage in *Dit* helped unlock Virdung's complicated prose to find his idea that gut strings belong with gut frets, while metal strings belong with metal or wood frets (*Mus. get.*, sig. I4v; p. 152 below).

Whereas some amplifications of Virdung's material are merely decorative (such as the description of a semibreve as a diamond, "just as are in glass windows" [sig. C2v]),[57] others in *Dit* reveal subtleties of thought and attitude. For instance, the preparer of this translation and adaptation of *Musica getutscht*, though

85

following Virdung in his differentiation between those who can sing from mensural notation and others who cannot, nevertheless departs from the original German text when he calls those in the latter category "all ordinary people" (sig. A2).[58] By this he implies an even more popular avenue of approach to the playing of musical instruments than even Virdung had intended. On weightier topics, *Dit* provides a few nuances not present in the parent treatise. For instance, in connection with the doubling of each lower course with a string that sounds an octave higher, the author of *Dit* evidently refers to the rhythmic or harmonic foundation (or both) provided by the bass notes when he states that, were these courses not so constituted, "they would not be able to support the excellent measure (*die edel mate*; [Fr.: *la noble mesure*]) on the other strings" (*Dit*, sig. F2v; *Livre*, sig. E3v).[59]

Some passages having the appearance of amplifying Virdung's material, however, in reality constitute conflations of several different parts of the original treatise. This can be seen in the discussion of the little cloths wound among the strings on a clavichord (*Mus. get.*, sig. Fv). *Dit* has the following: "Without this [cloth] it would give no proportions to the resonances, but it would continue ringing and [would] buzz (*cresselen* [= Ger.: *kesseln*]) all similar tones. And by means of the braided cloth it has the full resonance of thirds to thirds, or fifths to fifths, of octaves to octaves, and also successively according to its property" (sig. A4v).[60] This incorporates Virdung's statements regarding the avoidance of harsh sounds on the clavichord plus material he had presented on sig. E3 pertaining to measurements of the notes on the strings and relating to the consonances sounding together on several strings.

Another passage that at first glance seems to expand on Virdung's information turns out to be a mistranslation based upon a misunderstanding of Virdung's terms. The text (*Mus. get.*, sigs. E2–E2v) concerns the monochord, and in *Dit* (sigs. A2v–A3) it reads as follows (with the misinterpreted words here indicated in bold typeface and the French equivalents from *Livre* following the Netherlandic in brackets):

I believe that the clavichord is the instrument that Guido of Arezzo called "monochord," surely because of its single **side** [N.: *eender siden*; from Ger.: *eyner aynigen saiten*; Fr.: *l'ung des costez*]. And this is divided or measured, written and ruled according to the diatonic genus alone, about which I find enough written **in their books** [N.: *haerlieder boecken* (from Ger.: *obdon geschriben*); Fr.: *leurs livres*] that such a monochord is a long, rectangular box, like a chest or coffer, on which box one **side** [N.: *side*] is stretched, which is divided with all the consonances by means of the proportions which bring forth all things in their essence and size, which divisions are indicated by little points. Moreover, on the interior floor of this monochord there is fashioned a **circle** [N.: *cirkel* (from Ger.: *zirckel*); Fr.: *cercle*] out of which the tones ring or give their sound. The divisions that are on the side in back of this monchord are called the "stick" [N.: *steeck*; Fr.: *la perchure*]. And this has much to do with whether the monochord is good or bad. For the stick [Fr. adds "or point"] is the tone [N.: *thoon*; Fr.: *ton*] that holds its proportions. A key will be placed on each of these above-mentioned little points, for which I am inclined to think this instrument is now named "clavichord."[61]

Misinterpretations of the indicated terms in this passage has resulted in a serious mistranslation of Virdung's text. In the first place, the word "side" should read "string."[62] In the second place, the phrase "in their books" should read "in the writings of Odo" (i.e., the medieval theorist). Thirdly, "circle" should properly be "dividers" (Ger.: *zirckel*). Here the divisions of the string on a monochord (indicated by points) have been interpreted in *Dit* as divisions marked on the *side* of the monochord; and the means of arriving at these measurements, dividers, has become the round soundhole on the same instrument. In addition, a third mistake occurs in this paragraph regarding the proportions. In *Dit* they "bring forth all things in their essence," an ancient idea and popular at the time, but one not present in the original German text.

Quite a startling mistranslation occurs in the passage concerning types of strings appropriate for different instruments (*Mus. get.*, sig. I4v). *Dit* has the following: "For [gut strings] are put on harps, on viols (*vedelen*), on hurdy-gurdies (*lieren*), on shawms [*sic*] (*scarmeyen*), and on other instruments similar to these" (sig. F3).[63] *Scarmeyen* may be an incorrect rendering of *drum scheits* ("trumpet marine") in the original German, and *lieren* may translate *clainen geigen*, therefore conveying the meaning of "rebec." In any case, the French translator wisely omitted both these instruments from this sentence in *Livre* (sig. E4v).

Although *Dit* and *Livre* are charming little illustrated books filled with much useful information, those who adapted the Netherlandic work from the German original, as well as the person who then translated the Netherlandic into French, did not do their tasks with the kind of care we would hope to see. Where the language and concepts challenged the translators beyond their expertise and ability to cope, these workers did the best they could. The result is often compounded confusion. It is heartening to know, however, that some of the most convoluted or obtuse sentences in *Musica getutscht* gave to translators in the sixteenth century difficulties similar to those we experience today.

Sebastian Virdung's idea of producing a picture book for musical amateurs with instructions and diagrams useful for learning how to play three of the basic instruments of the indoor or "bas" variety had far-reaching consequences. The success of this idea inspired adaptations and translations of *Musica getutscht* into four languages (Latin, German, Netherlandic, and French). These derivative works in turn enjoyed enough popularity for them to go through multiple printings, spanning six decades after the initial publication in 1511 of Virdung's treatise – that is, from *ca.* 1517 to 1568.[64] By comparing these offspring with the parent work, we see fascinating reinterpretations and misinterpretations of the original material. In addition, we gain insights into changing attitudes toward musical instruments and their use in the sixteenth century.

Virdung's idea caught the spirit of the time, and his accomplishment impelled this very spirit into the future. For the two basic assumptions behind *Musica getutscht* – that playing musical instruments is beneficial to both the individual and society and that one can teach oneself the fundamentals of these skills – lived on in the treatises that Virdung's work inspired; and, indeed, these assumptions still hold sway today.

PART TWO

Musica getutscht

A note on the translation

Sebastian Virdung wrote *Musica getutscht* in his mother tongue, a language known today as Early New High German (*Frühneuhochdeutsch*). Virdung's particular use of this language falls between two well-researched linguistic eras: that of its precursor, Middle High German, and that of its more standardized offspring, the Early New High German cultivated by Martin Luther and his literary contemporaries in the decades following publication of *Musica getutscht*. Virdung's German presents difficulties to the modern reader. These arise in connection with archaic vocabulary and grammatical constructions, as well as colloquial inconsistencies and orthographic variety. Then too, the convoluted ordering of elements in some of the more lengthy sentences, especially when further obscured by unreliable punctuation and capitalization, makes necessary "much effort and careful examination" (*vil müe und übersehens*) to quote Virdung himself (sig. A4v, p. 100 below).

In this English version of *Musica getutscht* I have followed the original text very closely, electing where feasible to render the German into English as accurately as possible *per verbum* rather than more casually *per sensum*. To this end I have consulted coeval dictionaries to check meanings of virtually the entire vocabulary employed in the treatise. I hope thus to have captured some of the flavor of Virdung's language and to have retained subtle insights into modes of thought characteristic of his time and place.

In preparing the edition of this work I have found the modal auxiliary verbs to be the most problematic to translate. Virdung employs future auxiliaries other than the modern *werden*, preferring those prevailing in his time and earlier, *sollen* and *wollen*. In certain contexts, furthermore, the verb *müssen* also connotes futurity in addition to obligation. In translating these modals I have attempted to reproduce original shades of meaning by often rendering the German *soll* (*sollen*) as the English cognate "shall" (which likewise at one time conveyed a sense of duty, or the result of a decision, along with futurity), and *will* (*wollen*) as "will" (which connotes determination or volition along with futurity). For these verbs as well as *müssen* I have been influenced by the sixteenth-century translations of this work into Netherlandic and French and by my English ear. Although I cannot claim absolute consistency in this matter, each decision is the result of thought and of consideration.

Many German nouns ending in *n* during this period were not plural, as they appear to readers of today, but singular in meaning. In most instances the terminal *n* reveals a now obsolete case ending. An example occurs on the title page, where *Orgeln*, *Lauten*, and *Flöten* refer to single instruments. (See also n. 40, p. 228 below.)

Because *Musica getutscht* represents a pioneering effort on the part of its author to wed the Latin-bound, scholarly subject of music (*Musica*), one of the seven liberal arts, with common instrumental practice and a local vernacular terminology, I have chosen to indicate Virdung's use of Latin in his conversation – at least the first time each Latin term occurs.

While largely adhering to Virdung's paragraph structure, I have nevertheless on occasion separated the information into somewhat smaller units to make reading more convenient for the modern reader. I have divided sentences for this reason as well. I have transliterated *u* and *v* to modern usage and supplied missing letters indicated by tittles (marks of abbreviation) without comment. Similarly, I have transliterated the typographical symbol for *s* and *z* (*es zet*: *ß*) as *ss*.

Minor misprints abound in *Musica getutscht*, especially those involving inverted letters (e.g., *u* for *n* and *vice versa*). Only the major ones – those affecting the substance of the text – will be noted in the translation.

Readers wishing to follow the original text of *Musica getutscht* in any of the several facsimile editions of this work (see below, n. 72, p. 202), can consult the documented glossary found in the doctoral dissertation that led to this book – Beth Bullard, "Musical Instruments in the Early Sixteenth Century: A Translation and Historical Study of Sebastian Virdung's *Musica getutscht* (Basel, 1511)" (University of Pennsylvania, 1987), pp. 125–42. This glossary offers meanings of archaic words as Virdung used them in *Musica getutscht*. Also included are sixteenth-century definitions of modern equivalents that were familiar to Virdung and his contemporaries but that may never or rarely be used today.

(Sig. [A]) *Musica*,[1] written in German and extracted [from a larger work] by Sebastian Virdung, priest from Amberg, with [instructions] for learning how to transcribe all song (*alles gesang*)[2] from the notes into the tablatures of the three instruments named here: the organ,[3] the lute, and the recorder; [instructions] presented in brief form, to honor the illustrious noble prince and lord, Lord Wilhelm, Bishop of Strassburg,[4] his gracious lord.

(Sig. [Av]) [Arms of the Bishop of Strassburg]

(Sig. A2) To the illustrious noble prince and great lord, Lord Wilhelm, Bishop of Strassburg and Landgrave of Alsace, his most gracious lord: Sebastian Virdung, priest from Amberg, offers his willing [and] humble service. Noble prince, excellent in [the sight of] God the Father, gracious lord: because at the last Imperial Diet held at Augsburg a year ago[5] your princely grace saw and desired [a copy of] my versified treatise on music in German (*mein gedicht der deutschen musica*);[6] and [because] from that time on I have also been repeatedly sought out by your princely grace's chaplain,[7] my old school fellow, who exhorted me and asked me – in letters or else by word of mouth – when I would finally be finished with the book so I [could] publish it; but because a great deal of trouble and expense arises for me daily, due to which this work has been delayed and kept back for so long a time, I thought of extracting a small, abbreviated treatise out of the complete book [to give] pleasure and [to be of] service to a good friend named Andreas Silvanus,[8] who almost overwhelmed me with entreaties to do so. Now that I have completed this task, I shall honor your princely grace with this [book] – before [I have brought out the other one] – by dedicating, entitling, [and] inscribing it to your princely grace, and by having published in your princely grace's name and honor that which I herewith present and offer to your princely grace. Here I beg you, with your princely grace, to accept in all graciousness, this, my little book, until I have finished the other one, at which time I shall send it as well to your princely grace.[9] With this I commend myself to (sig. [A2v]) your princely grace, as always in all meekness and humility.

Dated on Tuesday, St. Margaret's Day [15 July], 1511, at Basel.[10]

Beatus populus qui scit iubilationem. Psalm 88.[11] David, the holy prophet spoke these words in the psalm indicated above. And the words in German are as follows: "Blessed is the people (*das volck*) that knows how to make the joyful sound (*die iubilierung*)."[12] In these words the prophet promises that this people or those persons who know how to rejoice will be blessed. Then too, in Psalm 94,[13] he summons all of us and says, "Come exult in the Lord, and rejoice in God our Salvation and rejoice in Him with psalms." Upon consideration of such words, I find that there are two kinds of rejoicing. The first is called *Iubilatio contemplativa,* or the ardent rejoicing of the heart in God. The second is called

Iubilatio activa, that is, an active rejoicing. Christ spoke about the first type of rejoicing – that is, the ardent rejoicing of the heart in God – in the Gospel concerning Mary Magdalen.[14] Mary chose the better part, and for that reason we too should consider this rejoicing more valuable and more important than the active [rejoicing]. But the first [type] has more to do with theology than with music. Therefore, I shall write no more about it here at this time. Rather, I shall entrust [this subject] to the scholars (*den doctoribus*) of the Holy Scriptures and to the clergy in holy orders. Nevertheless, Christ the Lord also accepted the active good deed of Martha; and to this end, in the Holy Scriptures we are often and frequently admonished, required, and even almost compelled to serve and praise God; and [we are] told precisely who should always praise Him: (Sig. [A3]) In the psalm *Laudate dominum de c[a]elis,* [number] 148,[15] [the psalmist] begins with the angels and says, "Praise the Lord all His angels. Praise Him all His host (*kreffte*). Praise Him, sun and moon. Praise Him all stars and lights." [In Psalm] 149:[16] "Sing to the Lord a new song. Let Him be praised in the entire Holy Christian Church.[17] Let them praise His name in the *chorus* (*in Choro*);[18] let them sing praises to Him in the *tympanum* (*in Tympano*) and in the psaltery (*in dem psalter*). Then is the Lord pleased with His people." And after that [in] Psalm 150:[19] "Praise Him in the sound of the trumpet.[20] Praise Him in the psaltery and the harp. Praise Him in the tympanum and chorus. Praise Him in the stringed instruments and organ. Praise Him in the sonorous [? chime] bells (*in den wollautenden Zymeln*).[21] Praise Him in the [? chime] bells of rejoicing."[22] And then [in] Psalm 97:[23] "Sing sacred songs to the Lord in the harp and in the sound of the psalm. Praise Him in the slide trombone (*in den zehenden Busaunen*)[24] and in the sound of the trumpet [made] of horn." Then, in Psalm 91,[25] he says we should praise Him in the psaltery of ten strings, with song and with the harp. And in another place he says [that] He should be praised in the trumpet of the new moon (*in Neomenia tuba*),[26] that is, with the trumpet of the waits (*mit dem Turnerhorn*) with which daybreak and nightfall are announced. From all these words of the prophet, we can note how he exhorts all creatures to praise the Lord. And he tells with what kinds of instruments the Lord should be praised, enumerating them and calling some of them by their own [individual] names. And he speaks in particular to priests and those in holy orders: "You who stand in the house of the Lord and in the antechambers of the house of Our Lord should lift up your hands day and night unto the Lord (sig. [A3v]) and praise God the Lord."[27]

Since, however, we are all frail beings by God's creation, we cannot all of us experience continuously the ardent rejoicing. Therefore we are bidden and commanded in so many [Biblical] passages to rejoice in God the Lord actively, that is, with instruments. And [He] demands and requires this from an entire people, whereby we should understand that He desires this not only from one person but from all who believe in Christ. And [as noted] at the beginning [of this introduction], [He] calls those who are able to do this blessed. So that there will be even more of these [blessed people] who learn this [kind of rejoicing], I have begun a brief little treatise, writing a small amount about these instruments, from which those who wish to share in such promised blessedness may take some small or tiny bit as a foundation or introduction to the instrument with which to learn [it], thereby gaining the promised eternal blessedness. Therefore we shall say with the prophet Isaiah in the thirty-eighth chapter:[28] "Oh Lord, make me blessed. And thus shall we sing our psalms all the days of our lives in the house of the Lord." To this end help us all, thou majestic maiden, eternally chaste and pure, the tender virgin and mother of God, the heavenly queen, Mary, Amen.

Below, Herr Bastian[29] is welcomed by Andreas Silvanus,[30] the musician (*dem musico*)[31] with words such as the following:

(Sig. [A4]) [Woodcut portrait of the interlocutors]
    Andreas Silvanus   Sebastian [Virdung]

(Sig. [A4v] My dear Herr Bastian! In [the name of] God, I welcome you a thousandfold! *Se*[*bastian*]: Thank you, my dear friend. *A*[*ndreas*]: How are you my dear Bastian? *Se*: God bless you for asking. I am still well, by the grace of God. *A*: I pray you (*lieber*), tell me where you have been for so long. *Se*: I have researched, investigated, and made discoveries about that [subject in pursuit of] which I have been wandering about for a long time. *A*: What is it [you have learned]? *Se*: About theoretical, practical, and instrumental music. *A*: I have been well aware that for a long time you have occupied yourself with preparing something new and unusual, but I did not know what it was. So, unless you are keeping it as your own personal secret, I would like to ask you to tell me about it and to show it to me. *Se*: I would be most favorably inclined to grant you this request – and even larger ones – as long as it were to bring me no disadvantage. *A*: Dear friend, by [my] faith I tell you, it shall be without any detriment to you whatsoever. Let me see it. *Se*: It will take much effort and careful examination [on your part]. Then too, you do not have as much knowledge of German writings and verses (*des teütschen gedichts, und der reymen*) as [you do] of Latin works (*als der latinischen poetrey*). Still, if you want to have a brief view of the drawings for the illustrations, I cannot very well refuse you this. If you wished to read through all of it, however, that would take much too long. *A*: I pray you, just let me glance over it briefly. *Se*: Very well. Take it then, and have a good look at it.

A: Dear friend, you have many attractive pictures in the book. What is their purpose? *Se*: There are many illustrations with stories about the discovery or about the origin of music, from the Bible, and the poets,[32] [and] the Christian teachers as well. *A*: Why, then, are the organs, wind instruments (*Pfeiffen*), lutes, bowed stringed instruments (*Geigen*), and other instruments pictured in the book?

(Sig. B) *Se*: The [subject of] music has many divisions, and one of the parts concerns the music of instruments. These [instruments] are therefore pictured along with their names so that they will become known so much the better to each person who looks at the book.[33]

A: How many of these instruments are there then? *Se*: You must divide the part of music that has to do with instruments into three categories; then you will be able to understand me. *A*: What are these three categories? *Se*: The first consists of all the instruments that are strung with strings, and all of these are called stringed instruments. The second category consists of all the instruments that are sounded or piped by means of air. The third category consists of all the instruments that are made of metal or other resonant substances. *A*: I cannot understand that very well; explain it to me more fully. *Se*: Very well, I will make a second[-level] division for you [in each category].

In the first category, [that] of the stringed instruments, some of them have keys. For [these instruments] one can formulate rules (*mag man sie regulieren*) with reference to these [keys], and then, by following the rules, learn to play all the instruments with keyboards in the same way.[34]

Clavichord (*Clavicordium*)[35]

Virginal

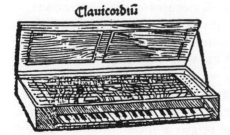

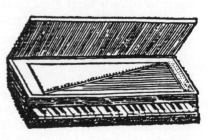

(Sig. [Bv] *Clavicimbalum* [harpsichord?])[36]
Clavicytherium[37]

Hurdy-Gurdy (*Lyra*)

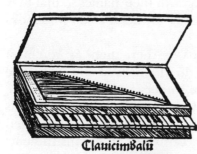

which?.. *clavicymbalum.*

That [instrument] is just like the virginal, only it has other strings made of sheep's gut, and nails [i.e., brays] that make it [sound like a] harp. Like the virginal, it also has quills. It is of recent invention, and I have only seen one of them.[38]

Stringed instruments of the second kind do not have keys, but [they do have] frets (*bünde*) and otherwise fixed bounds or boundaries[39] where one can have [a] secure touch – always on the courses and frets. By means of these [courses and frets], one (sig. B2) can also formulate rules and write out [intabulations] for these [instruments] from which to learn to play them. All of the instruments that follow here have [courses and frets]:

Lute(s) (*Lauten*)[40]   Viol(s) (*Gross Geigen*)[41]

Quintern[42]

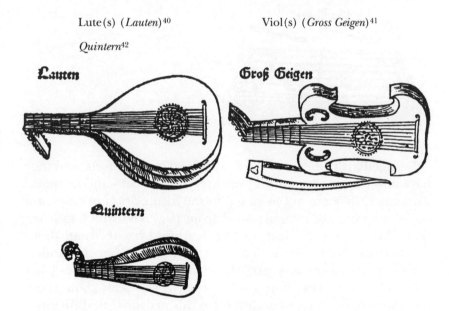

Lauten   **Groß Geigen**

Quintern

Stringed instruments of the third kind also have courses of strings, and one can formulate rules and write out [intabulations] with reference to these courses from which to learn to play them as well. All of the following instruments are [of this type].

Harp(s) (Harpffen)[43]   Psaltery (*Psalterium*)

Hammered Dulcimer (*Hackbrett*)

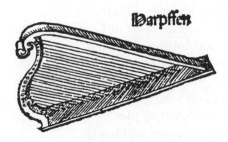

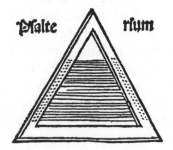

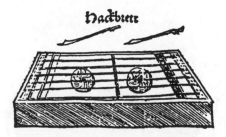

Stringed instruments of the fourth kind have no frets, and they have only one or two courses – or three at the most – and no more. Therefore, they are not as suited to the formulation of rules and the writing out [of intabulations] from (sig. B2v) which to learn them. For [with these instruments, learning] has to come about much more from a great deal of practice and from the understanding of song (*des gesangs*)[44] than it does by means of rules [that are] written out. Therefore I shall write the very least about these instruments; because, in addition [to this pedagogical difficulty], I consider and deem as unprofitable instruments (*onnütze instrumenta*) those such as the rebecs (*dye cleinen Geigen*) and the trumpet marine.

(Sig. B3) Trumpet Marine (*Trumscheit*) and Rebec(s) (*clein Geigen*)[45]

Trumscheit vnd clein Geigen

The instruments of music (*instrumenta der Musica*) in the second category are the kind that are [made] of hollow tubes through which air is blown.[46] And I find these to be of two types. There are some tubes for which a person can provide sufficient air, that is, which a person can play by blowing. [There are] some, however, [that] no one is able to sound by blowing. For these, one must have bellows.

Hollow tubes of the first kind – those that a person can sound by blowing – are likewise of two types. Some tubes have holes that one opens and closes with the fingers, and the more holes they have, the better and with more certainty one can formulate rules for them, though a pipe seldom has more than eight holes. But there are some that have only three holes, some four, some five, some six, some seven, some eight.

(Sig. [B3v]) Shawm (*Schalmey*)   Tenor Shawm (*Bombardt*)

Schwegel [Tabor Pipe = three-holed, vertical, one-hand, fipple flute][47]

Fife [and Transverse Flute?] (*Zwerchpfeiff*)

Recorders (*Flöten*) [bass, two tenors, discant]

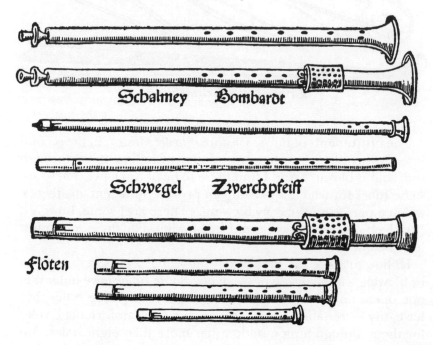

(Sig. [B4]) *Russpfeif* [~~"noisy~~ (?) pipe"][48]

Krum horn ["curved horn": a curved four-holed cornett?]

Gemshorn (*Gemsen horn*) ["chamois horn"]

Cornett(s) (*Zincken*) [= straight cornett(s)][49]

Bladder Pipe (*Platerspil*)

Crumhorns (*Krumhörner*) [apparently discant, alto, tenor, and bass][50]

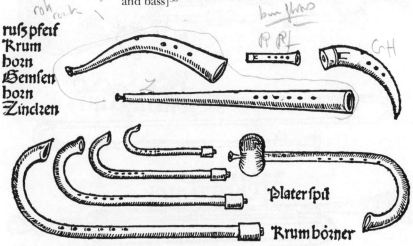

ruſspfeif
Krum
horn
Gemſen
horn
Zincken

Platerſpil

Krumhözner

The second type [of the first division] in the second category [– that of the wind instruments –] includes the hollow tubes that have no holes, but which a person can play by blowing. As for which of these can have rules formulated for them and how one will be able to learn to play them, however, I will say no more about that here. Rather, in the other book I will say and write something on this subject [that is] new and not [generally] known.

(Sig. [B4v]) Bagpipe (*Sackpfeiff*)[51]

Trombone(s) (*Busaunen*)[52]

Military Trumpet (*Felttrummet*)[53]   Field Anget.

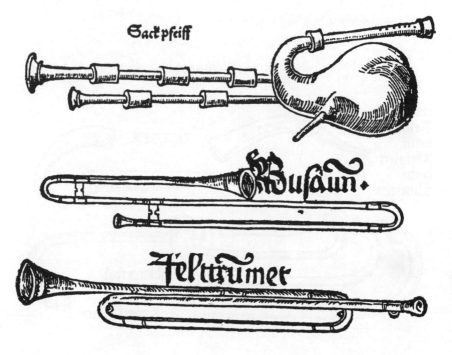

(Sig. C) *Clareta*

Trumpet of the Waits (*Thurner Horn*)

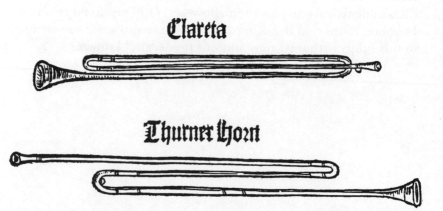

In this second category, that of hollow tubes, is the second kind of these instruments: those for which a person by oneself cannot provide enough air, that is, those that no one can sound by blowing. These are all the instruments for which one must have bellows:

(Sig. [Cv]) Organ (*Orgel*)

Positive [organ]

Regal (*Regale*)

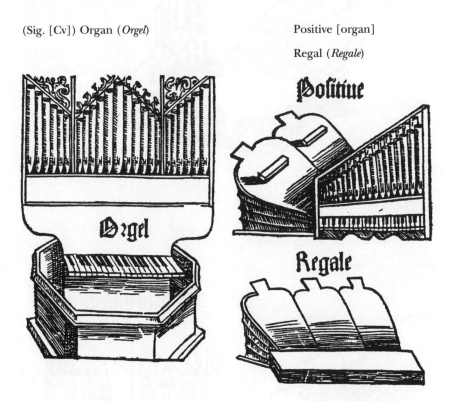

(Sig. [C2] Portative [organ]

Anvil and Hammers (*Ampos und hemmer*)[54]

Chime Bells [tuned bells (on a frame?) to be struck with a hammer] and crotal-shaped sectioned bell(s) ([both =] *Zymeln*)[55]

and Clapper Bell(s) (*Glocken*)[56]

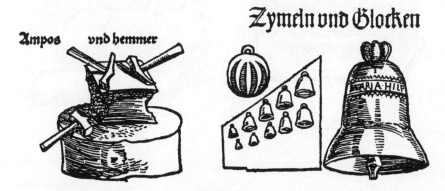

A: Then what is the third category of the instruments: *Se*: That one includes all those kinds of instruments that resound like the hammers on the anvil, from which the proportions were discovered for the first time by Tubal:[57] the little bells and chime bells. To write about these ringing instruments and also about organ pipes, I would choose Boethius,[58] because these have to do with the *mensur*, that is, [with] the (sig. [C2v]) measurement of the tubes and the weight of the metals (like the hammer), and that is expressed through the theory of the proportions. [I have] written nothing at all about these [here], but [I am] saving [this subject] for the complete work. It seems to me, therefore, that enough has been said to you for now about the instrumental [aspect of] Music and also about the categories of these instruments and their members.

A: It seems to me that the distribution of all the instruments into three categories is much too abbreviated, because I have seen quite a few other *instrumenta Musicalia* described and pictured. When I obtained the works of St. Jerome (*opera sancti Hieronimi*), I found a treatise therein that the holy father wrote to Dardanus (*ad Dardanum*) – in the sixty-first letter – about the kinds of Music (*de generibus Musicorum*), [with] many more unusual shapes or forms of instruments and with many more unusual names other than [those] you have given to the instruments of the present day.[59] Therefore, if you are indeed going to write separately about each and every instrument, then it will be proper that you not leave behind, pass over, or conceal these [instruments]. *Se*: I too have seen a few of these instruments pictured and described by my master, the late Johannes von Soest, Doctor of Medicine,[60] in a large parchment book that he himself composed (*co[m]poniert*) and wrote out.[61] But to tell the truth, at that time I took no notice of them, and I have not been to the place where the book is for a long time. I believe, furthermore, that no one is alive now who has made, heard, or seen these instruments, for they are no longer in use. I would certainly like to see them, even more (sig. C3) to hear them, and most of all, to know what they represented; because whatever Jerome wrote about things, it always had to have a second, spiritual meaning. Therefore, etc.[62] *A*: I can show you none of the actual instruments. But I will put before you an old book in which they are illustrated and also described to some extent. If you trouble yourself to examine this [book], I will give you [my] approval, to be sure. Since you have otherwise come to know so much [about musical instruments], if you occupy yourself with them [i.e., the instruments of Jerome], [then] you can perhaps imagine how they were used better than I could accomplish this [task]. *Se*: Yes, my friend, I beg you, kindly show me the old book so I may see how they were shaped.

A: I find three forms of harps, of which none is pictured like the one you showed me. Here they are:

Cythara of Jerome
(*Cythara Iheronimi*)

Another Cythara of Jerome
(*Alia Cythara Iheronimi*)

(Sig. [C3v]) Another Cythara of Jerome (*Alia cytera Iheronimi*)

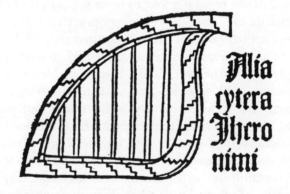

Se: The form and shapes of the three kinds of ancient harps, and of the new ones as well, are all of them triangular; and although, owing to their form, they [i.e., the old] are not exactly the same as our modern harps that are made at present, this could perhaps be the fault of the illustrator in former times (*etwan*). For [harps] are nevertheless also still built in the triangular shape, though the three parts, pieces, or sides of these [modern] instruments are found [to be] unequal – so that one [side] is longer than the other – and [they are] not [built in the shape of] an entirely true triangle. Yet the old and new harps do have quite a bit of difference with regard to the strings, because the new ones have more strings than the old ones. In addition, they are also far superior in resonance, and they are made more artfully and beautifully in form for their use – for learning and playing them. And that may perhaps be the case as well regarding the other instruments about which Jerome wrote.

A: I find the psaltery depicted in two ways, [which] likewise differ from the one you showed me, as appears here:

Psaltery of Ten Strings
(*Psalterium decacordum*)

Psaltery of Ten Strings
(*Psalterium decacordum*)

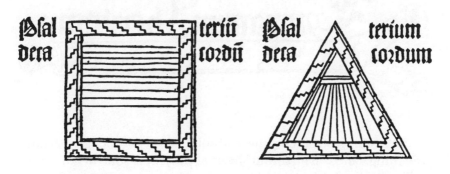

Se: I have never seen the psaltery that is still in use in a form other than triangular. But I believe and am of the opinion that the virginal was first thought to be made from the psaltery, so that nowadays it is touched and struck with keys and is made with quill feathers. In spite of the fact that this [instrument, the virginal,] (sig. [C4] is fastened into a long case just like the clavichord, it still has many other characteristics that make it more comparable to the psaltery than to the clavichord. [For example,] since one must have a separate string for each key, any string must be tuned higher than another. Therefore, in like manner, any string must be longer than another.[63] Because of this, from the cutting off and shortening of the strings, there will be [a shape] like a triangle inside the case. I will have more to say about this later. But it is not strange that you show the psaltery of Jerome as a square. For the [external] shape of an instrument does not matter much; rather, only the stringing and tuning [are important].[64]

A: In your division [of musical instruments] you have said nothing to me as yet about the *Tympanum,* to which the Holy Scriptures make frequent reference [regarding] how it was used to praise Almighty God. I find it pictured like this: (sig. [C4v]) as a long pipe that has a mouthpiece at its upper end into which one blows, and two apertures at the lower end out of which the sound and air are expelled. And it is known that a woman was able to carry it in one hand.[65] It appears here:

Tympanum of Jerome (*Tympanum Iheronimi*)

Se: Of this instrument I have absolutely no knowledge, because the thing called "tympanum" by us at present is [one of] the large military [kettle]drums (*die grossen Herpaucken*) made from a copper cauldron with calfskin drawn over it that one beats with drumsticks, so that it makes a very loud and clear noise. When the royal court summons [soldiers] to the [battle]field with trumpets (*zů den felt trummeten*),[66] when trumpets are sounded at table (*wann man zů tisch plaset*),[67] or when a prince rides into a city, or musters for war, or marches into the [battle]field, [these drums] are enormous tubs of great noise.[68] Besides these there are also other drums that are generally beaten to [the music of] fifes (*zů den zwerch pfeiffen*), like the soldiers have. Moreover, there is yet another small drum that the French and Netherlanders use a great deal along with one-hand flutes (*zů den Schwegeln*), especially for dances[69] or for festivals (*hochzyten*).[70]

(Sig. D) Military [Kettle]drums (*Herpaucken*), Drum(s) (*Trumeln*), and Small Drum (*clein paücklin*)[71]

All these drums are there if you want them. They greatly disturb the peace of honorable, virtuous, old people; of the sick and ailing; of the religious in cloisters, who have to read, study, and pray. And I believe and consider it the truth [that] the devil invented and made them, for there is absolutely nothing pleasant or good about them. On the contrary, [they cause] a smothering and a drowning of all sweet melodies and of the whole of Music. I can well believe, therefore, that the tympanum which was used in the service of God must have been an object entirely different from our drums that are made today, and [I believe] that we have given that name undeservedly to the devilish instrument, which is surely not worthy of being used for Music, (sig. [Dv]) much less [worthy] of even being admitted as an instrument of this noble art. For, if beating or making a loud noise is supposed to be Music, then the hoopmakers or the coppersmiths or the coopers must be musicians as well. But that is pure nonsense. As for the Tympanum of Jerome that you are showing to me, I cannot imagine what it could be or how one used it.

A: What kind of instrument, then, is the *Chorus*, which I find like this: it has a mouthpiece, into which one blows, and two tubes in the middle. After that, at the lower end, it has one aperture from which the sound or air exits. [It was] formed like this:

Chorus[72]

(Sig. D2)[73] Farther on Jerome says that the *Tuba* consisted of three mouthpieces, through which the air entered. These signify the Father, the Son, and the Holy Spirit in the Trinity. And the main part, where the air or sound went out again, signifies the four Evangelists. [It was] formed like this:

Tuba of Jerome (*Tuba Hieronimi*)

He describes [the] *Fistula* and draws it in the following manner: as a thing made like a carpenter's square, which is supposed to signify the holy cross, having a four-cornered object hanging from it, which is to signify Christ on the cross, with twelve pipes, which are to signify the Apostles, as do likewise the twelve pipes in the organ and also the twelve pipes in the *Cymbalum* (*in den zymbalo*). [They] appear here:

(Sig. [D2v]) Fistula of Jerome (*Fistula Hieronimi*)

Organ of Jerome (*Organum Hieronimi*)

Fistula Hieronimi

Organū Hieronimi

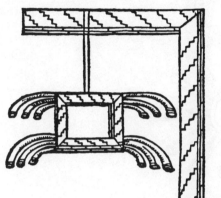

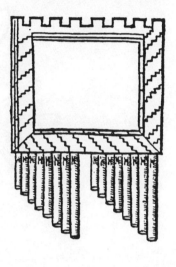

(Sig. D3) Cymbalum of Jerome (*Zymbalum Iheronimi*)

Zymbalū Jheronimi

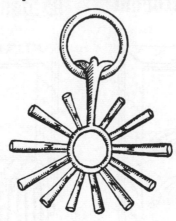

Se: Dear friend, that is enough said here about these things for the present. I can give you no further answer, because I have neither heard nor seen the instruments, nor do I know how or for what purpose they were used. *A*: Therefore you have not adequately looked into this subject, and [you have not] fully set forth in writing all that you took upon yourself [to cover] in your introduction [i.e., sigs. A2v through A3v – pp. 97–9 above]. *Se*: What I undertook [to deal with] is the instruments that are now used by us in our land and nothing more. The poets [of antiquity] also had many other instruments with strange names about which they wrote. I can discover nothing about these other than that they were musical instruments (*instrumenta Musicalia*). But how they were formed or shaped, [whether] they were better or worse, more beautiful or more ugly, more refined or more crude than ours, no one writes precisely about this. Indeed, I could mention [these instruments] by name, (sig. [D3v]) except that what one [writer] has defined as a harp, another calls a lyre, and vice versa, and the same [is true] for many [other ancient instruments]. I believe, moreover, that in the past hundred years, all instruments have been made [to be] so refined, so beautiful, so excellent, and so well formed, that neither Orpheus, nor Linus, nor Pan, nor Apollo, nor any of the poets [of antiquity] would have seen or heard [the likes]; nor [if they had,] could they have thought it possible that anything better could be constructed or invented.

On the other hand, one also finds many more *instrumenta* [that are] foolish, which are also considered or regarded as *musicalia,* like these:

Jew's Harp(s) (*Trumpeln*); Bell(s) (*Schellen*); Hunting Horn (*Jeger horn*);[74] Field Horn (*Acher horn*);[75] Cowbell(s) (*Küschellen*); Beater(s) on the Pot (*Britschen, uff dem hafen*);[76] [Clappers – with bell].[77]

Trumpeln/Schellē/Jeger horn /Acher horn/küschellen.Britschē/vff dem hafen

[There are] also many others, such as little whistles [made] from quill feathers; the fowler's bird calls, [like] quail calls, lark whistles, titmouse calls; whistles made from blades of straw; whistles [made] from the juicy bark of the tree [or] from the leaves of the tree, which, when blown,[78] (sig. [D4]) one calls mouth or lip flutes (*Schwegeln mit dem mund oder mit den lefftzen*); blowing in the hands as well as in keys; the xylophone (*hültzig gelechter*) [lit., "wooden laughter"]; and many other similar ones. All these instruments, whatever they are named or [whatever] names they might acquire, I consider tomfoolery (*göckel spill*) [lit., "juggler play"]. Therefore it irks me to name them, even more to illustrate them, and above all to describe them. Thus, at the present time, I will take leave of them altogether and speak only about those instruments that any peasant (*eyn ietlicher paur*) might know of and call by name [and] those that are serviceable to sweet melody. Nevertheless, however, you might persuade me later on – as a result of [considering] the illustrations of the old Hebrew instruments that you showed me – that I must look into [this subject] further [in order] to write something more explicit about it in the other book.

A: [Well] now, if you will not speak about them in more detail here at this time, then I shall have to be satisfied with the very division [into categories] of the recognizable and serviceable instruments that you made at the beginning [of our conversation]. But, I beg you, tell me how I can learn to play the instruments. Do they all have a similar principle, so that were I to learn to play wind instruments, I would then also know how to play the lute, [the] organ, or other stringed instruments in exactly the same way?

Se: All instruments of Music as a whole are not very different when it comes to melody that is written down in notes, and whoever knows how to sing these [notes] can very easily learn to play them exactly the same on all instruments, and this [kind of] person needs no other rule. But for the others, [those] who are not able to sing [from notes], for them a (sig. [D4v]) method (*modus*) has been devised – tablature – to teach them how to learn the instruments separately, according to the type and properties of each individual instrument. *A*: I too cannot sing anything [from notes], but I do have a strong desire to learn [to play] the instruments. Could you teach me [how to play] wind instruments, [how] to strike [the] lute, or [how to play the] organ, without [teaching me] mensural notation (*das gesang*)?[79] *Se*: I cannot teach you [how to play an instrument] entirely satisfactorily without [teaching you] mensural notation. You must learn to understand at least something of what the system (*das gesang*) is all about. At the very least you must learn to know the notes and the keys[80] and to call them by their names. Beyond all that, [to be an instrumentalist] you would need to learn the *modus componendi*, that is, the art of counterpoint and of composition. I write more about this in the other book, for [in the case of counterpoint and composition], one cannot write for you in advance how you should or must apply your fingers to the holes of the pipe, or to the frets and courses of the lute, or to the keys of the keyboard instruments.[81] Moreover, I do not believe that it could all be put into writing in this [book] (*einer*), owing to the complexity of counterpoint and diminution.[82] But if from the first (*vor hin*) you were to have a little [instruction in the] application of the fingers [to the various instruments],[83] then with good reason I believe you capable of learning [them] right now by means of the tablature that was previously prepared. But as for learning counterpoint and playing along *ad placitum* upon chant (*korgesang*) or some other [cantus firmus], I will present that in the other book. Therefore, at this point, you may undertake whatever you wish.

A: I would like to know everything about [playing] all instruments.[84] *Se*: I think it will not be possible to learn all [of them] at once. You must practice one after the other, each one for a while [before beginning another]. (Sig. E) As I previously stated, because of the various types and properties of the instruments, except for mensural notation (*das gsang*), a tablature cannot be made that is completely appropriate and suitable for all instruments. Therefore, because of this difference or distinction [between the instruments], there was invented and discovered for each its own tablature that is suitable and practical for learning. And although these tablatures are not all of them quite exactly the same – that is, they are [not] one single tablature – nevertheless, they still all have many similarities with measured music (*mit der regulierten Musica*) and also [many similarities] among themselves. If, therefore, you have the desire to learn how to set music written in mensural notation (*das gsang*) from the notes into the tablature, then I will introduce you to three instruments. When you can [play] from these three tablatures, then it will be easier for you to learn all the other [instruments] later on. *A*: Very well. I pray you, to which ones will you introduce me?

Se: First take up the clavichord, after that the lute, and thirdly the recorder. For, whatever you learn [to do] on the clavichord you [will] then have [as a foundation] for learning how to play well and easily the organ, the *clavizymell*,[85] the virginal, and all other keyboard instruments; next, whatever you learn about fingering and plucking on the lute you [will] have [as a foundation] for easily learning the harp, the psaltery, or the viol; [and] then, whatever you learn [to do] on the recorder you [will] have [as a foundation] for learning all the more easily later on all the other wind instruments with finger holes.

A: What do you have to say, then, about the remaining instruments, such as the trombone, [the] trumpet, and the like?[86]

Se: As I told you, I have written "A German *Musica*" in diverse kinds of verses and stanzas, just as the texts of German poetic *Lieder* are composed. In (sig. [Ev]) this book I teach singing, solmization, and mutation by the scale of Guido (*Gwidonis*), and about the eight modes, as well as figured song (*das figuriert gesang*) and singing counterpoint on the book.[87] In addition, I teach composition and whatever concerns Music and [whatever] is known to me. *A*: From what you are saying, this will be very comprehensive. Do tell me something about it without getting into the subject too deeply – [something] in ordinary terms. *Se*: I will also write about all proportions – theoretical and practical – in the whole of Music, and about all instruments, not only how one is to learn them, but also what is necessary in order to learn them. And [I] will provide so many examples of these, that – I know full well – no great thanks will be earned [by me] from some who have preferred not to show or present such things to their students. But since I have come to know and understand such [subjects], I am more inclined out of compassion to lighten the burden of these youths (*den selben iungen*), because many a youth – who would otherwise be eager to learn something – attains [knowledge] with great difficulty; and that can possibly make it not worth the trouble. For that reason – so that in future (*mer*) none of these youths [will] have to tire themselves for as long a time as I myself was worn out, impeded, and also delayed – I will therefore make a path for them to get easily to wherever they wish; and whatever I cannot make sufficiently clear in my writing, owing to its brevity, I will make up for by the multifarious and almost numberless examples or illustrations; and [I will] present as many of these as I am aware of [that] have not yet been publicly distributed.

A: Then won't you also give these examples and rules to me and write them out [for me] right now? *Se*: I (sig. E2) cannot ruin the complete book [i.e., give away the contents of the larger *Musica* before its publication] for your sake. But by the time you have learned the tablatures, God willing, the rest [of the examples] will also be ready [i.e., in print]. Since I will present all examples in mensural notation alone (*allein in dem gesang*), whoever wishes to may then transcribe them into whichever tablature is desired, [whether] it be for the organ, for the lute, or [for] another instrument, whichever one wants to have. For now, therefore, I can teach you no more than how to intabulate, [and that] in a few words. Then, if you wish, you may later obtain the other book as well. *A*: Very good. You are undertaking a large project. Take care that you follow through to its conclusion. *Se*: I know I can carry it out to the end, because everything – as much as I have to do for this [project] – is already prepared. *A*: Good, I am glad to hear it. Since you are going to extract a little treatise from this complete book – to please me, as you said; and [since] in telling me about the three instruments for which you will teach me to intabulate, you named the clavichord as the first; [tell me,] what kind of instrument is it, and how shall I learn to make one?

Here begin the lessons
Se: I will not describe how the clavichord and other instruments should be made, for that has more to do with architecture or the craft of the wood worker than it has to do with Music. However, learning the instruments according to the tablature does concern Music, and I will gladly give you instructions about that. *A*: That is what I would like. *Se*:[88] I believe that the *clavicordium* is what Guido of Arezzo (*gwido aretinus*) (sig. [E2v]) called the monochord (*monocordum*), because of its one single string. [He] divided or measured this [string], writing and giving rules [for these divisions or measurements] according to the diatonic genus alone.[89] On this subject, I find in the writings of Odo (*durch den obdon geschriben*), that such a monochord is a long, rectangular box, like a chest or a coffer.[90] Over this a string is stretched, which, having been apportioned [into measured segments] by dividers, produces all the consonances, [which are] demonstrably known by means of the proportions. But who it was who subsequently discovered or figured out that at every point designated by this measurement, a key [could be] made that would strike the string at exactly this place or point and thereby produce just this pitch and no other besides the one of its measure given by nature at this point, that I could never discover; and who it was who thus christened or named the instrument "clavichord" after these keys, I [likewise] do not know. *A*: Won't you also tell me how the monochord is to be measured? *Se*: Enough is written about that in the complete book [i.e., Virdung's yet unpublished manuscript, "A German *Musica*"]. In my opinion you need not know this now. For, at the present time I will teach you no more than how to intabulate for the instruments. *A*: Then what

[information] will you give me so that [I may] learn these tablatures?

Se: First, I will tell you about the keys and strings of the clavichord; after that, how these are to be represented in writing; and then, [how] to use these symbols in the tablature. *A*: Do proceed: tell me how many keys and strings a clavichord will have. *Se*: I cannot specify for you an exact sum that it actually must have; (sig. E3) [it has] as many as [it has], or that many and neither fewer nor more [than it has]. But since the instrument derives from the monochord, I think that it can be strung with as many strings as are desired. *A*: If it has more than one string, then it can no longer be called a monochord. Instead, one must name it for the number of the strings – for example, "tetrachord" for [an instrument with] four strings, "pentachord" for [one with] five strings, etc. *Se*: It does not matter that there are many strings; the important thing is that, [whether] the strings of the instrument be few or many, you see [to it] that they all are in unison (*unisonum*) with each other – that is, [they all have] the same pitch, not one higher or lower than the other. *A*: Why must that be so? *Se*: Because the division of the entire monochord is valid only on one string, and if there were more [strings] and [if these] were not of the same pitch, then the measurements would all be false on these strings and [this] would produce an untrue tuning. *A*: So it also suffices for a clavichord [to have] one single string. *Se*: No, you must of necessity have more than one. *A*: Why [is] that? *Se*: Because on one string alone no consonances can be made to sound *simul et semel*, that is, with each other at the same time, even though they can be heard well [when the pitches are sounded] one after another. Therefore it is necessary that there be many of these [strings], in order that one may hear on [the clavichord] the sweetness of the consonances with two pitches, with three, four, and with even more pitches [sounded] together, which one cannot do on one [string] alone.

A: How many keys will it have then? *Se*: When Guido wrote about the monochord, he considered only the diatonic genus, and for a long time the clavichord – in accordance with this [genus] – had no more than twenty keys,[91] like this:

(Sig. [E3v]) [Woodcut of Virdung's idea of an early keyboard]

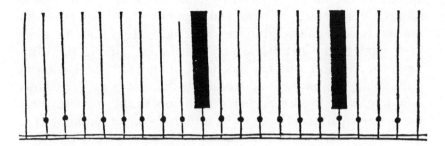

There were others coming along later, however, who made it more refined, and who, [having] also read Boethius,[92] divided the monochord according to the second genus, called the chromatic. *A:* You are telling me a lot about the strange genera. Do tell me what the diatonic genus is, and then [tell me] about the others as well, so that I may understand even better what you are saying to me. *Se:* As Boethius explains it in the first book of his *Musica,* in the twenty-first chapter,[93] the diatonic genus is [that which results] when one makes any diatessaron – which we call a fourth – out of two whole tones and one minor semitone, or out of four keys or four pitches. *A:* How am I to understand that? *Se:* Do as follows. Choose one of the keys among those that are pictured for you above, whichever you wish, and begin (sig. [E4]) to count them, either from below up to the highest, or from above going down to the lowest. Each time count four keys as a fourth. Thus, four of these keys always give you the [diatonic] diatessaron. [This] is correctly made from two whole tones and one minor semitone, except that I am omitting *b fa h mi.* I will speak about this later on, because that [note] has two keys that are counted as only one.

A: What, then, is the chromatic genus? *Se:* [The word] *c[h] roma* is just another word for "color," and *c[h] romaticum* [means] simply a colored thing. Then too, at times, something painted or nicely embellished is also called ["chromatic"]. So is it here as well in the art of Music, and the instrument is even more artfully decorated and made more beautiful by the semitones of the genus named *c[h] romaticum.* And it is [formed as follows]: One makes this [kind of] diatessaron – any one of them – from five species (*speciebus*) of the minor semitone, and this [type of] diatessaron must have

125

[within it] every one of the six pitches or keys that make up five species of the minor semitone.[94] Thus, according to the genus named "chromatic," thirteen more minor semitones (*semitonia minora*) have been added to the other raised keys [i.e., the black keys; namely, the two B♭ s] and distributed [among the white keys]. In addition, one key was made underneath the *gamma ut*, and, going up, one was added above the *e la* [i.e., f"].[95] Thus, counting from the lowest key directly up to the highest, three octaves are spanned. Some add another key and a semitone [i.e., g" and f#"]. Therefore [the clavichord] will generally be found nowadays with both genera [and] with thirty-eight keys, like this:

(Sig. [E4v]) [Illustration of a clavichord keyboard]

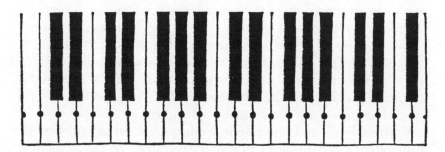

A: Then what is the third genus?[96] *Se*: It is called [the] *en[h]armonic* [genus]. But since it is not in practice or in use by organists and organ builders,[97] I will say nothing about it here at present. Rather, [for now, I will] only [speak] about practical matters and nothing more.

And one thing occurs to me that I can well understand: that some who call themselves illustrious learned masters, [thus] leaving themselves open to reproach, are not able to say very much about the three genera. For I recently read a small treatise that is entitled or named *The Mirror of All Organists and Organ Builders*, in the second chapter of which I find that [the author] says that the organist will in that case [i.e., when transposing] be playing by means of *musica ficta* (*per fictam Musicam*).[98] If this man knew what he was talking about regarding the three genera, he would not call it *musica ficta*, because what he deems to be *musica ficta* is the chromatic genus (*Cromaticum genus*); and, in the words of

Boethius (*secundum Boetium*) (sig. F) in the above-mentioned passage, [this genus has been] explained by a formula (*reguliert*) and by a description [that are easy] enough [to understand].[99] [The author] should be pardoned, however, because he over-looked [this passage]. [Either] his eyes are to blame, or the mirror has become dim. It would be better if it were polished clean by organists and organ builders.[100]

Then too, even though many newer clavichords are found nowadays that are even larger or longer – having four octaves or even more keys – still, these [keys] are nothing other than the equivalent of a repetition of the first pitches of the three octaves; and because of this, the majority [of these larger clavichords] are made in such a way that hanging pedals (*pedalia*) can be added to them, and [thus] of late another category of clavichords (*clavicordia*) [has been] made. Because of [these variables], I have not wanted to give any total number of strings at the outset. But, in general, three strings make up one choir (*uff einem kor*) so that if one string should suddenly snap [lit., "leap off"], as happens occasionally, [the player] need not stop playing on that account. Then too, each of most of the choirs has three keys that touch or strike it. Take great pains never to strike two [of these] at once, for they generally make a dissonance. Several empty choirs are also added to [the clavichord] which no keys touch at all. *A*: Why [is] that? And with what kind of strings is [a clavichord] strung? *Se*: Some think the empty choirs produce a good resonance on the instrument. Some say it is done for the sake of beauty or decoration, as if, when the white iron (*stehelin*) strings[101] and the yellow brass ones[102] are strung together, that will look good. I cannot believe that it is done for the sake of beauty, but rather out of necessity. *A*: What necessity? *Se*: (Sig. [Fv]) Because by nature the brass strings sound full (*grob*) and the iron ones thin (*cleyn*),[103] and since [clavichords] are now made to have as many as four octaves and even more, therefore the lower choirs are strung with brass strings and the upper ones with iron strings.

A: Then what is the purpose of the little strips (*zöttlin*) [lit., "tufts"] of woolen cloth on the instrument, those that are inter-laced among the choirs of strings? *Se*: These take the noisy ringing or the coarse, unpleasant sound or tone away from the strings,[104] [assuring] that they ring no longer than [the time] during which [the player] is holding down the key – for approximately one *tempus* and no more. But each time, as soon as he stops [holding down the key], even in runs, the string stops sounding immediately. This is what the little cloths do. Well then, let that be enough said to you about the first instrument, the clavichord. Now, if you wish, ask for more information that will be useful to you in your learning, and I will answer you as best I can.

A: You have told me enough about the instrument. Now how do I learn to intabulate for it? *Se*: I have told you that since you are not skilled at singing [i.e., reading mensural notation], I will try to teach you by means of the tablature. For this purpose you must know that Guido of Arezzo (*Guido Aretinus*) prescribed and established ten lines and as many spaces (*spacia*), and that he labeled these for the first time with the first seven letters of the alphabet. Then [he] named these letters "keys" (*claves*),[105] and to these keys [he] added the six notes – *ut, re, mi, fa, sol, la*. And he repeated these or set them again seven times. Thus is is that he has (sig. F2) made an entire word as a name proper [to each note] out of the letters of the keys and out of the repetition or resetting of the six notes, so that he might christen or name the lines and spaces. [He] labeled the first line with a Greek *gamma* (*Gamaut*) and set the first syllable of the notes [i.e., *ut*] to this letter, naming this line *gamma* and the note *gamma ut*. Then [he] called the first space above *gamma ut*: *a*,[106] and the second note: *a re*. After this [he] named the second line *h* and the third note *h mi*,[107] the second space *c fa ut, etc.*, going on upwards, as you can see in the following illustration.

There follows the musical scale or hand of Guido of Arezzo (*Sequitur Scala musicalis, sive manus Guidonis aretini.*)
(Sig. [F2v])

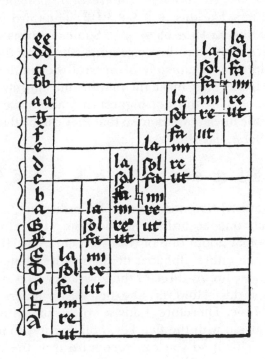

Thus, following Guido's arrangement [as shown] in the illustration, the organists[108] also have their keys (*claves*)[109] labeled with the first seven letters, as they are set out on the far left of the illustration, so that the first letter will always indicate the entire name. *A:* You are speaking to me about no more than seven letters? With those you want me to recognize five times seven keys and even more? How can I recognize and name so many keys from only these? *Se:* The organists generally have the practice of calling all of the lowest little boards "keys" (*claves*) [i.e., white keys],[110] and the others, which are elevated a little above and [are] shorter than

129

the ["keys"], they call "semitones" (*semitonia*) [i.e., black keys]. It was the practice of Guido that he (sig. F3) notated the first seven letters of the keys with capital letters, as shown here: 𝕬𝕭𝕮𝕯𝕰𝕱𝕲. He notated the second alphabet in plain lower-case letters, like this: a b c d e f g. The third [octave] he doubled, like this: aa bb cc dd ee ff.[111] Some organists also adhere to this practice. However, there are some who make the letters of the lowest alphabet completely plain, and they underline them with a small stroke. They make the middle one entirely bare, without any addition. The third or highest they also make plain, and they draw a little line above them so that they can be distinguished [from the others], like this:

a̲ b̲ c̲ d̲ e̲ f̲ g̲   a b c d e f g   ā b̄ c̄ d̄ ē f̄ ḡ [112]

Thus, [organists] have various ways [of indicating the different octaves], each one according to his taste. Therefore, if you wish, you too may adopt one of your own choosing, [either] the numerals or the entire alphabet of twenty-three letters,[113] since there are likewise twenty-three of the lowest keys [i.e., white keys] on the keyboard.[114] However, the first seven letters are more suitable for Music. Therefore, I advise you to stay with the usual practice and begin with the first key, notating it with a capital *F*, like this: 𝕱. This is so you can recognize it as the deepest or lowest tone of the clavichord, and [so that] you can distinguish it from or from among the other *f*[s], since you will have more than just one of them. And whenever you see a note in the song that is in the next space below the *gamma ut*, put the capital 𝕱 in the tablature to represent that space and that note [F].

(Sig. [F3v]) *A*: Then who will tell me if these notes should be long or short: *Se*: Later on I will give you information so that you can also recognize the *valorem notarum*, that is, the value of the notes. But first learn to recognize, name, and notate the keys. *A*: Then how do I notate the second and the other keys that follow one after the other, going up from the capital *F*? *Se*: Some make a semitone going up immediately after the first key, but that is not the case for all organists. I will therefore keep to the arrangement of the above-mentioned number of thirty-eight keys, and these according to the keyboard [I] showed [you] [i.e., the diagram on sig. Ev4, p. 126 above]. Thus, going up after the first key, there follows a second [key], which is named diatonic *gamma ut* [G] according to the system of Guido. Some organists notate [this] with a Greek gamma (*Gamaut*), others with a large capital letter, as appears here: **Ϭ**. Still others make a lower-case *g* with a little line under or through it, like this: **ꬶ**.

The third key going up will be a semitone, and that makes or brings the chromatic *fa* of *a re* [A♭]. Organists call it the great *post sol*, and they notate it just like the *gamma ut*, except that they make a loop at the end of it, like this: **Ϭℓ**, or like this: **gℓ**.

The fourth will be a diatonic *a re* in the space [A], which is notated with a capital *A* or made as a lower-case[115] *a* with a little line below it: **ﬃ**.

The fifth will be another semitone, *fa* of chromatic *h mi* [B♭], and it is notated (sig. [F4]) with a capital *B* or a lower-case *b* with a line drawn under it, like this: **♭**.

Now when the[se] five keys are counted one after the other, from the first to the fifth there will be [the interval of] a perfect fourth, but not [a] chromatic [one], that is, [one] in accordance with the colorful genus, since for that, one more minor semitone is needed [i.e., F#]. However, [starting] from the second key, named *gamma ut*, counting upwards six contiguous keys – beginning on whichever [white] key or [black] semitone you wish, from [*gamma ut*] up to the [top] end [of the keyboard] – you always find a perfect fourth in accordance with the chromatic genus.

The sixth key will be *mi* of diatonic *h mi* [B], and it will be notated with a large capital letter *H*. This is also called *h mi*. Alternatively, it is made with a lower-case *h* and is underlined with a little line: **♭**.

The seventh will be diatonic *c fa ut* [c], and it is notated with a large capital letter, but some make it with a little line under a plain *c*: **ꞓ**.

The eighth will be another semitone, *mi* of chromatic *c fa ut* [c#]. It is notated just like *c fa ut*, except that a loop is added at the end, and it is called the first *post ut*, like this: **ꞓℓ** or **ꞓ**.

The ninth will be diatonic *d sol re* [d], and it is notated with a large capital letter *D* or with an underlined lower-case [letter], like this: **ꝺ**.

The tenth will be *fa* of chromatic *e la mi* [e♭], which is notated [with a large capital letter *E* or a lower-case *e*] with a little line under it and a loop after it, like [this]: &?. It is called the first *post re.*

(Sig. [F4v]) The eleventh will be *mi* of diatonic *e la mi* [e], which they notate with a bare capital letter, like this: E, or an underlined lower-case letter, like this: ⅇ.

The twelfth will be *fa* of diatonic *f fa ut* on the line [f], which they notate with a bare [capital] *F*, or they make a little line underneath [lit., through it] like this: ƒ.[116]

The thirteenth will be *mi* of chromatic *f fa ut* [f#], a semitone that the organists call the first *post fa,* and they notate it with a loop after the letter, as appears here: ℱ or ℱ.[117]

The fourteenth will be diatonic *g sol re ut* in the space [g], and it is notated with a plain, entirely bare *g,* without any addition, like this: ℊ.

The fifteenth will be *fa* of chromatic *a la mi re* [a♭], and it is notated with a *g,* like the *g sol re ut,* except that it has a loop at the end, like this: ℊℯ, and it is called the second *post sol.*

The sixteenth will be *mi* of diatonic *a la mi re* on the line [a], [and it is] notated with a completely bare lower-case *a.*

The seventeenth will be a semitone *fa* of *b fa h mi* in the space [b♭], and it is notated with a plain, rounded *b.*

The eighteenth will be *mi* of *b fa h mi* in the space [b]. [It is] notated with a plain *h* and is named the second *h mi.*

The nineteenth will be *fa* of diatonic *c sol fa ut* [c'], and [it is] notated with a plain *c.*

The twentieth will be *mi* of chromatic *c sol fa ut* [c#'], and it is notated just like the other, with a *c,* except that it has a loop on the end: ℯ. It is called the second *post ut.*

(Sig. G) The twenty-first will be diatonic *d la sol re* [d'], notated with a plain *d.*

The twenty-second will be a semitone, *fa* of chromatic *e la mi* [e♭'], and it is named the second *post re* and notated with a *d* with a loop on the end, like this: &?.

The twenty-third will be *mi* of diatonic *e la mi* [e'], notated with a plain *e.*

The twenty-fourth will be *fa* of diatonic *f fa ut* in the space [f'], and it is notated with an *f* with a line drawn above it, like this: f̄.

The twenty-fifth will be a semitone, *mi* of chromatic *f fa ut* in the space [f#'], and it is named the second[118] *post fa.* It is notated with an *f* and a loop with a line drawn above it, as: ℱℯ.[119]

The twenty-sixth will be a diatonic *g sol re ut* on the line [g'], notated with a plain *g* with a line above it, as: **ḡ**.

The twenty-seventh will be a semitone, *fa* of chromatic *a la mi re* in the space [a♭'], and it is named the third *post sol*. It is notated with a *g* with a line above it and a loop at the end: **ℊℓ**.

The twenty-eighth will be a diatonic *a la mi re* [a'], and it is notated with a lower-case *a* with a line above it, like this: **ã**.

The twenty-ninth will be a semitone, *fa* of *b fa h mi* on the line [b♭'], notated with a rounded *b* with a line above it, like this: **b̄**.[120]

The thirtieth will be *mi* of diatonic *b fa h mi* on the line [b'] notated with a lower-case *h* with a line over it, like this: **h̄**.

The thirty-first will be diatonic *c sol fa* [c"], and [since] all the letters from here on up are doubled, this is notated with a double *c*, like this: **cc**.

(Sig. [Gv]) The thirty-second will be a semitone, *mi* of chromatic *c sol fa* [c#"], and it is called the third *post ut*. It is notated with a double *c*, to which a loop is added at the end: **ccℓ**.

The thirty-third will be diatonic *d la sol* [d"], notated with a double *d*.

The thirty-fourth will be a semitone, *fa* of chromatic *e la* [e♭"], named the third *post re*, and it is notated with a double *d* with a loop at the end, like this: **ddℓ**.

The thirty-fifth will be *mi* of diatonic *e la* [e"], notated as a double *e*.

The thirty-sixth will be a semitone, *fa* above chromatic *e la* [f"],[121] notated as a double *f*.

The thirty-seventh will be the last *post fa* [f#"], notated with a double *f* [and] a loop at the end: **ffℓ**.

The last is notated as a double *g*. [It] is one octave above *g sol re ut* [i.e., g"]. There you have the symbols of all the keys, and you [will] find them written out in the following drawing of the keyboard:

[Illustration of a keyboard with tablature letters][122]

(Sig. G2) Now [that] I have instructed you [in this], I shall also teach you how to recognize which notes you should make long or short; and the same [things] I am now going to tell [you] *de valore notarum* – that is, about the value of the notes – will then also apply to all other tablatures of all the instruments. Therefore I have to set it forth for you all the more clearly, so that I will not have to write it out again later for the other instruments as well – that is, for the lute, pipe, or others – since it is enough to write it out once in a book. *A:* Well, I hope to improve greatly with daily practice. For that reason, tell me more. How are the notes of figured song (*des figurierten gesangs*) made? *Se:* You need to know that singers have four kinds of four-sided figures (*quadratur*) out of which they form all notes. These are taken from the liberal arts of geometry and of metrification – that is, the art of making verse. *A:* What are these quadratic figures? *Se:* The first is called a *quadrilatera* [i.e., a square], the second a rhombus. The third, a rhomboid, is a *patronomicum* [i.e., a name derived] from the [word] "rhombus." The fourth is a *quadratur altera parte longius et rectangulum* [i.e., a rectangle]. *A:* What are you saying? How do you come to use geometry and poetry [in connection] with music? *Se:* I pray you, do not be surprised if you and many others do not understand much about this yet. For this reason I will reveal it and tell something that forms the foundation [for this theory]. If this [foundation] is unsound, then the whole [argument] built upon it falls. *A:* Then, what kind of figure or note in the song is the first *quadrilatera? Se:* The stonecutters call it a square (*ein gantz fireckte figur*), [one] that is equal on all sides. Singers have taken it over into music and have named it a *breve* for the reason that, because they made the old ones all black, and since they are thus made the most simply and quickly, therefore they are called *brevis*. (Sig. [G2v]) But, in order [to see] that this is so – that they are made or written the most quickly – take a dull, wide feather [pen] in your hand and pull it a bit forwards. This way, in one little stroke, the pen gives you the square (*quadratur*), like this: ▪. [The reason] that little lines are put on the sides, sticking out, is only in order that the sides be seen so much the sharper in appearance, like this: ▉. But as for why the notes are now made white in the middle, the reason may be that, as music in mensural notation (*das gesang*) has become so popular, were everything written with black notes, then parchment could not everywhere be had; moreover, since [ink] soaks through paper very readily, it would be necessary always to make the notes at all times on only one side, which takes too much paper.[123] Another reason may be that when black notes were used for those that we make white today, at that time all the notes that we now color [black] – as is [a] necessary [notational] symbol now and then in perfect or triple time – [all these] were written in red ink, and thus the notes were made with two colors. Since not everyone can carry red ink with them at all times, [white notation] was therefore considered useful and came into practice. Then too, the main reason may be [that] these and the other shapes or forms of the notes [were made] according to the pleasure of the founder [of white notation]. As Juvenal put it, "*Sic volo, sic iubeo, sit pro ratione voluntas.*" ["I wish it, thus I command it; let my will stand in place of a reason."][124]

But [as for] why the note called *brevis* is (or is worth) one *tempus*, that is [explained] as follows: When the consonances were discovered, a [length of] time also had to be devised for how long or how short any of them should or had to be held. (Sig. G3) Thus [one *tempus*] was considered a proper [length of] time to endow with sound, neither too long nor too short, but taking up a medium length. So, precisely the note *brevis* was fixed as the middle, always constant, like the *positivus* in comparison (*in comparatione*) with the larger and also [in comparison] with the smaller or shorter. [As an] example (*exemplum*) in comparison with the greater or larger, take the breve for the *positivum* as the lesser in comparison, the *longa* for the *comparativum* as the greater, the *maxima* for the *superlativum* as the very largest. On the other hand, take the breve as the greater or larger in comparison with

the smaller, the semibreve for the *comparativum*, that is, for the
lesser or smaller, the *minima* for the *superlativum* as the very
smallest or the [very] least. There you find that in all positions the
breve is the middlemost among the notes, and that it most fittingly
[has] the name "tempus," that is, the measured time belonging to
it. Just as this note ◨ is considered and written as the simplest in
mensural notation (*in dem gsang*),[125] so it is also notated in the
tablature as the simplest and smallest little dot [put] over the
letters of the keys of the clavichord, like this:

A: You are telling me about strange things. What kind of shape
is a rhombus? *Se*: The geometers call it a diamond. Following
them, the singers have found that when a square [placed] upright
like a diamond inside a second square (sig. [G3v]) is measured
with dividers, then the diamond will be exactly half of the perfect
square. And if the other four parts of the whole square that remain
next to the diamond are put together, then these four parts will be
exactly as much as, as big as, and not less nor more than the
diamond. So they have named this diamond a semibreve because
it is the half part of a square. Two of them make one tempus, or
one measured duration, or one beat, as some say.

These semibreves, and all other notes of this name that are
made or found in ligatures or elsewhere, are always notated in the
tablature with a plain stroke above the letters of the keys of the keyboard. For example (*Exemplum*):

A: What kind of shape, then, is a rhomboid? *Se*: It is just as if
two or three diamonds following after each other downward in
succession were fastened together. Geometers have called it
oblique-angled (*geschmiget*) [i.e., a ligature], and the singers have
considered it as two notes. *A*: Why should these oblique figures

represent two notes, unlike the others? *Se*: For the reason that the figure hangs below itself and cannot be situated on [only] one line or space; [thus] it has to touch another one as well. If this were not the case, it could not be recognized as oblique, and then it would have no differentiation from the oblong shape [i.e., the maxima]. These [two kinds of notes] would be too similar or alike, so that one could hardly distinguish one from the other. But since these oblique [notes] and also the oblong quadratic [ones] are not used in our tablature, for the reason that no (sig. [G4]) maxima or longa is set as a whole in the tablature (instead these are always divided into as many *tempora* as they are made up of or are worth), I will therefore say no more about this [kind of note] either, until I come to write about the formation of the notes (*de formatione notarum*). Owing to its [durational] value, however, nothing will be found in the tablature that is longer or larger than the symbol of a tempus – that is, of a breve – as represented by a little dot in the tablature. And after this dot [comes] the symbol for a semibreve, which is a plain, long stroke. Since I still have to show you as well how to recognize the remaining large notes of polyphonic music (*des gesangs*) in ligatures (so you can divide them [into separate tempora] and transfer them or put their equivalents into the tablature), I must therefore begin again to speak about the first four-sided figure, [telling] what notes are formed one from the other and how [they are formed]. You will thereby also meet with the remaining oblique-angled and oblong notes, [as well as with] matters that concern them. And so once more, I will take into consideration this first quadratic figure. I find that three kinds of names and notes are formed out of [the square].

The first case is that in which one puts a tail on a breve [i.e., on a square-shaped note]. One must notice initially on which side of the note this tail is situated. If you find it appearing on the right side as it faces you, [whether] the tail is above it or below it, then this is a longa, like this:

(Sig. [G4v]) However, if you find a tail on the left side of the breve [i.e., on a square note], then you must consider whether the tail is made to stand above or below [the note]. If it stands above

it, then another note must be attached to it. This attached
note may either go above or below the first note with the tail. [In
either case,] these first two notes are always two semibreves, like
this:

Furthermore, if the first note with the tail above it is a square
note, and the next following after it is an oblique-angled one, and
[if] there are as many notes as desired attached to one another,
in that case the first two would still always be two semibreves: like
this:

And this is also true with respect to the tail going upwards on the
left side above the oblique-angled notes; for the first and second
[notes] would both together constitute [one] oblique-angled
note, and [no matter how] many more notes are attached to them,
the first two would always be two semibreves, like this:

On the other hand, if you find a tail on the first square note
(which is one tempus or one breve), [and if] a tail descends at the
start [of the ligature] on the left side, then another note must
always be attached to the first – either a square note or an oblique-
angled one – and it must be attached below it and not above it. In
this case the first note is always a breve, [whether] many or few
square or oblique-angled notes are attached to it, like this:

(Sig. H) And this is also true of the tail when it descends on the left side at the beginning of oblique-angled notes. In this case, the first is always a breve, like this:

But when the first square note, the breve, stands alone, then it always remains what it is – a breve. If one attaches another note to it, however, and if this second attached note stands lower than the first square note, then the first is always a longa, like this:

And this is also true of the oblique-angled notes when they stand completely free without a tail. Then the first is always a longa, like this:

I must tell you one more thing about the first of the four-cornered quadratic figures, which is a breve. Whenever you find one of these square notes as the last note in a ligature, and this note hangs down below the previous one which is square, then this last [note] is always a longa:

In addition, you should know that in any ligature the third, fourth, fifth, sixth, seventh, eighth, etc. are always breves except if it is [the case] that the last note is a square note and it hangs down below the previous [one]. Then this late [note] is always a longa, like this:

(Sig. [Hv]) Then too, if the first two notes at the beginning [of the ligature] are two semibreves, and the third note, a square one, hangs below them, then this third note would be a longa, like this:

When, however, the last note in a ligature is square, and it rises above the penultimate note, then this late [note] is always a breve, like this:

And although I have said above that there is nothing in the tablature longer or larger than the tempus alone, nevertheless I consider that this [tempus] is the same as if it were something of a continuous quantity (*de quantitate continua*), which in increasing or augmenting becomes finite, but [which] by diminishing becomes ever smaller the longer [it is diminished], almost up to infinity (*Infinitum*).[126] Therefore, I must speak again about the diamond, which the singers call a semibreve; and [I] will form the other notes from it, as [I formed] the diamond from half the perfect square. Each [type of note] is reduced progressively by half. And [I will] explain [it] as follows: if you find a tail on a diamond (that is, on a semibreve), whether it is above it or below it, [the note] is worth the same. This is named a minim (*minima*) by the singers, and it is notated by instrumentalists with a little hook. The little hooks, then, have the value of one quarter of a beat or [one quarter of a] tempus, like this:

(Sig. H2) Then, if you find this minim blackened, it is called a semiminim (*semiminima*) by the singers. Instrumentalists notate them with two little hooks, and they have the value of one eighth of a tempus, like this:

But if in the music (*in dem gsang*) you find black diamonds, with a tail and a little hook on [each one], the singers call this a fusa (*fusele*). Instrumentalists notate them with three little hooks. These, then, have the value of one sixteenth of a tempus, like this:

Then, if in the music (*in dem gsang*) you find this fusa with two little hooks, the singers call them half[127] a fusa [i.e., a semifusa]. So instrumentalists notate them with four little hooks, and they have the value of one thirty-second of a tempus, like this:

You can now recognize all the notes, whether they be of the simple or of the figured [variety], single or in ligatures. Yet [for these] you have no more than the six kinds of symbols that you can use for all instruments and their tablatures, like this:

A: You have told me about four shapes of quadratic figures, and you have written enough about the first three of these [that is, the square, the rhombus, and the rhomboid]. What happened to the oblong quadratic figure? Which notes are formed out of this [one]? And, although you (sig. [H2v]) have just now named all of them for me, and [thus] I am quite familiar with them, who will tell me the value or worth of each one [of these long notes]? *Se*: Your question is well put, because I have told you nothing in particular about this oblong figure. You should, however, notice that the singers hold this figure sometimes three [longas] or [sometimes] four breves [i.e., two imperfect longas] in length. [They] make a tail on the right side of this [note], [either] below it or above it, as that stands for the same thing. [They] call this note a maxima. No other notes are formed from it, because it always stays what it is:

They should always be divided into tempora (*per tempora*) in the tablature [when transcribed] from the staff notation (*aus dem gesang*). But as you are asking for more information, [namely] how you can recognize what each of the notes is worth, I [will] tell you that this cannot be known without certain special external or internal signs. In addition, there is a great deal more that you would need to know concerning figured music (*de musica figurativa*), all of which I am saving for the other book. It will require a full ten chapters about modus, tempus, and prolatio (*de modo, tempore, et prolatione*), as well as other things. Were I to tell you about all these things here, then what would I have left to write about in the complete book for you and [for] others after you? Therefore, since at this time I cannot bring everything into the little treatise – owing to its brevity – let this suffice for the time being; and, in the meantime, choose no composition (*keinem gesang*) to intabulate other than one that is notated in imperfect time (*de tempore imperfecto*), in which [case] each maxima is worth four tempora, like this:

(Sig. H3) Any longa [is worth] two tempora; and that is taken from the art of metrification.

Any tempus [sic] [is worth] two semibreves, like this:

Any semibreve [is worth] two minims, like this:

Any minim [is worth] two semiminims, like this:

Any semiminim [is worth] two fusae, like this:

Any fusa [is worth] two semifusae, like this:

You also have four kinds of rests. A breve rest is notated in the tablature with a stroke down from the line, like this: **T**.

A semibreve rest is made with a little stroke going up from the line, like this: **⌐**.

(Sig. [H3v]) A minim rest is made with a little hook on the line, like this: **⌐**.

A semiminim rest is made with two little hooks on the line: **⌐**.

One can hardly rest for a shorter length of time; therefore at this point I will take leave of this [subject]. I will [proceed by] giving you brief instructions about the dots in mensural notation (*des gesangs*).

First [you should] know that [this] notation has two kinds of dots. The first is called *punctus additionis* [dot of addition], the second, *punctus divisionis* [dot of division]. The first, *Punctus additionis*, is always worth half of the note after which it is placed.

143

If it is put after a maxima, then it is worth a longa; if it is put after a longa, then it is worth a breve; if it is put after a breve, then it is worth a semibreve, and so forth. And it must always be sung.[128] The second dot, *divisionis*, has no place here, because it only [is used] in perfect time. It is never sung, and it should always be placed before the note that it separates [from other notes].

Some people, however, assign three or four different names to the dots, saying that one is the *punctus perfectionis* [dot of perfection], the second *punctus divisionis*, the third *punctus alterationis* [dot of alteration], and the fourth *punctus additionis*. They make many words [i.e., complications] for [all] this. On this subject I say that, as far as I am concerned, the two dots, *divisionis* and *additionis*, are entirely sufficient. For, the *punctus divisionis* is not to be used or set anywhere except in *modo majori perfecto* [i.e., where the maxima equals three longas], in *modo minori perfecto* [i.e., where the longa equals three breves], or in *tempore perfecto* [i.e., where the breve equals three semibreves], or in *prolatione perfecta* [i.e., where the semibreve equals three minims], and also in several proportions about which I shall speak later on. Since what is divided [by a *punctus divisionis*] needs no further alteration [by a *punctus alterationis*], and [since] a perfection is always (sig. [H4]) recognized by the *punctus divisionis* [thereby requiring no *punctus perfectionis*], and [because] there are even more of these [notational] symbols [in these time signatures] than little dots – for example, the symbol for coloration, that is, the blackening of the notes, and also of rests, and of the ligatures as well – therefore I will leave it at the two [types of] dots. Someone else may call them whatever he pleases. Let that be [enough] said to you about the notes as well as about the rests and dots of imperfect time signatures. This [should] satisfy you until the other book is completed.

Now, I will place before you a short song (*eyn kurtz lidlin*), [written] in notes, and after that [I will] transcribe the same [composition] into organ tablature. Let that be enough said to you about the organ or about the clavichord.[129] Now look at the little song and do likewise with a second composition (*mit dem andern gesang*) that you wish to transcribe.

The following little song (*liedlin*)[130] was made from the three responsories of Our Lady. The first verse is the responsory "Sancta

et immaculata virginitas."[131] The second is "Suscipe verbum virgo
Maria."[132] The third is the responsory "Felix namque es sacra virgo
Maria."[133]

(Sig. [H4v]) [Tenor part of the musical example]

O Holy, immaculate, tender virginity of Mary!
With what praise and elegant [words] shall I speak of thee; for truly thou
    hast
Carried to birth, there within thy womb, in corporeal weakness,
The very One whom even the heavens could never contain.

Receive the word, thou most precious treasure, Mary, pure virgin,
Which Saint Gabriel announced from God to thee alone: that
Thou wouldst give birth to God, Our Lord, with all grace. Therefore we
    rightly say
That of all women everywhere, thou art the most blest.

Blessed and holy art thou, O Virgin Mary;
Thou art also the most worthy of all praise: thus do I esteem thee!
For from thee, beloved [maiden] has now arisen the sun of righteous-
    ness,
Even our Lord God, Jesus Christ. Pray for us, as I trust [in thee].

(Sig. I) [Cantus, Altus, and Bassus parts of the song]

(Sig. [Iv]) [Keyboard intabulation of the preceding song][134]

147

(Sig. [I2]) [Conclusion of the keyboard intabulation]

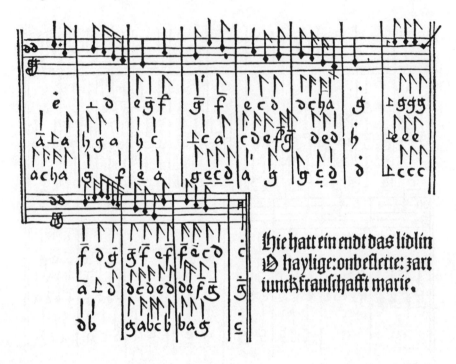

The little song, "O Holy, immaculate, tender virginity of Mary," ends here.[135]

(Sig. [I2v]) [Woodcut of a lutenist, signed by Urs Graf][136]

(Sig. I3)[137] *A*: Since you are breaking off [the discussion] so abruptly, and, as always, referring me to the complete book, I too must therefore leave it at that. But how shall I learn to intabulate for the lute? *Se*: The first thing you must know in learning how to intabulate for the lute and how to play [it] is how many strings or courses you wish to have on it. Secondly, [you must know] how many frets you will have on it. Fourthly, you must learn to write out or notate [the symbols for] the neck. Fifthly, [you must] learn how these [alphabetic] symbols [stand] for the letters in the scale or in the hand of Guido, according to the two genera of music [i.e., diatonic and chromatic]. Lastly, [you must learn] everything that you will encounter in a composition in imperfect time (*in dem*

gesang de tempore imperfecto), in order to transcribe it from the notes into the symbols or the letters that you find written out on the neck and in the [Guidonian] hand or scale, following the length or shortness of the notes, just as you have previously heard with reference to the clavichord [sigs. G3–H3v, pp. 135–44 above]. All this I will teach you in very few words, after which I will show you this in illustrations for [your] inspection, so that you can easily understand me.

A: Then tell me, how many strings or courses will there be? *Seba*: Some lutenists play on nine strings, which have only five courses; some play on eleven strings, which have six courses; some play on thirteen strings, or fourteen, and these have seven courses. You may decide for yourself whichever of these you wish. As I have four types of tablatures in the large book, you may also select the one out of all of them that you [would] like.[138] I will teach you according to that one. (Sig. [I3v]) *A*: I pray you, advise [me] about this. How many strings should I choose? And, after that, which is the best of the tablatures to learn? You are in a better position to inform me about this than I am to choose. Therefore, I suggest that you present one of these to me, and I will learn according to that one. *Se*: It seems to me that nine strings are too few to learn; [and] not all lutes have thirteen and fourteen strings. I advise, therefore, that you take up a lute with eleven strings, [a type] that is found almost everywhere. I will present to you a tablature for it that is the most common and best known.

A: I am most satisfied with this. Tell me at once about the lute with eleven strings. *Se*: First you must know that the eleven strings are distributed among six courses, always two strings for each course, with the sole exception of the sixth course (*die quintsaitte*) [lit., "the fifth string"],[139] which normally has only a single string to its course. Each of these six courses has its own name. *A*: What are the names of these courses? *Se*: The first course is named the "great rumbler" (*der gross prummer*), and it is strung with one large or thick string. The second course is called the "middle rumbler" (*der mittler prummer*), and it is also strung with a coarse or thick string, but [one that is] somewhat thinner than the first. The same is also true of the third course [which is] strung with a coarse string, but somewhat thinner still, and it is called the "small rumbler" (*der clain prummer*). For these three [courses called] rumblers one adds to each large string another string of middle size, and one stretches or tunes each of these [middle-sized strings] one octave above the [large] rumbler [string] with which it is paired. *A*: Why is this done? (Sig. [I4]) Because, although they are coarse and big, one cannot hear at a distance the large strings sounding nearly as loud or as strong as the small or the higher [strings]. For this reason one adds the octaves, so [the lower three courses] are heard the same at the other ones. *A*: How, then, are the other three courses made? *Se*: The fourth course is strung with two middle-sized strings, of which neither is larger or smaller [than the other], and neither is tuned higher or lower than the other. Rather, they must be in unison (*unisonum*), that is, have the same pitch. And this fourth course is called the "great singing string" (*die gross sancksaytt*). The fifth course should also be strung with two equal strings. And it is not bad if these are somewhat thinner than the strings of the fourth course, and both should also have the same pitch. This fifth course is named the "small singing string" (*die claynen sancksaitte*).

A: How, then, does one string the sixth course? *Se*: With one pure, good, even string. And, you may recognize it [i.e., a good string] in the following manner. When you open a little bundle of strings, choose the string that it as long as you need it for the lute, and stretch a bit of it between both of your hands. Then hit the string with your thumb so that it vibrates and rumbles. Then, as it vibrates, the less you see the repercussions or [multiple] appearances of this string, the better it is; the more you see it, the worse it is. It has a course of its own, which is called the "quintsait." [This string is tested] like this:

(Sig. [I4v]) [Woodcut of two hands testing strings]

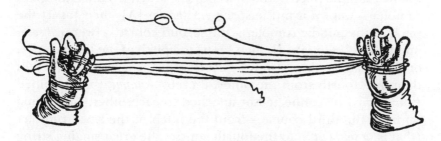

All these strings of the lute should be strings that are made from the gut or from the intestines of sheep, although Boethius and other *musici* call them *nervis*, as if they were made from the sinews of the animals. It may, perhaps, have been [the case] in former times that they were made out of sinews, but at the present time these strings for the lute, as well as [those] for the viol and the rebec (*der grossen und clainen geigen*), and for the harp, and for the *harpfentive*,[140] [and] also for the trumpet marine, are all made solely from sheep's gut. But some other instruments have brass strings, and some [have] iron strings (*stehelenen saiten*).[141] It will not be possible for these [metal strings] to be used on the lute. For if one presses down [metal strings] on the [gut] frets with bare fingers, [the metal strings] will not sound as good as if one stopped them with iron or wood [frets]. You must therefore know the difference [between kinds of strings] and give to each instrument [the type] that belongs to it and no other.

(Sig. K) *A*: Very well, you have told me how I should string[142] the lute, [and] also how to name the strings and the courses with their own individual names. Now tell me as well how I should set or tune them. *Se*: Some lutenists set the first course (which they name the great rumbler) a fifth below the middle rumbler. But [since] this is not the practice of all lutenists, I will therefore not bother to write it out. Instead, [I shall speak about] the practice that is current in our time. And this practice is found as follows: each course is always tuned a fourth above the other, except for the small rumbler and the great singing string. Only these two are tuned or placed a diatone away or apart from each other; that is, [they are separated by] a major third, which is made up of two whole tones. And so that you understand this correctly, tune it as follows: as if the pitch of the first course – which is named the great rumbler – were *a re* in the space (*in spacio*) [A], then [as if] the pitch of the middle rumbler – the second course – [were] *d sol re* on the line (*in linea*) [d], then [as if] the pitch of the third course, or the small rumbler, [were] *g sol re ut* in the space [g]. Each of them is a fourth from the other, thereby *synaphe*, that is, joined (*coniunctim*) or connected or attached to each other. Now going on from the third course – from the pitch of the small rumbler (that is, *g sol re ut*) – to the fourth course, the great singing string should be [tuned] a third higher than the small rumbler. This will be *mi* of *b fa h mi* [b] and is *diezeüsis*, that is, disconnected [*disiunctim*] from the other. After that, tighten the small singing string [so that it is] a fourth higher than the great singing string, which brings you *e la mi* on the line [e']. After that, tighten the last course [so that it is] a fourth higher than the small singing string, which brings you *a la mi re* in the space [a']. The six courses are strung in this way, as you can see in this illustration:

(Sig. [Kv]) [Woodcut of lute strings with relative pitches and the intervals between them]

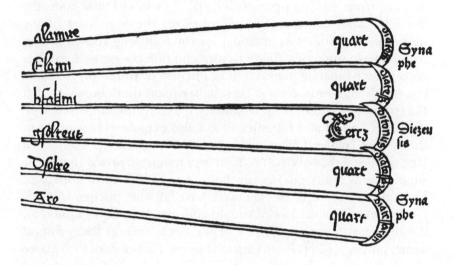

a la mi re			
	fourth	4th	conjunct
e la mi			
	fourth	4th	
b fa h mi			
	third	3rd maj.	disjunct
g sol re ut			
	fourth	4th	
d sol re			
	fourth	4th	conjunct
a re			

(Sig. K2) *A*: I now understand this very well. Do go on and tell me: how do I learn to intabulate for the lute? *Se*: To begin with, you must know about the number of frets. In addition, [you need to know] how the neck is notated, and [you should know] what [strings] one must finger or not finger, strike or pluck. *A*: I can certainly bear these things in mind; therefore, I wish to be instructed. *Se*: Lutenists generally have seven frets on the lute. With eleven strings on the seven frets, and also on the open courses, they have [available the notes] from *a re* [A] at the bottom going up to the *e la* [e"] including all the pitches of the two genera of music, named diatonic and chromatic, as I showed you before with reference to the clavichord. In addition, they have the unisons [of these pitches] several times, except for some of the very lowest ones, that is, the pitches of the biggest rumbler, namely, from *a re* [A] up to *d sol re* [d]. As you will hear later, the same [is true] of several upper ones on the high part of the quintsait. And [one has unisons] for the following reason: when, from time to time, one fingers a pitch on one course and another consonance must be played that would also be found on the same course, then, a unison must be sought on another course, so that the consonant [note] rings or sounds at exactly the same time with the other [note] and not after it, as I also explained before about the strings [played] in combination (*eynigen*) on the clavichord [see sig. E3, p. 124 above]. *A*: I am very much surprised that there should be as many pitches on the lute as on the clavichord, and both genera as well. *Se*: Yes, you have all the pitches of both genera on half of the neck. And, in addition [you have] almost all the unison pitches on the rest of the neck, and on the quintsait nearly an (sig. [K2v]) octave up to the rose (*biss zǔ dem stern*) above all [the] frets. *A*: Show this to me, and teach me how to write out the symbols for the neck.

Se: The practice of lutenists in this: They notate with five numerals the six courses that I have just set forth for you to learn. This [notation] was devised for nine strings. But for eleven strings they duplicate the [number] one and say that the number for the great rumbler is called the "large [number] one." To differentiate it from the "little [number] one," they make a long stroke with two little dots, like a crown, on top of the long stroke, like this: ⅄. And they do not press down with their fingers any of these courses, or the numerals [that represent them]. Instead, [lutenists] allow these courses to give the pitch that they have by nature when they are struck. Thus, this [written] stroke, which signifies one in numbers, ⅄, always signifies *a re* [A] in the tablature.

They do the same with the middle rumbler, [giving the open pitch] a plain or bare numeral that stands for "one" in numbers, like this: ı. And they call it the "little [number] one," which also signifies the [pitch] *d sol re* [d]. [It is] unstopped and unfingered in the tablature.

As for the third course, which is named the small rumbler and is *g sol re ut* [g], they notate it with a number that signifies "two" in numbers like this: ɪ.[143]

They notate the fourth course, which is named the great singing string and *b fa h mi* [b], with a numeral that represents "three" in numbers, like this: ȝ.

They notate the fifth course, which is named the small singing string and *e la mi* [e'], with a numeral that signifies "four" in numbers, like this: 4.

They notate the sixth course, which is the quintsait and *a la mi re* [a'] in the space, with a numeral that signifies "five" in numbers, like this: ꙅ.

And you see before your eyes [these numerals] applied to the neck [of the lute].

(Sig. K3) [Woodcut of the open courses of the lute with their names, relative pitches, and notational symbols]

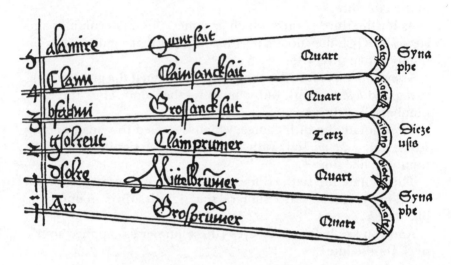

5	a la mi re	Quintsait				
			fourth		4th	conjunct
4	e la mi	Small singing string			4th	
			fourth		3rd	
3	b fa h m	Great singing string		maj.		disjunct
			third		4th	
2	g sol re ut	Small rumbler				
			fourth		4th	
1	d sol re	Middle rumbler				
			fourth			conjunct
ï	a re	Great rumbler				

(Sig. [K3v]) *A*: Now, how do I notate [the other positions on] the neck? *Se*: I hear that there was a blind man born in Nuremberg and buried in Munich, named Meister Conrad from Nuremberg,[144] who in his time was famous and praised above other instrumentalists. He directed that the entire alphabet be written [crosswise] on the five courses and on the seven frets of the neck. And when it had been used once, he started again from the beginning of the alphabet and doubled all these letters for the second alphabet. From this I can understand that he had no more than nine strings on the lute. But there are several other kinds [of tablatures] that [developed] after [this one] – which I have seen in part from reports of the earliest originators [of these updated tablatures], who also used this tablature in the same way as he [Meister Conrad] introduced it, but with two strings that is, a sixth course – added to it.[145] For the letters of the sixth course, which is now named the first [course] or the great rumbler, they have exactly the same letters as are notated for the middle rumbler, except that they have written these letters as large capitals (*grosse versalia*) on the [new] course and on the frets of the lute. These [letters] – for fingering, striking, and plucking – are named the "capital A," the "capital F," the "capital L," the "capital Q," the "capital X," the "capital AA," [and] the "capital FF," as you can see in the illustration:

(Sig. [K4]) [Woodcut of the neck of the lute with tablature symbols on the courses and frets]

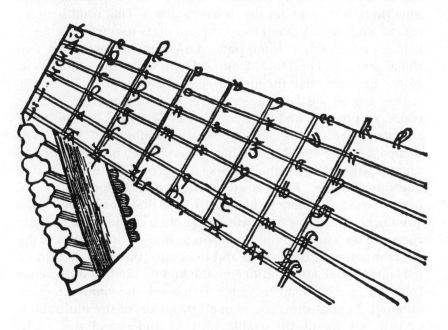

5	e	k	p	v	9	ee	kk	ll
4	d	i	o	t	ɾ	dd	ii	
3	c	h	n	s	z	cc	hh	
2	b	g	m	r	y	bb	gg	
1	a	f	l	q	x	aa	ff	
ï	A	F	L	Q	X	AA	FF	

157

(Sig. [K4v]) *A*: Thus far I have learned a number [of things] from you: about the six courses and the seven frets, and also [about] the writing out of the letters, the numbers, and the alphabets. Now, how am I to know where or how far from the others I should put or set each fret? *Se*: It is not easy to describe how far any [fret] should or must be from another. Although one may write out the measurement exactly according to the proportions, nevertheless [placing the frets] is entirely uncertain. For the neck usually has seven frets (and each course has its own open pitch as well), and according to some [people], [there is] a semitone (*semitonium*) between one fret and the next. But, as Boethius states, a tone (*tonus*) cannot be divided into equal semitones, because a tone is based on the sesquioctava proportion (*in proportione sesquioctava*) – that is, the relationship of nine to eight – and between eight and nine there is no number that is a mean.[146] *A*: That is difficult for me to understand; therefore, explain it better for me. *Se*: It belongs in school, as some state who otherwise cannot say anything about it. Therefore, I too will save it for the other book. Notice here only that the lute has seven frets.

Now [then], on [to] the seven frets and six courses: It is the common practice of lutenists that the first pitch of the great rumbler, [the] open, unstopped, and unfingered [pitch], is named diatonic *a re* [A], and that *a re*, or the pitch of the string, is notated with a long [written] stroke that properly carries two little dots upon it, like a little crown, which [symbol] represents "one" in the science of numbers, like this: ᛉ. And that is called the "large [number] one." Now from this lowest pitch of the great rumbler counting up, (sig. L) I will teach you to find all the pitches of the above-mentioned two genera and to notate [them] as they go up *gradatim* (or one after another) to the highest pitch of the seventh fret of the sixth course, which is named the quintsait. And, although I could show you enough by means of the illustrations or with my hands [to enable you] to understand this easily, nevertheless I must write these things out fully to please the others, so that anyone who cannot accomplish such [a task] for himself from the illustrations can put the illustrations in front of him and then read about them in the little book until he can understand this.

And now, if you wish to go up from *a re*, then finger and strike or pluck the first course, which is called the great rumbler, on the first fret [lit., "in the first zone"]. This gives you *fa* of chromatic *h mi* on the line [B♭]; and it will be notated with a big *A*.

After this, finger and strike the first course on the second fret, which gives you *mi* of diatonic *h mi* on the line [B], and which is notated with a *2* written in front of a big *f*, like this: [₂]ς; and it is called the "big 2F."

Finger and strike the first course on the third fret, which gives you *fa* of diatonic *c fa ut* [c] and which is notated with a *2* in front of an *l*, like this: ₂ℒ; and it is called the "big 2L."

Finger and strike the first course on the fourth fret, which brings you *mi* of chromatic *ca fa ut* [c#]; and it is notated with and named a big *Q*.

Finger and strike the first course on the fifth fret. With this you will hear diatonic *d sol re* [d]; and it is notated with a big *X* and is a unison [*unisonus*] with the "small [number] one."

Finger and strike the first course on the sixth fret. Thus you will find *fa* of chromatic *e la mi* [e♭] in the space; (sig. [Lv]) and it is notated with a doubled large *A* and is a unison with the small *a*.

Finger and strike the first course on the seventh fret. Thus you find *mi* of diatonic *e la mi* [e], which is notated with a doubled capital *F*, written following a *2*; and it is a unison with the small *f*.

THE SECOND COURSE

Now, going on, strike the open, unstopped second course, and do not finger it. This produces diatonic *d sol re* [d], and it is notated with a small[147] [number] "one," like this: ı.

Finger and strike the second course on the first fret. This brings you *fa* of chromatic *e la mi* [e♭], and it is notated with a small *a*.

Finger and strike the second course on the second fret. This brings you *mi* of diatonic *e la mi* [e], and it is notated with a plain small *f*.

Finger and strike the second course on the third fret. This brings you *fa* of diatonic *f fa ut* on the line [f], and it is notated with a plain small *l*. It has no unison.

Finger and strike the second course on the fourth fret. This brings you *mi* of chromatic *f fa ut*, on the line [f#], and it is notated with a small[148] *q*. It has no unison.

Finger and strike the second course on the fifth fret. This brings you diatonic *g sol re ut* [g], and it is notated with a small *x*. It is a unison with the independent number that signifies "two" in numerals [i.e., the open third course].

Finger and strike the second course on the sixth fret. That brings you *fa* of chromatic *a la mi re* [a♭], and it is notated with two small *a*s. It is a unison with the small *b*.

(Sig. L2) Finger and strike the second course on the seventh fret. This brings you *mi* of diatonic *a la mi re* [a], and it is notated with two *f*s. It will be a unison with the small *g*. And there you have the second course.

THE THIRD COURSE

The unstopped, unfingered third course produces diatonic *g sol re ut* [g] in the space, and it is notated with a numeral that represents "two" in numbers like this: **2**.

Finger and strike the third course on the first fret. This brings you *fa* of chromatic *a la mi re* [a♭], and it is notated with a small *b*.

Finger and strike the third course on the second fret. This brings you *mi* of diatonic *a la mi re* [a], and it is notated with a small *g*.

Finger and strike the third course on the third fret. This brings you *fa* of *b fa h mi* [b♭], and it is notated with an *m*.

Finger and strike the third course on the fourth[149] fret. This brings you *mi* of *b fa h mi* [b], and it is notated with an *r*.[150]

Finger and strike the third course on the fifth fret. This brings you *fa* of diatonic *c sol fa ut* [c'], and it is notated with a *y*, and will be a unison with the *c*.

Finger and strike the third course on the sixth fret. This brings you *mi* of chromatic *c sol fa ut* [c#'], and it is notated with a double *b*. It is a unison with the *h*.[151]

(Sig. [L2v]) There you [have] three courses with all the pitches of the two genera.

THE FOURTH COURSE

The unstopped, unfingered fourth course produces *mi* of *b fa h mi* in the space [b], and it is notated with a numeral that means "three" in numbers, like this: **3**.

Finger and strike or pluck the fourth course on the first fret.

This produces *fa* of diatonic *c sol fa ut* [c'], and it is notated with a small *c.*

Finger and strike the fourth course on the second fret. This brings you *mi* of chromatic *c sol fa ut* [c#'], and it is notated with a plain *h.*

Finger and strike the fourth course on the third fret. This brings you diatonic *d la sol re* [d'] and it is notated with an *n.*

Finger and strike the fourth course on the fourth fret. That brings you *fa* of chromatic *e la mi* on the line [e♭'], and it is notated with an *s.*

Finger and strike the fourth course on the fifth fret. This brings you *mi* of diatonic *e la mi* [e'] on the line, and it is notated with a *z.* It is a unison with the *4.*

Finger and strike the fourth course on the sixth fret. This brings you *fa* of diatonic *f fa ut* in the space [f'] and it is notated with a double *c.* It is a unison with the *d.*

Finger and strike the fourth course on the seventh fret. This brings you *mi* of chromatic *f fa ut* in the space [f#'] and it is notated with a double *h.* It is a unison with the *i.*

Thus you now have all the pitches of the two genera on four courses.

THE FIFTH COURSE

(Sig. L3) The unstopped, unfingered fifth course produces *e la mi* [e'], and it is notated with a numeral that represents "four" in numbers, like this: **4**.

Finger and strike the fifth course on the first fret. This brings you *a* of diatonic *f fa ut* in the space [f'], and it is notated with a *d.*

Finger and strike the fifth course on the second fret. This brings you *mi* of chromatic *f fa ut* in the space [f#'], and it is notated with an *i.*

Finger and strike the fifth course on the third fret. This brings you diatonic *g sol re ut* on the line [g'], and it is notated with an *o.*

Finger and strike the fifth course on the fourth fret. This brings you *fa* of chromatic *a la mi re* [a♭'], and it is notated with a *t.*

Finger and strike the fifth course on the fifth fret. This will be *mi* of diatonic *a la mi re* [a'], and it is notated with an 'et' sign [ℨ]. It is a unison with the *5.*

Finger and strike the fifth course on the sixth fret. This brings you *fa* of *b fa h mi* on the line [b♭'], and it is notated with a double *d*. It is a unison with the *e*.

Finger and strike the fifth course on the seventh fret. This brings you *mi* of *b fa h mi* on the line [b'], and it is notated with a double *i*. It is a unison with the *k*.

There you have five courses.

THE SIXTH COURSE

The unstopped, unfingered sixth course produces *mi* of diatonic *a la mi re* [a'], and it is notated with a numeral that represents "five" in numbers, like this: **5**.

(Sig. [L3v]) Finger and strike the sixth course on the first fret. This brings you *fa* of *b fa h mi* on the line [b♭'], and it is notated with an *e*.

Finger and strike the sixth course on the second fret. This brings you *mi* of *b fa h mi* on the line [b'], and it is notated with a *k*.

Finger and strike the sixth course on the third fret. This brings you *fa* of diatonic *c sol fa* [c"], and it is notated with a *p*.

Finger and strike the sixth course on the fourth fret. This brings you *mi* of chromatic *c so*[*l*] *fa* [c#"], and it is notated with a *v*.

Finger and strike the sixth course on the fifth fret. This brings you diatonic *d la sol* [d"], and it is notated with a **9** [a sign for "con" or "us"].

Finger and strike the sixth course on the sixth fret. This brings you *fa* of chromatic *e la* [e♭"], and it is notated with a double *e*.

Finger and strike the sixth course on the seventh fret. This brings you *mi* of diatonic *e la* [e"], and it is notated with a double *k*.

There you have all the pitches of both genera on all courses and frets. You can also go much higher beyond the frets, but for that there are no more fixed rules, especially for the quintsait. Therefore, I will not write further about this either. A: Very well. That is written out clearly enough for me. Nevertheless, I am still in need of a little more explanation, and it concerns this: You are speaking to me about several letters and numerals that I cannot distinguish from each other. Give me instruction about this, and then I will be content with it. *Se*: You are right. There are indeed several letters that are made just like the numerals, or the numerals like (sig. [L4]) the letters. And, as I think about it, I find three instances: first, when one writes the number "one" with a stroke; next, the *2*; and third, the *3*. In this regard, you should know that the lutenists have two forms of [the number] "one." They make the first with a long stroke and two little dots above it, as here: ï. And they call it the "large [number] one." They make the second [number] "one" as a plain little stroke, unembellished, without any addition at all, and they name this the "small [number] one," like this: ı. Furthermore, they make a small, short little stroke with one little dot above it. They call that a vowel, which is the ninth letter of the alphabet and the third of the five vowels. It is made like this: i.

In the second instance, the *2* and the *r* are also two different things. [Lutenists] consider as a numeral the one made like this: 2. And [they consider] as a consonant the one formed like this: ꝛ.[152]

Thirdly, they consider that which signifies "three" in numbers to be a numeral, made like this: 3. And that which is made a second way, like this: ʒ, they make as a consonant.[153]

And these are all the distinctions that may confuse you. Otherwise, I know of nothing more that you need for the tablature of the lute, except for reviewing which notes are long or short, as I have told you with reference to the clavichord. But since I have already said enough about it, it is not necessary to repeat it here. Therefore I will leave it at that, and [I will] show you [all] these things [in the form of] such beautiful illustrations, which I have written out for you, [illustrations] that I know have not yet been seen, heard of, or thought possible of being devised, like those that follow below. The first [is] the *Scala musicalis* [musical scale] with all the numbers and letters for the neck of the lute.

(Sig. [L4v]) [Woodcut of the notational symbols of lute tablature related to the notes of the musical scale, in four columns with the following typeset captions from left to right, above and below: "Diatonic notes," "Diatonic unisons," "Notes of the chromatic genus," and "Unisons of the chromatic genus."]

(Sig. M) I presume from this illustration you will understand well enough what each letter is and what it signifies on the neck of the lute, so that you will always put into the tablature the one letter for the line or for the space on which the written note stands. However, so that you will understand it even better, I will show you one additional illustration in which you also see all the letters that you [saw] before on the neck of the lute now written out [and] standing next to the hand or scale of Guido. In the following illustration you will find all of these [letters and notes], each one put on its own course and on its own fret, and on its proper line and space as well. I think you will make sense out of it if you look at the illustration very diligently; and [to clarify] whatever about it is difficult for you, simply reread the early section about the lute and put the illustration in front of you. I expect it will get to be easy for you. So, turn [the page], and look over the illustration. I think it is correct.

(Sig. [Mv]) [Woodcut of the six courses and the tablature symbols as they relate to the scale]

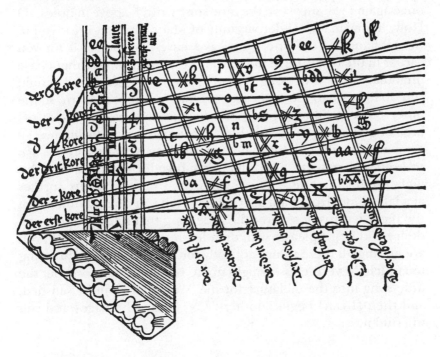

Letter names of notes
The numbers
are not pressed down.

the 6th course
the 5th course
the 4th course
the third course
the 2nd course
the first course

the first fret
the second fret
the third fret
the fourth fret
the fifth fret
the sixth fret
the seventh fret

165

(Sig. M2) I think you now have enough rules, for I can write no more about this tablature for eleven strings. But in the other book I will present three other kinds of tablatures for you, and [I will] teach you to intabulate for thirteen strings.[154] Consequently, I can think of nothing more that you would need for now, except that once again I will show you the little song written above in notes, "O Holy, immaculate, tender virginity of Mary," and set it for you in the tablature of the lute, [just] as I have likewise set it for you earlier in the tablature of the clavichord. And as you see that I have intabulated the little song following the notes exactly, so should you do likewise to the other [songs] that you want to learn. In the other book I will also give you a better way (*modum*), [that of] breaking up some of the pitches (*ettliche stymmen zů diminuiren*),[155] so that [the music] does not proceed so very simply (*so gar schlecht*). For now [though], let this suffice for you regarding this tablature for the lute. Then, if you wish, you may inquire further at a later time, [for] I am also going to tell you what I know about the recorder. Just look over the little song that follows, and if you desire and [if] it pleases you, then learn to play it.[156] *A*: Well, you are ending all these things abruptly for me, and you are hurrying too much. Nevertheless, I ought not to vex you. Therefore, put the little song into the tablature for me. With that I will be satisfied, and then [I can] begin another.[157] *Se*: Turn [the page] and you will find it.

(Sig. [M2v]) [Woodcut of the song found on sigs. H4v–I2 as intabulated for lute(s)][158]

(Sig. [M3]) [Woodcut of lute tablature, continued]

(Sig. [M3v]) [*The chapter*] *on the recorder begins here*[159].

A: Now tell me about the recorder. How should I set about to learn it? *Se*: In learning to play the recorder you must first know how many [finger] holes this [kind of] pipe will have; secondly, how the fingers are to be placed on the pipe; thirdly, how the pipe is to be labeled; fourthly, which hole or how many of the holes must be opened or closed so that they produce exactly the pitch you intend, from the two genera – diatonic and chromatic. Then, when you know the fingering, you must also learn to apply the tongue – which is also used on the recorder – together with the fingers [so that] they move with each other exactly [at the same time] up and down [the scale] or with leaps, as the case may be.

A: Then, tell me how many holes the recorder has, [holes] that must be opened and closed. *Se*: Recorders generally have two holes at the lower end situated directly opposite each other. They are made directly opposite each other because some players (*ettliche pfeiffer*) are accustomed to having the right hand above and the left hand below on the pipe, and these [players] close the hole on the right side with wax. Others are accustomed to having the left hand above and the right hand below, and they therefore close the hole on the left side with wax. Thus, the two holes are made equivalent, so that they can be serviceable to any [player], whether he wishes to use the left one or the right one. Therefore, (sig. [M4]) the two holes are counted as only one, because whichever of the two is opened, the other opposite to it must be closed. One of these side holes, whichever one wishes, is for the little finger. Thus, these two holes are made on the sides of the pipe and not in the middle like the others, so that they can be reached with the little finger.[160] After that, proceeding upward, on the second hole of the recorder belongs the *annularis*, which is called "the golden ring finger" by the erudite, or [simply] "the gold finger."[161] Then, going up from the bottom, on the third hole belongs the middle among the five fingers of the hand. After that, on the fourth hole of the pipe belongs the index finger of the lower hand. Now, going further up, on the fifth hole of the pipe belongs the ring finger of the upper hand. On the sixth hole of the pipe, going up, belongs the middle finger of the upper hand. On the seventh hole belongs the index finger of the second hand, which is the upper one. Then there is one more hole in the back of the pipe. The thumb of the upper hand belongs on this one, as you [can] see drawn in this illustration of the two hand [positions].

(Sig. [M4v]) [Woodcut of the hands on a recorder in two configurations]
The left hand below   The right hand above
The right hand below   The left hand above

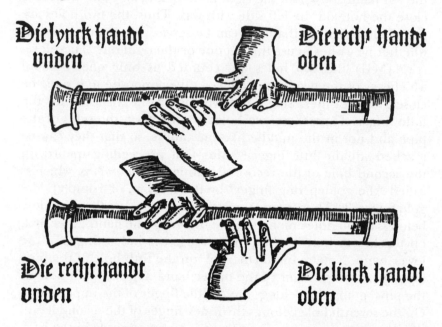

Die lynck handt vnden   **Die recht handt oben**

Die recht handt vnden   **Die linck handt oben**

(Sig. N) *A*: This too I understand well. Now, how shall I label the recorder? *Se*: In the other book I have made a special [fingering] chart and illustration for each [size of] recorder: a separate one for the discant [i.e., the size called "alto" or "treble" today, but one pitched a fifth rather than a fourth above the tenor], a separate one for the tenor, and also [one] for the bass (*basscontra*), according to the way [in which] the three sizes of recorders are tuned together [as a consort]. And these charts or[162] illustrations – on account of the letters that I have applied to the holes – are somewhat more like or similar to our music [i.e., to staff notation] than [are] the present numerical symbols.[163] Nevertheless, [in this instance] I am making the charts with only the numerals, so that they can be used for all recorders, be they tenor, bass, or discant. And since you have eight holes on the recorder, we will therefore take just the first eight numerals for this purpose, and [standing] for the lowest two holes (which, after all, are counted as only one, and on which the little finger belongs) we will put a numeral that represents "one" in numbers, like this: 1. [Standing] for the second hole, on which the ring finger belongs, we will put a numeral that represents "two" in numbers, like this: **ᴢ**. For the third hole, on which the middle finger of the lower hand belongs, we will put a numeral that represents "three" in numbers, like this: **3**. For the fourth hole, on which the index finger of the lower hand belongs, we will put a numeral that represents "four" in numbers, like this: **4**. For the fifth hole, on which the ring finger of the second hand ([the one] that is on top) belongs, we will put a numeral that represents "five" in numbers, like this: **5**. For the sixth hole, on which the middle finger of the second hand belongs, we will put a numeral that represents "six" in numbers, like this: **6**. For the seventh hole, on which the index finger of the upper hand belongs, we will put a numeral that represents "seven" in numbers, like this: **7**. (Sig. [Nv]) For the eighth hole, situated on the back of the recorder, on which the thumb of the upper hand belongs, we will put a numeral that represents "eight" in numbers, like this: [8].

[Woodcut of a recorder with all eight holes numbered]

A: Well now, you have told me enough about the placement of the fingers on the recorder, [and] similarly, how I am to label the pipe. Now tell me how and in what way I am to get and obtain the pitches on it. *Se*: You must know [that] when one tunes two or three recorders together, then the small recorder of the discant [part] must always be pitched a fifth above the middle-sized recorder of the tenor [part]; and in the same way, the recorder of the bass [part] must likewise be pitched a fifth below the tenor. Therefore, I will show you the lines and spaces, for they are the same in the three fifths. For example, if I begin on the *fa* below *gamma ut* [F] for the bass, [then] on the tenor [it will be] *c fa ut* above that in the space [c], [and] then on the discant it will be *g sol re ut* in the space [g], a fifth above the tenor.[164] In like manner, the first line for the bass will be *gamma ut* [G], the tenor

[will be] a fifth above that at *d sol re* [d], and then the discant, a
fifth above the tenor, will be *a la mi re* on the line [a]. And thus,
going on further up, one [size of] recorder is fingered and blown
almost exactly like the others, as long as in other respects they
have their correct measurements – of the length, of the diameter,
(sig. N2) and also of the holes – but not otherwise. Only the bass
cannot be made to speak as well in the shrill or high register as the
tenor or the discant. Therefore, I will give you an illustration later
on in which I will present you with three different sets of letter
names for the notes (*claves*),[165] setting them distinctly on the lines
and spaces: those of the discant in the first column [i.e., on the
right (see below pp. 179–80 – sigs. O3 and O3v)], those of the
tenor in the middle, and the letter-names of the bass last [i.e., on
the left]. And since these three recorders are thus almost all the
same in all pitches, by fifths [i.e., they have the same fingerings for
pitches that are a fifth apart], I will put the numerals of the holes
[only] once in these lines and spaces. For, if these are correct for
the tenor, then they will be correct as well for the discant and the
bass in all pitches.

   And so I will begin by telling you about the opening and closing
of the holes on the recorder. With this you can be sure to obtain
the pitches of the two *genera* discussed above. In the first place I
[will] tell you [that], when you close all the holes of the recorder
and blow into the recorder, then the lowest pitch of all will sound.
On the tenor you must consider this pitch as diatonic *c fa ut* in the
space [c], and on the discant as if it were diatonic *g sol re ut* in the
space [g]. But in the bass, you must consider it as the *fa* below the
gamma ut [F], [a] chromatic [note].[166] In the fingering chart as
well as in the tablature, you must notate this lowest or deepest
pitch with a round circle and a little dot inside it, or else, with a *0*
[i.e., a zero] and a little dot inside it, like this: ☉. *A*: Why must the
lowest pitch of the recorder have a special symbol in the tablature
and not a symbol for a numeral like the other holes? *Se*: Because,
just like the *0* in the science of numbers, it represents nothing at
all. (Sig. [N2v]) Rather, it only takes the place of a number. Therefore, in this case as well, it is not to indicate any of the numbered
holes, but only an open pitch of the recorder, as if it had no holes
at all. *A*: Then what is the purpose of the little dot in the middle of
the circle? *Se*: That differentiates it from the pitch that the recorder
produces when all the holes are open. This pitch is likewise not

notated with a numeral, but with an unembellished circle, or a *0*,
as [you see] here written on the [picture of a] recorder: **O** .

[Woodcut of a recorder with the two notational symbols marked upon it]

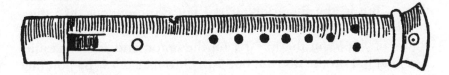

A: Now tell me more about the pitches [as you] go up on the
recorder. *Se*: Open now only the first hole, on which the little
finger [belongs]. [This pitch] is notated with a numeral that
represents "one" in numbers, like this: *ı*. This brings you one
whole tone above the first pitch of the recorder, when all [the]
holes are closed; and this must be *d sol re* [d] on the tenor, *a la mi
re* [a] on the discant, and *gamma ut* [G] on the bass. It is notated
in the following fingering chart, and also in the tablature as well,
with a plain stroke, like the one above.

Now going higher up: close the first hole once again and open
the second. That gives you a semitone that is *fa* of chromatic
e la mi [e♭] on the tenor, but it is *fa* of chromatic *a re* [A♭] on the
bass, and *fa* of *b fa h mi* in the space [b♭] on the discant. And this
pitch is notated in the following illustration [i.e., in the fingering
chart] as well as in the tablature with a numeral that (sig. N3)
represents "two" in numbers. But in addition, [in the tablature] a
little stroke must go through it, just as if it were crossed out [or
slashed] in half, like this: *✗*.[167] *A*: Why must that be? *Se*: So that
one can distinguish between the two numerals [in the tablature]
that represent "two" in numbers, or [so that one can tell] one
from the other. And since this [pitch] is no more than a minor
semitone, in order that such a [numeral] should represent such a
semitone, I will make a stroke through [the numeral] so that this
half part will indicate the minor semitone. And every time I make
a little stroke through a numeral, that will always indicate nothing
more than a semitone to me. But wherever there is an intact
numeral without a stroke or line through it, that will always
indicate a whole tone to me. Now, going further up [the scale]:

open the first two holes, to which the little finger and the ring finger are assigned. That gives you *mi* of the *e la mi* [e] on the tenor, but on the bass it will be *mi* of diatonic *a re* [A], and on the discant *mi* of *b fa h mi* in the space [b]. And that is notated in the tablature with a numeral that represents "two" in numbers, like this: **2**. But in the fingering chart I put two numerals, like this: **21**. After that, open the third hole and the first [one]. That gives you *fa* of *f fa ut* on the line [f] on the tenor, and *fa* of diatonic *c sol fa ut* [c'] on the discant, but *fa* of chromatic *h mi* [B♭] on the bass. That is notated in the fingering chart with two numerals, the first of which represents "three" in numbers, and the second of which represents "one" in numbers, as here: **31**. But in the tablature it is notated with only one numeral that represents "three" in numbers, with a little stroke drawn through it, like this: **♯**.

A: Wait! Wait! I cannot understand that. Should I open the third hole and the first [hole] and keep the second [one] closed? Earlier you said I should open the second hole and keep the first one closed, and you notated it like this: (sig. [N3v]) **♯**. But now you are talking about two [holes], and you skip over the middle one. And since I see that you open sometimes three, sometimes four, sometimes five, sometimes six holes, [and] sometimes all [of them], how will you let me know how to notate these pitches with one single numeral so that I [can] find the correct pitch? Set me straight about this so I need question you no further about it.

Se: I will give you a very concise rule for this so that you need ask nothing further, and it is this: every time you put a numeral into the tablature that stands for the pitch and [for] one of the holes, whichever it may be (notice immediately if the pitch is a whole tone), then all the other holes underneath this one – that is, the holes with numerals that are lesser or smaller – must always be opened. For example, if the sixth hole is to be open, and if it is a whole tone, then the fifth, the fourth, the third, the second, and the first must all be open. Or, if the fifth hole is a whole tone, and if "five" is put into the tablature, then the fourth, the third, the second, and the first must be opened. But, if it is a semitone, then the next hole below the one that the numeral designates must always remain closed, while, moreover, the others below it [are] all open. So if the sixth hole is a semitone, then this sixth hole must remain open and the fifth [one] closed, and then the fourth, the third, the second, and the first all remain open. If the fifth is a semitone, then the fourth must always remain closed, and the fifth, the third,[168] the second, and the first [must] be opened. You must therefore merely watch for the semitones and keep the rules. Moreover, it is not necessary to put into the tablature all the holes that should be opened for any pitch [along with] all their numerals. (Sig. [N4]) For then, many pitches will have as many as five, six, or seven numerals, as I show in the following fingering chart. But that would not be intelligible [in a tablature]. Therefore, I am putting into the fingering chart the numerals alone, so that you can easily obtain, learn, and finger the pitches and also impress them upon your memory. And if you have understood them, then you will always put [just] the first numeral of the same pitch into the tablature. If it is a whole tone, then you need open no more than this hole of the numeral as well as all others underneath it, and [you] put into the tablature only the first numeral of this pitch, completely bare and without a slash. But if it is a semitone, then keep the nearest hole below it closed, and make a little line through the first numeral in the tablature.

A: Well, I think I will remember it. Now let us go on farther up [the scale]. Show me the fingerings in more detail. *Se*: Now open the third, the second, and the first holes, and blow [into the recorder]. On the tenor that gives you *mi* of *f fa ut* on the line [f#'], and on the discant, *mi* of chromatic *c sol fa ut* [c#']. But on the bass it gives you *mi* of diatonic *h mi* [B]. And that is notated in the fingering chart with three numerals, like this: **3 2 1**; in the tablature [it will be indicated[with only a *3*.[169]

Now take the lower hand completely away. Four holes are thus open: the fourth, the third, the second, and the first. Recorder players call this pitch "at the half-way [point]" (*zum halben synn*). It is *g sol re ut* in the space on the tenor [g], *d la sol re* on the discant [d'], and *c sol fa ut* on the bass [c]. In like manner, it is notated in the fingering chart with four numerals, like this: **4 3 2 1**, but in the tablature with only one numeral, like this: **4**. And in this way, by following the tenor, you can find the other pitches of the discant, (sig. [N4v]) and also of the bass, all of them together almost exactly the same on one pipe as on another, except that the bass cannot sound as good in the high register as the other pipes [do]. I will therefore give further instructions for the tenor alone. You will be guided by it for the other pipes as you put in front of you the fingering chart in which I clearly show you all the pitches. Therefore, for the sake of brevity, I will leave out the other pitches [i.e., of the discant and bass recorders], because the pipes will ordinarily be the same by fifths.

Now to proceed: There comes next a semitone [that] is *fa* of chromatic *a la mi re* [a♭]. For this you must open four holes: the fifth, the third, the second, and the first. And it is notated in the fingering chart with these four numerals, like this: 5321. But in the tablature [it is notated] with a numeral that means "five," with a little like drawn through it, like this: 𝟝.

After that comes the *mi* of diatonic *a la mi re* [a]. You must open five holes: the fifth, the fourth, the third, the second, and the first. And it is notated in the fingering chart with five numerals: 54321. But in the tablature it is notated with a single bare numeral that represents "five," as here: 5.

After that there follows the *fa* of *b fa h mi* [b♭]. You must open five holes: the sixth, the fourth, the third, the second, and the first. And it is notated in the fingering chart with the five numerals: 64321. But in the tablature [it is notated] with only one numeral that represents "six," with a little line through it, as here: 𝟞.[170]

After that comes the *mi* of *b fa h mi* [b]. For this you must open six holes: the sixth, the fifth, the fourth, the third, the second, and the first. And the pitch is notated in the fingering chart with the six numerals: 654321. But in the (sig. O) tablature [it is notated] with only one numeral that represents "six" in numbers, like this: 6.[171]

After that comes the *fa* of diatonic *c sol fa ut* [c']. For this you must open six holes: the seventh, the fifth, the fourth, the third, the second, and the first. And that is notated in the fingering chart with six numerals, thus: 754321. But in the tablature [it is notated] with only one numeral that represents "seven" in numbers, with a little line drawn through it, like this: 𝟟.

After that comes *mi* of chromatic *c sol fa ut* [c#']. For this you must open seven holes: the seventh, the sixth, the fifth, the fourth, the third, the second, and the first. And that is notated in the fingering chart with the seven numerals: 7654321; but in the tablature [it is notated] with only the numeral that represents "seven" in numbers, like this: 7.

After that there follows diatonic *d la sol re* [d'], and for this you must open all holes, lower and upper, and this is notated in the fingering chart the same as in the tablature. Thus, you should draw only a round circle without any addition, which will indicate to you an open pitch that the recorder produces without putting down any fingers. Therefore, one draws nothing at all except a bare circle: **O** .

A: Now do I have all the pitches of the recorders for playing in the higher and lower [registers], so that the indicated holes are all set in order in the fingering chart and [in the] tablature? *Se*: No, you have another perfect fifth to go up higher *gradatim* through all the semitones of the two genera discussed above. But [as for] how you are to put them into the fingering chart and then into the tablature, that requires special attention. *A*: I beg you, tell me about this as well. *Se*: Very well, I will present this to you – likewise with few words– and set down a rule about it, which is this: whenever you wish to go up higher from here, then you must always have the eighth hole – (sig. [Ov]) on which the thumb of the higher hand belongs – half open and half closed for all the pitches. These pitches are also called the pitches of the high register of the recorder, and they are discovered, obtained, fingered, and blown exactly the same as their lower octaves, except that the thumb hole on the back or underside of the recorder is always half open. Thus, going straight on, you have all the pitches as before an octave higher, up to the *fa* of *b fa h mi* [b♭'] on the line in the tenor, and up to the *fa* above *e la* [f"] in the discant; but you cannot reach this in the bass. And so that you understand this completely, we will go further up from the pitch that was *d sol re* [d'] and [for which] all holes were open. For the first [note of the upper register], make the thumb hole half open, and, in addition, [open] the second hole once again. That gives you *fa* of chromatic *e la mi* [e♭'] on the line, and you will find it notated in the fingering chart with two numerals next to one another. The first is *8* [and] the second "two," like this: **8₂**. But in the tablature it has another notation, and it is this: In place of the numeral that represents "eight" in numbers, you should always draw a little half-circle, with a little dot [and put it] above the [written] numeral. The little half-circle with a little dot in it indicates the half part of the eighth hole that must always be open. And the small dot within it means that the first holes, going up from the full circle (that is, from the bottom up), must be opened exactly as before. And thus, you notate this *fa* of *e la mi* [e♭'] in the tablature with a numeral that represents "two" with a little line through it, to which is added above the numeral a half circle with a small dot, like this : ⚡.[172]

(Sig. O2) Now make the thumb hole on the back half open and half closed, and then [open] the second and the first holes. That gives you *mi* of diatonic *e la mi* [e'], and it is written like this in the fingering chart: 8 4 1, but in the tablature with a numeral that represents "two" in numbers and above it a half circle with a dot, like this: ⚡.[173]

Now make the thumb hole on the back of the pipe half open and half closed, and then [open] the third hole and the first. That gives you *fa* of diatonic *f fa ut* [f'] in the space, and it is notated in the fingering chart like this: 8 3 1. But in the tablature it is notated with a numeral that makes "three" in numbers, with a little line drawn through it, and above the number a half circle with a dot: ⚡.[174]

Now, once again, make the thumb hole on the back of the pipe half open and half closed. In addition, [open] the first three holes: the third, the second, and the first. That gives you *mi* of chromatic *f fa ut* [f#'], and it is thus notated in the fingering chart with four numerals,[175] but in the tablature with only a *3* and above it a half circle and a dot, like this: ⚡.[176]

Now make the back thumb hole half open and closed, and [open] the fourth, the third, the second, and the first hole[s] as well. These give you the diatonic *g sol re ut* [g'] on the line, which recorder players call the half-way point of the high register, and it is notated in the fingering chart with five numerals, like this: 8 4 3 2 1. But in the tablature it is notated with only one numeral, which represents "four" in numbers, and above this numeral [there is] a half-circle with a dot, like this: ⚡.

Now, once again, make the back thumb hole half open and closed. Then [open] the fifth, the third, the second, [and] the first as well. That gives you *fa* of chromatic *a la mi re* [a♭'], and it is notated in the fingering chart with five (sig. [O2v]) numerals, like this: 8 5 3 2 1. But in the tablature this pitch is notated with one numeral that represents "five" in numbers, with a half circle and a dot [drawn] above it [and a line through the numeral], like this: ⚡.

Now, once again, make the back thumb hole half open and half closed. Then [open] the fifth, the fourth, the third, the second, and the first hole[s] as well. That gives you *mi* of diatonic *a la mi re* [a'], and it is notated in the fingering chart with six numerals, like this: 854321. But in the tablature [it is notated] with one single numeral that means "five" in numbers. And above, it must have a half circle with a dot, like [this]: $\mathbf{3}$.

Finally, make this back thumb hole half-way open and half-way closed [once more]. At the same time you must also open five more holes: the sixth, the fourth, the third, the second, and the first. For you this will be the highest pitch of the tenor [recorder], and it will be *fa* of *b fa h mi* [bb'] on the line. It is notated in the fingering chart with six numerals, like this: 864321. But in the tablature it is notated with a single numeral that means "six" in numbers, with a little line drawn through it, and above it a half circle with a dot, like this: $\mathbf{6}$.

So, you now have all the pitches as well as how you shall obtain them on the recorder. I will put before you two illustrations of this. In the first [there are] the numerals of all the pitches on the three sizes of pipes. Then, in the second [there are] the symbols for the pitches in the tablature. With these we will end the little book.

(Sig. [O3]) [Woodcut of recorder fingering chart][177]

Bass   Tenor   Discant

(Sig. [O3v]) [Woodcut of simplified recorder fingering chart, the "tablature"]

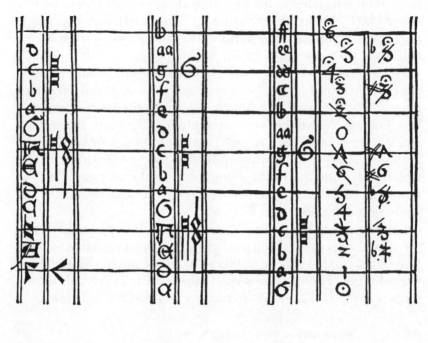

[Bass]   [Tenor]   [Discant]

(Sig. [O4]) If you now wish to set something for recorders into the tablature, then put the symbols of the latter illustration in front of you and pay attention to the measurement *de valore notarum*, or, of the value of the notes, just as I have taught you previously for the clavichord. It will be easy for you to learn. Let that satisfy you for now.

A: There is still one very little[178] [matter] about which I must inquire. Give me information about this and then [you can] happily conclude your little book. Earlier you presented to me a little song that had four voices. Since I now would like to set it for recorders into the tablature [that you] have shown [me], what kind of recorder must I have then for the alto part?

Se: You need to know that one generally makes four recorders in one chest (*in einen futeral*),[179] or six together, which is called a "coppel": two discants, two tenors, [and] two basses. You must observe [in] the alto part whether the range from top to bottom allows you to have another tenor or not. If you deem it [appropriate] for a second tenor recorder, then you need no other.[180] But if it goes too high, then you must take a second discant for the alto part.

And thus, so that you and I may also become those about whom the prophet David spoke [in the quotation] at the beginning [of this book]: "Blessed is the people that knows how to make the joyful sound"; and so that many a good companion who wishes to become one of the blessed [people may] improve himself in the future, I will herewith commend you to God, and contentedly conclude my little book. And I desire no more than [this]: that wherever I have erred, no one [will] blame me for my great, impudent lack of diligence and [my] oversight; and, if I have offended someone in it, may he forgive me, God willing. With that, may God keep you in good health. *A*: You too, my dear Bastian. May God be your reward. *Se*: Amen.

Appendix: transcriptions of documents pertaining to Sebastian Virdung and *Musica getutscht*

Document No. 8 (English translation on pp. 35–6 above)

This document is transcribed by Wallner in "Sebastian Virdung von Amberg," pp. 87–8, as follows (here omitting slashes that indicate changes of line in the original document but including Wallner's solutions to the abbreviations in parentheses):

Wie sich Her Sebastian virdung caplan der caplany stalburg halb v(er)schribn hett[:] Ich Sebastianus virdung von amb(er)g prister eystetter bistumb bekenn mit disser myner eygen Handgeschrifft, dwyl der durchluchtigst Hochgebornn furst vnd Her, Her philips pfalzgraue by Ryn Hertzog Inn bayern, dess Heyligen römischen rychs Ertzdruchsess vnd kurfurst etc, myn gnedigster lieb(er) Her, mir geliehen Sant peters altar Im Sloss stalburg, trier bistumb, der syner gnaden capell(e)n zu Heidelb(er)g Im sloss, dar Inn eyn person dem gotsdinst Zuhalt(en), Inncorporiger)t ist, mich mit versehen, das ich mit truwen an eydesstatt gelobt vnd versprochen Han, Syn fl. g. vnd syner gnaden erben Inn der capell(e)n zu Hoff oder, wo ich vff syner fl. gn. kosten Hin bescheid(en) wirdt, mit kunst der musigk vnd gesang, das mir gott verliehen Hett als eyn senger getruwlich, gehorsamlich vnd pristerlich dyenen vnnd gewartten, vnd zu Heyligen tagen zu mess lessen schicken vnd mess lessen, wan mich gott ermant. Ich soll vnd will auch vss Heydelberg nit oder von den enden, dahin ich bescheid(en) wurde, on sunder syner furstlichen gnad(en), vrlaub noch syn, es sy dan ey(n) nacht, dry oder vier ongeuerlich; Es wer dan das man mir den disch oder kost vnnd cleydung, [p. 88] wie ich bissher gehabt Han, abbreche, oder so ich kranck wurde, dasselb nit lieffern wolt. Ich soll vnnd will auch den altar Zu stalburg mit mess less(e)n nach lutt der Innstruction gnugsamlich versehen vnd belessen lassen, das dem gotsdinst das nit abgee, vnd wo ich das mit geuerd(en) nit Hilt od(er) on vrlaub vber eyn monat von Heydelb(er)g od(er) end(en), dahin ich verordent wer(e), oder ob ich schon vrlaub Hett, vnnd vber Zyt mir erlaubt, On sunderlich nuw vrlaub' vssblibe, alles onredlich lybs oder ander ehafft vrsach. So soll vff stundt on eynigen behelff die gemelte pfrimt syner fl. gn. als patron ledig

Heymgefallen syn vnd vacirn, das syn fl. gn. die lyhen vnnd daruff presentirn mogen, wem oder wen syn fl. gn. wolle on myn od(er) meniglichs Innredt. Ich will auch syn fl. gn. als dan, vnd dan, als itzunt so sich der fall begebe, die pfrimt freywillig vnd lediglich Zugestellt vnd resignirt Han, vnd Hiewidder soll und will ich nit erlangen annemen thun oder schaffen, auch mich dauon nit absoluir(e)n lassen. Sunder alle disse puncten stet vnd vest Halt(en), auch synen f. gn. getruw vnd Holt syn. Syner gnaden schaden warnen fromen vnd bestes getruwlich werben, auch syn(er) furstlich(e)n gnad(en) rett vnd Heymlicheit, wes ich der weyss od(er) erfure ewiglich verschweyg(en), alles getruwlich vnd ongeuerde, vnd Zu noch mer(er) sicherheyt Han ich myn signett Herby gedruckt. Datum vff freytag nach Sant Jacobs, des heyligen appostels tag. Anno dom(in)j millesimo quigentesimo.

Document No. 9 (English translation on pp. 36–7 above)

The original German text of this document is transcribed in Wallner, "Sebastian Virdung von Amberg," p. 90, as follows (see doc. 8, p. 182 above, for principles of transcription adopted here):

Dem durchleüchtigen hochgebornen fursten vnd hern hern[,] Ludwigen Pfaltzgrauen bey rein[,] hertzogen In beyern. Meynem gnedigen liben hern In seinr furstlichen gnaden eygen hent.

Durchleüchtiger hochgeborner furst, gnediger her. mein vnd her(n) hans kargl vnd hern Jacob vnd vnser(er) gesellen vndertenig dinst Zu vor an, mit aller vndertenickeit vnd gebett sein eürn fl. gn. allbeg bereitt, Nün so vns eur fl. gn. gnediclich haben bedacht grüss zü sagen, durch meister hanss hasfürt, der das fleissig than Hatt, des freüwen vnd trosten wir vns all vnd Itlicher, sunderlich das eür fl. gn. vnser In gnáden gedenkt, darinn wir auch all willig vnd vndertenig begern vnd bitten wellen eür fl. gn. heill vnd selig widerfart; it(em) Gnediger Her, m(eister) Hans Hasfürt Hatt ein müsick mit In herbracht, dye hatt man In geschenkt zu lügdüne, Ist also genent vnd Intitülirt von namen vnd tittel, wye eür fl. gn. In dem eyngelegten Zettell werden finden, auch ist noch ein müsick In franckreich gemacht, der namen auch darbey wirdt stan, bitt ich eür furstlich gnad underteniclichen eürn gnaden vnd hern vatter auch diesem fursten tüm zü eren, solichs hern niclasen eürn gnaden Caplan zu befelhen vnd mir oder vns allen In dye capellen, oder Zu vor an In eürs hern vnd vatters liberey Zu bestellen, da mit vns dye zu lesen oder zu sehen werden; vns In eür fl. gn. eren Zü bessern, das willich, wo ich täglich würdt vm eür fl. Gn. langleben albeg bitten vnderteniglich Zu verdynen. dat(um) vff Dornstag nach Dionisij Im 1503.

Eür fl. gn. vnderteniger caplan[,] Sebastian virdüng[,] Singer.

Appendix

Document No. 10 (English translation on pp. 37–8 above)

The original German text of this document is transcribed in Wallner, "Sebastian Virdung vom Amberg," p. 91, as follows (see doc. no. 8, p. 182 above, for principles of transcription adopted here):

Ludwig etc. Andechtigen, vnd lieb(en) besondern. Wjr hab(en) uw(er) schr(eiben) getruw(er) v(n)d gut(er) mejnung v(er)stand(en), Zu danknemig(em) gefall(en) angenom(en), woll(en) (uwer) erbiet(en) on vergess(en) hab(en). hab(en) zu vil mal(en) auch uw(erm) geschefft der sengerij, auch meist(er) Arnolt(en) v(n)d der orgeln, sampt vns(er) h(ern) v(n)d vatter tromettern her an hoff ein dag od(er) ij zu sin gewonscht. Dann wie woll der konglichen seng(er) vil v(n)d vo(r) wa(r) vns bedunken vast gud, so will vns doch das, so die orgeln v(n)d piff(en) da(r) zu djen(en), nit so lieblich und lustlich dunken zin als dusen, wisse(n) ab(er) nit, ob wjr recht hab(en) oder nit. die vfz(ei)chnis, jr her Bastjan vns g(e)schickt, haben wjr der Konglichen seng(er) ejn(em), der dutsch(er) v(n)d von Nuwenmarkt bürtig v(n)d gudt ist, seh(en) lass(en); der sagt, man fy(n)d solicher büch(er) in Frankrich nit, sondern zu B(r)abandi(en), da hinein wjr nit wa(n)d lo(n)g; wjr wolt(en) sie sust gern bestell(en) v(n)d schick(en), wie ir begert. Nit m(er) dan denk uns(er) zu ziten bij den guten drenk(en) auch z(um) best(en) und grust vns alle die, so in gutem nach vns fragen. Datum Leon, vff dinstag nach allerheiligen dag anno ect. XV. und III.

den andechtig(en), vnsern lieb(en), besond(ern) hern Sebastian Vijrdong, he(r)n Jacob(en) Salcz(ern) v(n)d her Hans(en) Kargen, sengern ect. sampt und sunder.

Document No. 11 (English translation on pp. 38–9 above)

The original German text of this document is transcribed in Wallner "Sebastian Virdung vom Amberg," pp. 97–8, as follows (see doc. no. 8, p. 182 above, for principles of transcription adopted here):

Dem durchleüchtigen hochgebornen fursten vnd hern hern Ludwigen Dem erstgebornen, vnd pfaltzgrauen bei reyn Hertzogen in beyrn meynem gnedigen liben Hern In seiner furstlichen gnaden eygenn hantt.

Durchleuchtiger hochgeborner fürst gnediger her. Mein vndertenig dinst sindt eurn furstlichen gnaden alzeitt willig bereitt. Gnediger her, den gesang, den vns eur furstlich gnade geschickt haben mit haberkorn, ein mütetlin mit fier stym[m]en, Der ittlich ein füg mit Zweyen stym[m]en ist qüintis, ein grosse künst auch da Zü ein meisterliche mess mit fieren zü gesellen zu syngen, darin auch fügen meisterlich vnd woll gemacht oder geschickt syndt, hab ich alsampt meim gnedigsten hern vber antwürt vnd solichs mit mein gesellen In seiner fl. gn. habitacion gesungen, hatt sein fl. gn. ein sunder verwundern gehabt, In dem als ob sich eür fl. gn. auch vm solch Ding an neme. Hab ich auch den brieff den mir eür fl. gn. zugesant Haben, offt vberlesen, darinen nicht vff erden ist, das anders dan güt ist, vnd erdacht, das das on eür fl. gn. schaden vnd allein Zu wolgefallen mag kümen eur fl. gn. Hern vnd vatters Halben; Hab sein gnaden vff sein verwunderung den brieff gezeigt, Den haben sein gnad aussen und Innen titell sigill vnd alle vmstend Zu merern maln woll besehen, aber ich wolt nitt vill nemen, dan er hett es woll besehen für eür gnad. Item gnediger her, ein meister aller c(om)ponisten, Hatt geheissen Johannes ockeghem, vnd als ich wen, der ist ein probst Zu thüren, da sant martin ligt oder bischoff gewesen ist, Der hatt ein mütett mit sex stym[m]en gemacht. Der stym[m]en itlich ist ein füg mit sex stym[m]en, vnd alzüsamen xxxvj stym[m], Auch Hatt er ein mess gesetzt p(ro)lacionüm, sind zwo stym vnd ittlich ein füg In vnisono, in tercijs, In quartis, In q(ui)ntis, In sextis, In sept(imis), In octauis, dye zwey Ding haben wir hye aussen bey vns vnd ein mess c(uius)vis toni, aber aller Ding vnge- [p. 98] recht geschrieben, vnd ich mein, wan eur gnad durch den singer vom neüwen marckt Zu wegen mochten pringen Zu bestellen gerecht, vnd das es eür fl. gn. zu meinem gnedigsten Hern zu schickte, eür gnaden solten auch sein furstlichen gnaden sunder gefallen daran then, dan nün kein ander freid noch kurtzwill mer ist, dan In der stuben vnd hinder dem ofen singen vnd frolich sein, vnd so vill michs nütz vnd lüst bedrifft, so sag ich eur furstlichen gnaden vber alle mass grossen dank desglich(en) auch mein gesellen vnd begeren nitt anders, dan das vm eur fl. gn. mitt aller vnderthenickeitt bitten Zu verdyenen, vnd befelhen vns auch all in eür furstlich gnad, als wir vns In allem güten Zu allen Zeitten eur furstlich gnad In vnserm gebett wellen befolhen haben. Datüm vff freytag nach den neuwen Jars tag Im 1504 Jar[.]

Eur furstlichen gnaden vndertheniger caplan[,]

Sebastianus Virdung[,] Singer

Document No. 22 (English translation on pp. 40–4 above)

The complete German text of this document can be found in the facs. edn. (Kassel, 1977). sigs. π2v–π4. (A transcription of these preliminaries into modern typography by Robert Eitner appears in his "Tabulaturen etlicher lobgesang und lidlein uff die orgeln und lauten von Arnolt Schlick dem Jüngeren [*sic*]," *MfM*, 1 [1869], 121–5.) On the symbol π, see n. 23, p. 206 below. The original reads as follows (my transcription):

Vetterliche Trewe lieber Sone, und
alles das mir got inn vernünfft verlawen, bin ich dir, zů der schůldt,

mitzůdeilen gůtwilligk. Aber du begerst an mich armen blinden, zůvil gross und beinoch unmüglich ding, die einem wolgesehenden, zůvolbringen schwer, und nemlich, do die leiplichen augen, mitsampt der vernůnfft, hohe grosse arbeyt thůn, unnd sich (an tag zůbringen, das in der welt vor nye gesehen noch gehort worden) uben müsten. Sunderlich in dem, die tabulatur uff die Orgel unnd lautten, mit zweyn und eyner Stim zů singen etlich lobgesangk und lidlein zůspiln und zwicken, orden zů Setzen, un[d] durch die Truckerey, uss zůspreitten, das vormals nitmer gesehen, gehort, noch understanden. Dan[n] das her Sebastian virdung priester vo[n] Ambergk (der scharpffs gesichts, un[d] hoher kůnst sich aussgibt) zů Basel fürgenomen, un[d] nitmer dan ein lidlein (dannocht nit durch die ware kunst Truckens, Sunder allein in holtz schniden lassen das gantz onfelen, auch wo das corrupt gemacht, den Truckern kein schult geben, und nit anders dan[n] wie ess geschriben getruckt werden mag) alss ich bericht den selben Truck Sogar onkünstlich, onartlich, onmöglich, un[d] korrupt do bei auch mich und ander verach, schumpffirt, angeben, trucken, aussgehen, und feiltragen lest, nemlich sein mir angetzeigt, in seinem lidlein das er auff die lautten tabuliert, und nit mer dan dreissigk Tempora lang ist, der selben sechtzehen ubersehen, darin fele, un[d] unmüglich griff [sig. π3] gesetzt und gelert, und der süssen gethön, nit geacht, oberhört, un[d] ga[n]tz wider art der seitte[n]cla[n]gk geschriben. Lieber son ker fleis an, besich das fiert, sechst, siebent, acht, 10. 11. 15. 18. 19. 20. 22. 23. 26[.] 27. 28. und das .29. Tempus, mir ist gesagt der selben iglichs, Sey ga[n]tz onartlich, onkünstlich und corrupt. Etwan in eim ein zeiffer und ein buchstab zweimol uff einen Chor gesetzt, als .0[.] 4. 0[.] in dem fierden tempuss, wo nu dem also, magstu und ein ieder mercken, das er des so er sich ussgeben ander zůleren, selbs gantz ongelert und onverste[n]dig dweil solichs zů greiffen unmöglich, und zů hören die oren der verstendige[n] nit fült, der gleiche[n] sein alle obgemelte[n] tempora bresthafftig onformig, onkünstlich, onmüglich zů greiffen, dissonirn, discordirn, unnd ist lautter pletzwerck, das furwar in einem soliche[n] kurtzen liedlein, einem der sich uber and[er] künstner erheben und ichts sunders zůmachen aussgibt meister zů sein (der er sich gantz nit schemen solt noch in die schul zů geen und lernen) zů grob ubergockt, ubergambt, und ubersehen, und zůvil kindisch un[d] onkünstlich gemacht. Ich bitt dich bei deinem lob, das zů hertze[n] zůfassen, un[d] nit so frevel in deinem fürnemen zů werden, und dich ichts aussgeben ander leut zů leren, das du noch nit gelernt hast, nit glaub deinem fürneme[n], vertraw deiner eige[n] vernunfft allein nit zůvil, veracht niemant so bleibstu auch unveracht. Ferrers hab uffmerckens in dem lidlin, das gedachter her Bastian uff die orgel tabulirt hat, sůnderlich des zehenden, zwolfften un[d] achtzehenden tempus, des gleichen der beschreibung des lautenkragens unnd des clavirs der orgeln, wirstu es auch als ich bericht gantz onmeisterlich und onartlich angeben (und mit seinem lernen und trucken, mer die zeit verderbt, dan nůtz geschafft) befinden, un[d] die weil sein onkünstlich onartlich wergk so gar am tag und offenbar ist, das es ein ieder wenigs verstants der musick, und art der instrument, selbs erkenne[n] mag, wil ich dich damit nit ferrer uffhalten, wo aber du her bastian oder iemant anderer an oben angezeigtem zweifelten und nit verstünde[n], wie dovo[n] geret wil ich uff des selben bit wes ich gesagt gern zeigen und underrichte[n], onangesehe[n] her Bastians schupffiren nochreden und trucken sůnderlich in dem do er mir den tittel in meinem orgelbuchlin verkert und zům schmelichsten ausslegt, den ich da[n]nocht dermos nit, sunder ander also [sig. π3v] zu trucken verordent haben, und auch als er setzt wo ich gewüst wz Chromaticu[m] genus gewesen, ich het in meinem büchlein fictam musicam nit gene[n]t. Glaub mir lieber son, will her bastia[n] das kriegisch wort Cromaticus gemeint haben als ess Tortellius und and[er] kriegischer sprach verstendig aussIege[n], ist er des vil bas geübt un[d] teglicher brauchen dan ich, wil er ess aber meine[n] als die musici, Und sunderlich die hochgelerten un[d] erfarne[n] unser auctores, Joha[n]nes de muris[,] Johannes de felle, Joha[n]nes de Susato, Franchinus Gafferus. etc. Die es ficta[m] musicam nennen, un[d] eygen capittel de ficta musica schreiben, aber nit als gelert gewesen sunderlich in krichischer sprach zů interpretirn als her Bastian. So ist als ich mein, gleich ein underscheit und[er] fictam musicam un[d] Chromaticu[m] genus als zwischen dem Rein und mein, do sie zů Meintz zusamen kome[n] under irer substantz des wassers, ich muss solichs ein wenigk anregen, doch niema[n]t zů schme sund[er] die warheit an tag zůbringe[n], und auch das der greůlich geacht wirt, der sein ere nit verantwort, wie wol ich disse schumpffiru[n]g (dertzeit zu wormbs uff dem grossen reichstag und an andern orten, do ich her bastian behülfflich unnd fürtreglich gewessen bin, do ym sein ere und gelimpff angelegen bei fürsten herren un[d] andern gemeine[n] person) umb her bastian nit verdint, und mir billicher bas gelont hett, aber das hiendan gesatzt, betracht ich dein ermanen mich nit rach zu sůchen, deweil ess auch weibisch ist, und will dem volgen und ferrer uff dein begern volnfarn, und ist dem also wie du mich gehörst, was zeichstu mich dan[n], mir uff zůlegen diesse schwere bürden, un[d] ob ich wol solichs mit vernu[n]fft anzůgeben geschickt were, wurde ich doch alleweg zweifeln, durch die trucker zu zeitten, ein weis not vor ein schwartz, ein breve vor ein semibreve, ein fusel vor ein semifusel, ein a vor ein b gesetzt, zu zeitten aussgelassen, ussgetzogen, onfleissig und unrecht ingesteckt un[d] getruckt werden, dardurch du un[d] ich schumpffirt un[d] villeicht on unser verschult veracht würden, aber von dem zulassen und uff dein bit und hohe ermanung, dir alss meinem liebe[n] son zu wilfaren, wil ich sovil mir müglich zu einem anfang und prob, etlich gesang und lidlein, leicht zu singen uff die orgeln und lauten zůsetzen un[d] tabulirn zůmache[n] understeen, und dir zů besichtigen, un[d] in den truck anzůschicken, hiemit bevolhe[n] [sig. π4] haben, wo du anderst inradt findest der verstendigen, und deren so dich gebetten, solichs von mir zuerlangen, das zu offenbaren, wirdig, dienlich, un[d] nütz sein, darnoch und nit ee aussgeen zu lassen, und so ich erfare das dem fleissig nochko[m]men wirt, und zugefallen und nůtz der welt und got furtreglich, wil ich nochvolge[n]d, ein ander werck von meren instrume[n]ten, und scherffer ubung notirn und tabulirn, auch neben dem selben, dz, so mir fürbracht, ursach clerlicher dan[n] in dissem truck erzelen, waru[m]b, wo, wie, und in[n] welchen punckten, her bastian, in seiner newen engellische[n] music, gefelt, onkünstlich, onartlich, onmüglich und corrupt werck gemacht hat, auch mich darin unvereint, onworlich on allen grundt schumpffirt und gestupfft, verantwůrten trucken und aussgee[n] lassen, und bit dich und allen denen dis mein erst prob furko[m]pt nie uber die achseln sund[er] mit fröliche[n] augen und dapfferm gemüt anzusehen, zuhören, wol ergründen und ussörtern, un[d] wo ichts ungeschickts, onartlichs oder corrupt von mir angeben gesatzt und an tag bracht, oder von setzern, truckern, und correctorn ubersehen, brüderlich un[d] nie mit nidischem rach zů straffen und bessern, und mer mein gemüt gegen dir meinem son dan[n] etwas newes gemacht, achte[n], un[d] zu gůttem bede[n[ken un[d] beschirmen, domit wöllest mich deiner bit quitire[n] sei got bevolhen, der dir dein lebe[n] in ere[n] lang wöll friste[n]. Datu[m] Andree apo. a[n]no 1.5.1.1.

Schlick appended the following verse to his dedication in *Tabulaturen* (sig. π4v) (transcription mine):

Ir Musici senger orgler / Und dartzů ir lauten schleger / Die liebhaber sein warer kunst. / Kumpt her, ich bit umb ewern gunst / Mich zů schwawen und lern mit fleiss. / Ir schöler und auch meister greiss. / Wo ich gefelt das corrigirt. / Un[d] nit als bald neidisch schumpffirt / Als Bastian virdung hat gethon. / Sein eigen werck gibt im den lon. / Das erzůlern so schwer gemacht. / Das see ein ieder selbs un acht. / Ob er uff lauten greiffen möcht. / L. c. 4. kk. das er döcht / Und der gelichen fint man vil / Do er geschoseen hat vom zil. / In seiner musick die er acht. / Sich selbs von[n] kunst un[d] art gemacht. / Und michel furtern trucken lan. / Zů Basel als ich das verstan / Zum ersten facht mein Salve an.

Document No. 23 (English translation in pp. 44–5 above)

The original text to Othmar Luscinius's dedication in *Musurgia seu praxis musicae* (Strassburg, Johann Schott, 1536; repr. 1542) – with spellings modernized and abbreviations supplied – reads as follows:

[Sig. a2] Magnifico viro Domino Andreae Calvo Mediolanensis. Ottomarus Luscinius, Argentinus, S.D. Cum ob alias insignes virtutes tuas, magnifice Andrea, summamque eruditionem, plurimus tibi honos ab omnibus jure optimo debeatur: tum in primis ingens praeconium, et favorem immensum apud studiosos cura tibi tua conciliat, qua veterum monumenta librorum, per chalcographiam ab interitu vindicas: et novam ingeniorum foeturam, divite semente spargis in orbem. Nam (ut mea fert opinio) sicut non minoris est meriti, res praeclaras gessisse, quam gestas foelici stilo exarasse, adeo, ut non paucos invenias (si alterum expetendum sit) qui Homeri esse malint quam Achilleis: ita non minus consultum universae reipublicae literariae crediderim, per eos qui ceu Iupiter ex capite partum edunt, novis quibusdam inventis literas illustrando, quam illos demum qui partum huiuscemodi in sinum excipiunt ac confovent. Denique mille exemplis sua ope, aut impensa excusum, protrudunt in lucem: tantaque librorum propagatione id demum agunt, ne sit (quod aiunt) τυφλὸγπλϕτογ. Itaque nescio, cuinam potissimum referamus acceptum, quod quam plures (ut in proverbio dicitur) mutos magistros domi habemus, quibus cum vegetandi ingenii gratia, diurnum nobis existat nocturnumque commercium: an ne authoribus ipsis, qui ea nobis peperere: an iis, quorum ope ad haec usque tempora integre servata sunt. Tuo igitur ductu, cum subinde alii atque alii insignes libelli, ex officina Joannis Schotti chalcographi impendio solertis, haud secus, quam ex durataeo equo fortissimi armati prodierint: superioribus diebus be-[sig. a2v] nigne me adhortatus es, ut libellum Sebastiani Virdung de Instrumentis Musicis, ex Germanico Latinum facerem: sic enim fore, ut etiam ab exteris Musicae studiosis legi possit. Ea tamen lege, ut liber essem ad hac fide, quae abs quovis interprete exigitur: liceretque nobis (si modo ex re lectoris id futurum speraremus) ab authore longo intervallo dissentire. Nam quo licentius id fieret, multorum nobis proponebas exemplum: qui in alienis libris restituendis non sine gloria laborassent. Id quod in hoc libello operae precium existimabas: cui, ut ex certis conjecturis deprehendere licet, propter ereptum praemature e vivis Sebastianum, supremam manum constat haud quaquam contigisse. Igitur tantum abesse dicebas, ne quis interim vicio mihi vertat, sicubia Sebastiani sententia tota ratione descivero: ut etiam gratiam non mediocrem hac occasione a studiosis sim reportaturus: vix enim futurum arbitraris, vi haec qualia cunque sint, diligentius quispiam amplexetur, ob id, quia summa cura sint translata, quam que ex aliqua saltim parte videantur utilia. Ego quamvis primo contra officium arbitrarer futurum, ut meo nutu in alieno solo aedificium extruerem. Deinde, ut tempus severioribus studiis destinatum, in his levioribus sarmentis legendis perderem. Vicit tandem apud me ratio, tibi vir optime, atque omnibus simul Musica studiosis gratificandi. Et quidem in ipso statim operis ingressu (quo votis tuis responderem) satis affabre Sebastiani perpendiculum aequando aedificio nostro congruebat. Verum cum subinde alias atque alias quaereremus excursiones, quibus utile dulci commisceremus, nescio quomodo sit, ut amphora incepta, iam tandem urceus exie-[sig. a3]rit. Caeterum nihil moros ob id amicum lectorem: neque admodum magni refert, sub cuius nomine legantur dialogi isti, nostro marte utcunque concinnati, sive Sebastiani et Andreae: quando illis libelli congruit principium: sive Ottomari et Bartholomei Stoffleri: est is enim municeps noster, vir in literis et re Musica non parum exercitatus: cum illo enim eodem freti contubernio, succisivis horis de Musicis multa iucundissime fabulamur: quae necque nos unquam scripsisse pudebit: neque, uti considimus, lectorem (nisi sorte magnopere delicatus fuerit) onerabunt. Quod idcirco admonui, ne Sebastiano adulterinum quasi partum supposuisse viderer, vulgando eius nomine id quod ipse haud quaquam scripsisset. Bene valeto vir praestantissime. Argentorati anno Christi, 1536.

Notes

1 Why study "Musica getutscht"?

1 Two chapters on musical instruments in an illustrated Korean treatise antedate *Mus. get.* in print by almost two decades. *Akhak Kwebŏm* (*Guide to the Study of Music*), written in literary Chinese, was published in Seoul, Korea, in 1493 (facs. edn., Seoul, 1968). The relevant chapters (Chapters 6 and 7) include fingering charts for wind instruments in a notation like that used by Ganassi in his treatise on the recorder (*Opera Intitulata Fontegara* [Venice, 1535; facs. edn., Milan, 1934]; Eng. trans. Dorothy Swainson, ed. Hildemarie Peter [Berlin-Lichterfelde, 1959]. Other chapters in the Korean work treat aspects of music such as theory, philosophy, and performance practice, as well as the related arts of dance, costume, and ceremony. See Robert Provine, *Essays on Sino-Korean Musicology: Early Sources for Korean Ritual Music*, Traditional Korean Music, II, ed. Korean National Commission for UNESCO (Seoul, 1988), pp. 54–9

2 At least three of these phenomena had appeared in manuscript before 1511: German keyboard tablature, German lute tablature, and recorder fingering charts. On earlier examples of this type of keyboard tablature, see Willi Apel, *The Notation of Polyphonic Music, 900–1600*, 5th edn. (Cambridge, MA, 1953), pp. 22–6; Thurston Dart and John Morehen, "Tablature," *New Grove*, vol. XVIII, p. 508; and John Caldwell, "Sources of Keyboard Music to 1600," *New Grove*, vol. XVII, pp. 724–5. On this kind of lute tablature, see Hans Tischler, "The Earliest Lute Tablature?," *JAMS*, 27 (1973), 100–3; and David Fallows, "Fifteenth-Century Tablatures for Plucked Instruments: A Summary, a Revision and a Suggestion," *LSJ*, 19 (1977), 7–33. On previous recorder fingering charts, see Martin Staehelin, "Neue Quellen zur mehrstimmigen Musik des 15. und 16. Jahrhunderts in der Schweiz," *Schweizer Beiträge zur Musikwissenschaft*, Publikationen der Schweizerischen Musikforschenden Gesellschaft, ser. III, vol. III (Bern and Stuttgart, 1978), pp. 62–4,

and Plates 4 and 5; Arnold Geering, *Ein tütsche Musica, 1491: Festgabe der literarischen Gesellschaft zur Feier ihrer 500. Sitzung,* Schriftung der literarischen Gesellschaft Bern, IX (2 vols., Bern, 1964); and Beth Bullard, "Musical Instruments in the Early Sixteenth Century: A Translation and Historical Study of Sebastian Virdung's *Musica getutscht* (Basel, 1511)," Ph.D. diss. (University of Pennsylvania, 1987), pp. 359–61.

3 Two citations from the sixteenth century, one to the original treatise and the other to one of its offspring, identify the work in question by the illustrations rather than the text. First, the bibliographer Conrad Gesner listed *Mus. get.* in his catalogue of 1548 not under its proper title but as "Pictures of various musical instruments in a little book in German by Sebastian Virdung" (*Picturae variorum instrumentorum Musicorum, in libello Germanico Sebastiani Wirdung*) (listed by Lawrence F. Bernstein in "The Bibliography of Music in Conrad Gesner's Pandectae [1548]," *Acta,* 45 [1973], 149). For the second citation, this time to a related treatise, see above, pp. 32–3.

4 *Musica getutscht,* like other early printed works, has no numbers for pages or foliation. Instead, the typesetters labeled some of the pages with "signatures" (abbreviated as "sig." or "sigs."). Signatures usually have the form of a letter representing the single, large unfolded sheet of paper upon which two, four, eight, etc. pages of the book were printed, depending upon the format chosen. This letter is followed by a number indicating the order of pages for purposes of collating and binding them. *Mus. get.,* in quarto format (i.e., each sheet of paper was folded twice after having had four pages printed on each side of the sheet), consists of fourteen sheets labeled A to O in alphabetical order. Using sheet B as an example, three leaves – recto sides only – carry signatures, as follows: B, B2 (indicated in the print itself as "Bii"), and B3 ("Biii"). Normally only two or three of the leaves on each sheet have signatures, it being unnecessary to indicate the fourth. Nevertheless, all unprinted signatures are understood. Thus, the order of signatures for all eight pages of a sheet (still using sheet B as the example) will be: B, Bv, B2, B2v, B3, etc. to B4v. All references to pages of this treatise, as well as other coeval works, will be in signatures – as they are printed or as they are understood.

5 These instruments, having been named in the Bible, described in a letter attributed to St. Jerome, and subsequently depicted in various medieval manuscripts, are now recognized as fictitious. Virdung, too, correctly identifies these as allegorical rather than as realistic objects (sig. C3). For a discussion of the Jerome instruments, see Reinhold Hammerstein, "Instrumenta Hieronymi," *AfMw,* 16

(1959), 117–34; and Christopher Page, "Biblical Instruments in Medieval Manuscript Illustration," *EM*, 5 (1977), 299-309.

6 Virdung uses the capitalized Latin term *Musica* in the broad sense in which it was understood at the time. Music, as one of the seven liberal arts and as an integral embellishment to the liturgy in Christian worship, held high status. To retain Virdung's meaning when used in this sense, therefore, the word will be capitalized here as well.

7 For a use of this term in the sixteenth century, see above, p. 44.

8 Pitch names like these indicated precise relationships between the various sizes of instruments as well as their approximate ranges in the gamut rather than the absolute pitches we expect today. Virdung expresses this situation when he directs the learner to "consider this pitch as . . . " (p. 000 above – sig. N2).

9 On Virdung's sources for *Musica getutscht*, see Bullard, "Sources of Influence in *Musica getutscht*," Chapter 4 of "Musical Instruments," pp. 325–62; and Martin Staehelin, "Bemerkungen zum geistigen Umkreis und zu den Quellen des Sebastian Virdung," *Ars Musica, Musica Scientia: Festschrift Heinrich Hüschen zum fünfundsechzigsten Geburtstag*, ed. Detlef Altenburg (Cologne, 1980), pp. 425–34.

10 For a discussion of the perceived relationship between past and present in that era, see Leo Schrade, "Renaissance: The Historical Conceptions of an Epoch," *International Musicological Society Congress Report, Fifth Congress, Utrecht 1952* (Amsterdam, 1953), pp. 19–32; repr. in Schrade, *De Scientia Musicae Studia atque Orationes* (Stuttgart, 1967), pp. 311–25, Interestingly, in his "Nachwort" to his facs. edn. of *Mus. get.* (Kassel and Basel, 1931), Schrade misinterprets Virdung's statement to mean the opposite – that the instruments in the next century would reach perfection surpassing that of antiquity. And Schrade rightly expresses surprise that Virdung would have this attitude. Schrade's misinterpretation stems from his taking Virdung's word *nechst* to mean future time, as it does now; in Virdung's language the concept of "next" could point either forward or backward in time. Virdung's phrase was actually *in hundert jarn nechst vergangen* ("in the past hundred years").

11 On the ensuing controversy, see above, pp. 30–1 and 42.

12 Since this city played such an important role in German culture in the sixteenth century, the German spelling will be retained in the present study. Use of the French form, adopted into English because of this city's subsequent inclusion within the borders of France, would be anachronistic in this context.

13 Wilhelm Honstein (b. 1475) served as the eightieth bishop of Strassburg from 1507 until his death in 1541. For more on his

career, see Richard Wolff, *Die Reichspolitik Bischof Wilhelms III. von Strassburg, Grafen von Honstein. 1506–1541*, Historische Studien, LXXIV (Berlin, 1909; repr. Vaduz, 1965); Edouard Sitzmann, *Dictionnaire de biographie des hommes célèbres de l'Alsace* (2 vols., Paris, 1909–10; repr. Paris, 1973), vol. I, pp. 797–8; and Bullard, "Musical Instruments," pp. 197–202.

14 The controversy was finally resolved by papal decree in 1854, in favor of the side on which Virdung cast his lot. For more on this issue in the early sixteenth century, see Staehelin, "Bemerkungen," pp. 431–3.

15 On this topic see James McKinnon, "Musical Instruments in Medieval Psalm Commentaries and Psalters," *JAMS*, 21 (1968), 4–20. For strong echoes of this theme in the writings of early reformers and the light these may case on the use of instruments in German liturgical contexts at the time of Virdung, see Leslie Korrick, "Instrumental Music in the Early Sixteenth-Century Mass: New Evidence," *EM*, 18 (1990), 359–70.

16 On this topic, see Bernd Moeller, "Religious Life in Germany on the Eve of the Reformation," *Pre-Reformation Germany*, ed. Gerald Strauss (New York, Evanston, San Francisco, and London, 1977), pp. 13-43, esp. pp. 19, 23, 29-30.

17 Phillips Salman has written on this subject in his "Instruction and Delight in Medieval and Renaissance Criticism," *Renaissance Quarterly*, 32 (1979), 303–32, esp. pp. 331–2.

18 This type of conversational dialogue in written form was cultivated by humanists of the day as a vehicle for didactic exposition. On this subject, see Marcelle Derwa, "Le Dialogue pédagogique avant Erasme," *De Gulden Passer*, 47 (1969), 52–60; and Rudolf Hirzel, *Der Dialog: Ein literatur-historischer Versuch* (2 vols. in one, Leipzig, 1895), vol. II, pp. 385–93. It is possible that the interaction between Virdung (Sebastian in the dialogue) and Andreas mirrors a type of conversation that might have taken place in a humanistic academy, for both Virdung and Andreas Silvanus had lived and studied at Heidelberg, scene of a very active *sodalitas litteraria*.

19 Thoinot Arbeau (pseudonym for Jehan Tabourot), *Orchésographie* (Paris, 1588), facs. edn. (Hildesheim, 1980); trans. Mary Stewart Evans, ed. Julia Sutton (New York, 1967); facs. edn. of 1589 edn., ed. Laure Fonta (Paris, 1888; repr. Geneva, 1970).

20 Thomas Morley, *A Plaine and Easie Introduction to Practicall Musicke* (London, 1597), modern edn., ed. R. Alec Harman (New York, 1973).

21 See above, p. 29.

22 Franchinus Gaffurius told readers of his Italian translation of the

Practica musicae (*Angelicum ac divinum opus musicae*, 1518) that he had prepared this work with nuns in mind (among others), for they would not know Latin well enough to read the original language. See Irwin Young's *The Practica Musicae of Franchinus Gafurius* [*sic*] (Madison, Milwaukee, and London, 1969), p. xxxii.

23 A study of the ruling class of Strassburg (Basel's sister city), for example, reveals that from 1520 to 1555, only 13.5 percent of these men had a university education; therefore the vast majority of citizens at all levels there spoke and read only German (Miriam Usher Chrisman, *Lay Culture, Learned Culture: Books and Social Change in Strasbourg, 1480–1599* [New Haven and London, 1982], p. xxix). As for literacy in German, a signboard advertisement for a teacher of reading dated 1516 (painted by Hans Holbein, now in the Kunstmuseum, Basel) gives evidence that reading skills in the vernacular were being taught to men and women at the lower as well as the upper levels of society (see Chrisman, *Lay Culture, Learned Culture*, pp. 68–9).

On the complex subject of hybrid forms of communication – of which *Musica getutscht* is an example, combining as it does the printed text to be read (in the guise of an oral form of communication, a dialogue) with the visual form of the woodcuts – see R. W. Scribner, *For the Sake of Simple Folk*, Cambridge Studies in Oral and Literate Culture, II, ed. Peter Burke and Ruth Finnegan (Cambridge, 1981), pp. 1-3.

24 For a definition and discussion of the social class "peasant" (*paur*) in German society of the time, see Gerhard Benecke, *Society and Politics in Germany, 1500–1750*, Studies in Social History, ed. Harold Perkins (London and Toronto, 1974), pp. 19, 49, 76–8, 147–8. For information on all four elements of society – clergy, nobles, burghers, and peasant-plebeians – see pp. 10-22 of the same work.

25 On this subject, see Iain Fenlon, "Music and Society," Chapter 1 of *The Renaissance: From the 1470s to the End of the Sixteenth Century*, ed. Iain Fenlon (Englewood Cliffs, NJ, 1989), pp. 35–9, 42; and Chrisman, *Lay Culture, Learned Culture*, Chapter 3: "The Reading and Book-Buying Public," pp. 64–74.

26 On the complex issue of what constituted "Germany" at the time, see Benecke, *Society and Politics*, pp. 5–9. On emerging national pride, see "Heinrich Bebel's Oration in Praise of Germany Given Before Maximilian I (1501)" in Gerald Strauss, comp., *Manifestations of Discontent on the Eve of the Reformation* (Bloomington and London, 1971), pp. 64–73.

27 Presumably, Virdung means here the time-honored academic method of teaching music as wedded to mathematics, under the

umbrella of philosophy – as expressed by Gregor Reisch in his *Margarita philosophica* (1503), for example. See John Ferguson, "The *Margarita philosophica* of Gregorius Reisch," *The Library*, 4th ser., 10 (1929), 194–216; and see below, n. 20, pp. 205–6.

28 One of these men, Rudolph Agricola, had been at Heidelberg (see below, n. 4, p. 203) at the time Virdung was there. Agricola left a foundation upon which reformers in the mid sixteenth century rebuilt the German educational system. On the turn from scholastic methods in German lands, see Terrence Heath, "Logical Grammar, Grammatical Logic, and Humanism in Three German Universities," *Studies in the Renaissance*, 18 (1971), 9–64.

29 Reported by George Sarton, *Introduction to the History of Science* (3 vols., Baltimore, 1931; vols. I and II repr. Baltimore, 1950), vol. II, pt. 2, p. 5; and vol. III, pt. 1, p. 127. Knowledge of arabic numerals in Europe came via a treatise, *Algorismus vulgaris*, by John of Sacrobosco (thirteenth century). More commonly known as *De arte numerandi*, this work circulated in manuscripts and prints from the fourteenth to the sixteenth centuries. For a translation of the relevant passage, see Edward Grant, ed., *A Source Book in Medieval Science*, Source Books in the History of the Sciences (Cambridge, MA, 1974), pp. 94–5.

30 Virdung's wording here is almost exactly that of Sacrobosco. See Grant, ed., *A Source Book*, p. 95.

31 The term "Netherlandic" will be used here to denote the sixteenth-century language used as native tongue by inhabitants of areas now in Holland and Belgium. This word is used in preference to "Flemish" or "Dutch" because it serves as a more inclusive and more historically accurate linguistic designation. This choice of linguistic nomenclature follows the plea of Coenraad Berardus van Haeringen in his *Netherlandic Language Research: Men and Works in the Study of Dutch* (Leiden, 1954), pp. 1–9. (For adjectival purposes the word "Netherlandish" will be used here, as in "Netherlandish composers.")

32 Surviving copies date from 1554 and 1568. Both were published by Jan van Ghelen the younger. A facs. edn. of the 1568 print, ed. John Henry van der Meer, appeared in vol. IX of Early Music Theory in the Low Countries (Amsterdam, 1973).

33 The sole surviving copy dates from 1529. It was published by Willem Vorsterman. This treatise appears in facs. along with its twin, *Dit is een seer schoon Boecxken*, in vol. IX of Early Music Theory in the Low Countries, ed. van der Meer.

34 Editions of this work appeared in print in 1529, 1530, 1532, and 1542. A facs, edn. of most of the 1529 printing was brought out as an

appendix to the facs. edn. of Agricola's *Musica Figuralis Deudsch (1532)* (Hildesheim, 1969). A somewhat misleading diplomatic facs, edn., ed. Robert Eitner, is found in PäptM, XX (Leipzig, 1896; repr. New York, 1969). See the trans. of *Mus. inst. deudsch* by William E. Hettrick, *Musical instrumentalis deudsch: A Treatise on Musical Instruments (1529 and 1545) by Martin Agricola* to be published by Cambridge University Press.

35 A similarly misleading diplomatic facs. edn. of this work, ed. Robert Eitner, also appears in PäptM, XX. See Hettrick's translation of the actual 1545 print, included with his translation of the 1529 edn., to be published by Cambridge University Press.

36 See n. 2, p. 223 below.

37 See n. 3, p. 223 below.

38 Our author chooses to treat winds without finger holes (i.e., lip-blown brass instruments) in his forthcoming work (p. 109 above – sig. B4). He mentions no tablature for them. In his discussion of the instrumentarium, furthermore, he gives only passing reference to percussion instruments, including in this category only those capable of sounding discernible pitches (p. 110 above – sig. C2). He mentions no tablature for any of these instruments, although it is possible that one for chime bells existed. This could have had a pitch-letter name for each separate bell. Drums and timpani he excludes on the grounds that they make noise, not music (p. 115 above – sig. D).

39 For transcriptions of Virdung's musical example in mensural notation and his two intabulations of it, one for keyboard and one for lute, see Gerhard Stradner, *Spielpraxis und Instrumentarium um 1500 dargestellt an Sebastian Virdung's "Musica getutscht" (Basel, 1511)*, Forschungen zur Alteren Musikgeschichte, IV (2 vols., Vienna, 1983), vol. II, pp. 105-10. Christian Meyer, in *Sebastian Virdung. Musica getutscht: Les Instruments et la pratique en Allemagne au debut du XVIe siecle* (Paris, 1980), gives a transcription of the Lied (pp. 132–3) and lists the minor variants in Virdung's keyboard and lute intabulations of it (pp. 144–5).

40 Perhaps an example that Virdung had prepared had to be omitted, owing to the length of the treatise. An additional page for this purpose would have meant wasting most of an entire sheet of paper, an added expense for the printer. Since paper was the most expensive single item in the production of a book at the time, it would not have been worth the printer's trouble to include an extra leaf.

41 See n. 8, p. 193 above.

42 The one exception to this self-imposed restriction occurs in the

chapter on the lute. Virdung invites the learners to look over the intabulation he has made and then to learn to play it if they wish (p. 166 above – sig. M2). Given the author's frequent statements throughout the treatise that he means only to teach intabulation and nothing more, the latter invitation would seem to constitute a momentary slip from his intended focus. It may stem from the fact that, in contrast to his treatment of the clavichord and recorders, Virdung instructs his readers to actually pluck the strings of the lute as they go through the symbols. Nevertheless, at no time in the course of the treatise is it implied that a reader is to pause and make music before proceeding with further instructions from this book.

43 For the reaction of Schlick to this and other impossible doublings, see above, pp. 40–1. They are discussed and analyzed by Hans Lenneberg in "The Critic Criticized: Sebastian Virdung and his Controversy with Arnold Schlick," *JAMS*, 10 (1957), 1–6. Regarding Virdung's lute tablature, see also Ruggero Chiesa, "Storia della Letteratura del Liuto e della Chitarra: Il Cinquecento," *Il Fronimo*, 2 (1974), 23–8.

44 Johannes Tinctoris, writing in the 1480s (*De Inventione et usu musicae*), describes two virtuoso ways of playing the lute in his day: (1) playing the top part of a polyphonic piece of music and decorating it, and (2) playing an entire polyphonic composition of two, three, or four parts. The second of these he deems the more difficult. See the translation of this passage by Christopher Page in "The Fifteenth-Century Lute: New and Neglected Sources," *EM*, 9 (1981), p. 13. See also Keith Polk's article "Voices and Instruments: Soloists and Ensembles in the Fifteenth Century" (*EM*, 18 [1990], 179–98), in which Polk presents evidence found in German archives from 1421 to 1489 of three and four – even possibly five – lutes playing together (p. 188) as well as lutes played with other instruments (pp. 188–90). Consorts of two to four viols, documented as well in Polk's sources (pp. 190–1), also point to an instrumental practice mirroring the vocal one, i.e., one player per line of music. See also the same author's "Vedel and Geige – Fiddle and Viol: German String Traditions in the Fifteenth Century," *JAMS*, 42 (1989), 504–46.

45 Schlick's anger also stemmed in large part from Virdung's attack on him in *Musica getutscht*. See above, pp. 30–1.

46 Luscinius wrote in Latin for an educated international readership; Agricola wrote in German verse for boys in school as well as for amateurs; and van Ghelen and Vorsterman published their works for amateurs in Netherlandic- and French-speaking areas.

47 See n. 36, pp. 225–7 below.

48 As can be seen from the table of slight differences among the three versions of Virdung's Lied (see Meyer, *Sebastian Virdung*, pp. 144–5), most of the discrepancies derive simply from reiterated notes caused by the lack of ties over the bars in the two instrumental versions. Three instances involve simple variants consistent with sixteenth-century practice in vocal polyphony (Meyers's nn. 4, 8, and 12). None reflects idiomatic instrumental usage.

49 "Leider sind diese Holzschnitte, besonders was die technischen Probleme des Instrumentenbaus betrifft, in vieler Hinsicht unzuverlässig, manchmal seitenverkehrt, und verlangen eine sehr kritische Betrachtungsweise, um sich vor falschen Schlüssen zu hüten." This quotation comes from Stradner's article "Bemerkungen zu den besaiteten Tasteninstrumenten in Sebastian Virdungs 'Musica getutscht . . . '," *Der klangliche Aspect beim Restaurieren von Saitenklavieren*, ed. Vera Schwarz, Beiträge zur Aufführungspraxis, II (Graz, 1973), p. 79.

50 Noted by Stradner, "Bemerkungen zu den besaiteten Tasteninstrumenten," p. 80.

51 See especially the clavicytherium, p. 102 above (Sig. Bv).

52 Witness the large hurdy-gurdy compared with the clavicytherium next to it on p. 102 above (Sig. Bv); the almost same-sized shawm and tenor shawm on p. 106 above (sig. B3v); the trumpet that is larger than the trombone on p. 108 above (Sig. B4v); all the bellows instruments in unrealistic proportion to each other on pp. 109–10 above (sigs. Cv–C2); and the "foolish" instruments – of which the Jew's harp appears almost as large as the hunting horn – on p. 119 above (Sig. D3v).

53 These hand-colored pen and ink drawings of the pictorial woodcuts in *Musica getutscht* appear in the Rughalm Codex (Ms. B 200 – formerly 1463), fols. 126v–129v, found in the Universitätsbibliothek at Erlangen. For reproductions of some of these, see Heinz Zirnbauer, *Musik in der alten Reichsstadt Nürnberg: Ikonographie zur nürnberger Musikgeschichte*, Beiträge zur Geschichte und Kultur der Stadt Nürnberg, IX (Nuremberg, 1966), p. 16; and Stradner, *Spielpraxis*, vol. II, p. 116, Plate 10. See also Eberhard Lutze, *Die Bilderhandschriften der Universitätsbibliothek Erlangen*, Katalog der Handschriften der Universitätsbibliothek Erlangen, VI (Erlangen, 1936), pp. 69–70.

54 The impetus for these probably derived from printing B of *Musica getutscht*, for it has a new, more attractive title page with a decorative frame made up of musical instruments. See the facsimile of it in Edwin Ripin, "A Reevaluation of Virdung's *Musica getutscht*," *JAMS*, 29 (1976), p. 193. An example of a border almost certainly based on

this one can be found in a print from 1521, *Was man in Martino Luthers sachen handlen* (no place or printer given). The title page of this book is reproduced in Julius von Pflugk-Harttung, ed., *Kunstgewerbe der Renaissance,* vol. I: *Rahmen deutscher Buchtitel im 16. Jahrhundert* (Stuttgart, 1909), Plate 62.

55 The keyboard instruments in *Mus. get.* are in mirror image from what they should be, showing that the preparer of the woodcuts did not bother to reverse the images he was given to copy in order that they appear to the viewer as they would in life. The printer and cutter for printing B of *Mus. get.* went to considerable expense and trouble to maintain these mirror-image instruments in order that they conform to the original treatise. For Agricola's *Mus. inst. dedusch,* on the other hand, the printer and cutter reversed only parts of the images from *Mus. get.* they were copying, so that special features of the instruments would come out in the new print exactly as they had appeared in the original publication. Among the parts they reversed were, ironically, the keyboards; thus, they perpetuated an inaccuracy they were apparently intending to avoid. (There is one exception to their general policy of copying Virdung's keyboards exactly: Agricola's cutter put the keyboard from Virdung's *clavicimbalum* [*Mus. get.,* sig. Bv – see above, p. 102] on both the *clavicymbalum* [*sic*] and the virginal [*Mus. inst. deudsch,* sigs. D3 and D3v]. Then he or the typesetter apparently reversed the captions for these two instruments. See above, p. 74.) See Agricola, *Musica instrumentalis deudsch,* trans. Hettrick (forthcoming).

56 See below, n. 34, p. 213.

57 This point is crucial to Korrick's argument from iconographical evidence in her article "Instrumental Music in the Early Sixteenth-Century Mass."

58 George Sarton recounts the history of herbals in *The Appreciation of Ancient and Medieval Science During the Renaissance (1450–1600)* (Philadelphia, 1955), pp. 92–104.

59 Many examples could be cited here to support this point. Perhaps the most famous come from Hartmann Schedel's *Weltchronik* ("Nuremberg Chronicle") of 1493, in which the same woodcut illustrations were placed in more than one section of the text to stand for totally different persons, places, and events. See, for example, the woodcut of a medieval city that appears in this work to represent Damascus, and Ferrara, and Milan, and Mantua (reproduced by E. H. Gombrich in *Art and Illusion: A Study in the Psychology of Pictorial Representation,* 2nd rev. edn., Bolligen Series, XXXV, The A. W. Mellon Lectures in the Fine Arts, V [1956] [New York, 1961], Plates 41 and 42, p. 69, and text pp. 68–9).

60 On the proliferation of popular woodcuts as mementoes from pilgrimages and as aids for private devotion in German lands at the time, see Scribner, *Simple Folk*, pp. 4–6.

61 For detailed studies on this fascinating topic of relevance to all who use pictures as historical evidence, see Gombrich, *Art and Illusion*; and its sequel by Gombrich, *The Image and the Eye: Further Studies in the Psychology of Pictorial Representation* (Ithaca, NY, 1982); and Nelson Goodman, *Languages of Art: An Approach to a Theory of Symbols* (Indianapolis and New York, 1968).

62 Goodman, *Languages of Art*, p. 37.

63 Gombrich, *Art and Illusion*, p. 394.

64 For an analysis of these works in the history of book illustration and the development of visual consciousness, see William Ivins, *Prints and Visual Communication* (Cambridge, MA, 1953), pp. 36–44. Interestingly, Fuchs's work was printed in Basel, city of birth for *Mus. get.*, and Brunfels's was put to press in Strassburg, city of Virdung's dedicatee and one of his translators, Luscinius.

65 This would apply to readers of *Mus. get.* no less than to those who would peruse the manuscript of "A German *Musica*" to which this passage refers.

66 An analogous situation at the time was the use – especially by German printers – of woodcuts depicting scenes, landscapes, and persons that could be used for multiple purposes in a single printed work. See n. 59 above.

67 The distinction drawn here between illustrations that edify and those that inform derives from the work of William Ivins, as expressed in his *Prints and Visual Communcation*. Ivins traces the history of book illustration and the evolution of our visual consciousness from the early stages of book production up to the modern period. He observes that in the eras before the mid sixteenth century, the values of decoration and edification (as seen in the pictures in *Mus. get.*, for example) predominated, while from the end of that period to the present day, technically useful information (such as that given by means of the measuring stick provided by Praetorius in his illustrations for *De organographia*, for example) came to be demanded as a matter of course. See Michael Praetorius, *Syntagma musicum*, 3 vols., vol. II: *De organographia* (Wolfenbüttel, 1619; facs. edn., ed. Wilibald Gurlitt, Documenta musicologica, 1st ser., XIV, Kassel, 1958). *De organographia* has been translated by Harold Blumenfeld (Kassel, 1962; repr. New York [Da Capo Press Reprint Series], 1980) and by David Z. Crookes, Early Music Series, VII (Oxford, 1986).

68 Emmanuel Winternitz, "The Visual Arts as a Source for the

Historian of Music" in his *Musical Instruments and Their Symbolism in Western Art: Studies in Musical Iconology*, 2nd edn. (New Haven and London, 1979), p. 36 (text and fig. 3).

69 See n. 67 above and pp. 59–60 above.

70 Sir John Hawkins, *A General History of the Science and Practice of Music* (2 vols., London, 1776; repr. 1853; repr. of the 1853 edn. with intro. by Charles Cudworth, New York, 1963), vol. I, pp. 328–32.

71 Charles Burney, *A General History of Music* (4 vols., London, 1776; repr. 1789; repr. of 1789 edn., ed. Frank Mercer, 2 vols., New York, 1935), vol. I, pp. 203–4. (References here are to the modern reprint.)

72 Robert Eitner, ed., PäptM, XI (Berlin, 1882; repr. New York, 1966; Leo Schrade, ed. (Kassel, 1931); and Klaus Wolfgang Niemöller, ed. (Kassel, 1970; repr. Kassel, 1983).

73 Christian Meyer has provided a modern French translation in his *Sebastian Virdung* (1980). Gerhard Stradner offers a study of the entire treatise in his *Spielpraxis* (1983). See also the present author's Ph.D. dissertation, "Musical Instruments" (1987).

74 Besides those in the article by Ripin discussed above ("A Reevaluation"), two other examples of misunderstandings call for clarification here. First, in his important article "Vedel and Geige – Fiddle and Viol" (p. 509, n. 12), Keith Polk incorrectly concludes that members of Virdung's third category of stringed instruments (described on sig. B2) were "exactly like the 'Grossen Geigen' [i.e., viols] but without frets." Actually, this category consisted of instruments with a separate string or course for each note, i.e., those pictured on the next page (sig. B2v), namely, harp, psaltery, and hammered dulcimer.

Secondly, Margaret J. Kartomi misrepresents Virdung's text in her *On Concepts and Classifications of Musical Instruments* (Chicago Studies in Ethnomusicology, ed. Philip V. Bohlman and Bruno Nettl [Chicago and London, 1990]), pp. 149–50: The "Book" from which Virdung reads is not the Bible but his own treatise in manuscript on musical instruments ("A German *Musica*"); Virdung does not say that kettle drums had been used in church services, nor does he group percussion instruments "according to whether they were invented by the devil or were used in church services"; lutes and viols did not have "fretted keyboards," nor did trumpets marine and rebecs have "fretted fingerboards"; and Virdung does not group bagpipes with instruments having sacks instead of finger holes (they appear in the latter category).

In addition, the article on Sebastian Virdung in *New Grove* (vol. XIX, pp. 868–9) by Klaus Wolfgang Niemöller conveys misinformation regarding Virdung, his treatise, and the instruments he depicts. Examples of errors include: the translation of *Gross Geige* as "double bass" (*Gross Geigen* were viols, presumably of several different sizes); the assertion that wind instruments came in families of four sizes (those that came in consorts generally were of three sizes); the implication that recorder tablature was set forth by Virdung as a four-voice hymn (it was not); and the statement that Schlick's response to Virdung's criticism of him appeared in Schlick's *Spiegel der Orgelmacher* (erroneously cited as *Orgelbauer*) *und Organisten* (it appeared in Schlick's subsequent publication – see above, pp. 31–2 and 40–3).

75 Readers wishing to see Virdung's vocabulary as translated here may consult the annotated glossary in Bullard, "Musical Instruments," pp. 125–42, in conjunction with one of the facs. edns. (see n. 72, p. 202 above).

2 A *biography of Sebastian Virdung*

1 Unless otherwise noted, all translations in this study, whether of primary or secondary material, are my own. Transcriptions of phrases in foreign languages are here given in italics without quotation marks, even when taken from secondary literature.

2 Gerhard Pietzsch, *Quellen und Forschungen zur Geschichte der Musik am kurpfälzischen Hof zu Heidelberg bis 1622*, [Mainz,] Akademie der Wissenschaften und der Literatur, Abhandlungen der geistes- und sozialwissenschaftlichen Klasse, Jg. 1963, no. 6 (Wiesbaden, 1963), p. 669; Pietzsch suggests 19 or 20 January as Virdung's birthday, because the latter was St. Sebastian's Day.

3 The court singers at Heidelberg recruited members from the student body at the university nearby. See Fritz Stein, *Zur Geschichte der Musik in Heidelberg* (Heidelberg, 1912), pp. 5–7.

4 Virdung's tenure there coincided with a period of extraordinary intellectual activity at Heidelberg. His employer, Count Philip (b. 1448; reigned from 1476 until his death in 1508), surrounded himself with many of the greatest minds that the northern Renaissance had produced to date. These included Johann von Dalberg, Jacob Wimpfeling, Johann Reuchlin, Rudolph Agricola, Johannes von Soest, and Conrad Celtes. The latter three men contributed their considerable talents to music as well as to other humanistic fields of endeavor. (See n. 28, p. 196 above and the following: Lewis Lockwood, "Rudolph Agricola," *New Grove*, vol. I, p. 167; and Peter Bergquist, "Conradus Protucius Celtis," *New Grove*, vol. IV, pp. 155–6.)

5 During the period from 1499 through the year 1503, the governing of France took place at Lyons, for the king and his court had taken up primary residence there. Louis XII did this for military reasons, that city being located strategically for both defensive and offensive purposes, in light of his military ambitions in Italy. An alliance between King Louis of France and Virdung's employer, Count Philip of the Rhenish Palatinate, brought the latter's son to the French court on a diplomatic mission. For more on this period of French history, see Louis Bourgeois, *Quand la cour de France vivait à Lyon, 1494–1551* (Paris, 1980); and Roger Doucet, "Le XVI^c siècle," in Arthur Kleinclausz *et al.*, *Histoire de Lyon*, Publication de la société lyonnaise des études locales, 3 vols. (Lyons, 1939; repr. Marseilles, 1978), vol. I, pp. 357–549.

6 Virdung's acting in this role seems to be the root of the assumption by some biographers (following Gerhard Pietzsch in his article "Sebastian Virdung," *MGG*, vol. XIII, col. 1801) that Virdung had become Kapellmeister at Heidelberg, although none of the extant documents refer to him by this title.

7 Maximilian did not adopt the title "Emperor" until 1508.

8 This is the speculation of Christian Meyer in *Sebastian Virdung*, p. 17. For more on the Bavarian war, see Thomas A. Brady, Jr., *Turning Swiss: Cities and Empire, 1450–1550*, Cambridge Studies in Early Modern History, ed. J. H. Elliott, Olwen Hufton, and H. C. Koenigsberger (Cambridge, 1985), pp. 72–9.

9 From 1502 the choir at the Constance Cathedral included eight choirboys; more than that number may have received musical training, however. See Manfred Schuler, "Die konstanzer Domkantorei um 1500," *AfMw*, 21 (1964), 25.

10 Hermann Baier, "Vorreformationsgeschichtliche Forschungen aus der Diözese Konstanz," *Freiburger Diözesan-Archiv*, 41, n.s. 14 (1913), 36–8.

11 These dates are found in Schuler, "Domkantorei," pp. 39–41; and Christoph Friedrich Stälin, *Wirtembergische Geschichte*, 4 vols. (Stuttgart, 1841–73), vol. IV, p. x.

12 See the miniature of Maximilian's Hofkapelle in the Constance Cathedral (from the "Luzerner Bilderchronik" of 1513 by Diebold Schilling) reproduced in *New Grove*, vol. X, p. 180.

13 The cathedral chapter later commissioned him (in April 1508) to write parts of his *Choralis Constantinus*. See Otto zur Nedden, "Zur Musikgeschichte von Konstanz um 1500," *ZfMw*, 12 (1930), 455.

14 Schuler, "Domkantorei," p. 39.

15 Thus, Edwin Ripin errs in his assumption that Silvanus is fictitious. This name, furthermore, led him erroneously to assume that the

captions on the picture of the two interlocutors (sig. A4, p. 100 above) were inadvertently interchanged by the printer, since the person labeled "Sebastian" wears rustic clothes while the man labeled "Andreas Silvanus" (i.e., Andreas "of the woods") sports academic clothing that one would expect to find worn by the author of a book. As the dialogue makes clear, however, Sebastian has just arrived from travels, hence his appropriately rugged attire and his weapons. See "A Reevaluation," p. 190, n. 3.

16 Pietzsch, *Quellen*, pp. 683–4. Records of Virdung's and Waldner's matriculation at Heidelberg show them as coming from the same diocese – Regensburg. Pietzsch's assumption that Silvanus/ Waldner and Honstein's chaplain are one and the same, however, is untenable, as the context in which both are named makes plain (sig. A2, p. 97 above).

17 p. 99 above. Four sections of a Mass by a man named "Andreas Sylvanus" survive in the *Dodecachordon* of Glareanus as Ex. 94 (*Heinrich Glaren: Dodecachordon*, trans., transcribed and with commentary by Clement A. Miller, Musicological Studies and Documents, VI [2 vols., American Institute of Musicology, 1965], vol. II, pp. 270, 514–16).

18 Silvanus does, however, play the more pedantic role in the dialogue, for Virdung portrays him as well versed in Latin writings and decidedly less familiar with vernacular literature (sig. A4v, p. 000 above). His role is not, therefore, "to lighten the tone of the exposition," as Ripin suggests ("A Reevaluation," p. 190).

19 "Tuesday, St. Margaret's Day" (*zinstag Margarethe*) (sig. A2v, p. 000 above was 15 July in Basel and Strassburg (not 20 July as celebrated elsewhere) according to Hermann Grotefend, *Taschenbuch der Zeitrechnung des deutschen Mittelalters und der Neuzeit*, 10th edn., ed. T. Ulrich (Hannover, 1960), p. 77.

20 Michael Furter came to Basel from Augsburg in the early 1480s. He died in 1517. During his lifetime he produced a variety of books in both Latin and German – many of them illustrated – to match the tastes and interests of differing audiences for his products. Among his Latin offerings were numerous textbooks and erudite works for university students and scholars. These included two dealing exclusively with music: *Lilium musica planae* by Michael Keinspeck (with some of the earliest examples of music printed from wood-blocks), which Furter produced in 1496; and *Clarissima plane et choralis musice interpretatio . . . In alma Basileorum universitate exercitata* by Balthasar Prasberg, which Furter brought out in 1501, 1504, and 1507. In addition, in 1508 and 1517, Furter printed editions of Gregor Reisch's *Margarita philosophica*, an encyclopedic work that

incorporated a chapter on music (both theoretical and practical). For the earlier version of this work he collaborated with the Strassburg printer Johann Schott, who later published Othmar Luscinius's Latin version of Virdung's treatise, *Musurgia seu praxis musicae* (see above, pp. 65–6). For more on Furter see Bullard, "Musical Instruments," pp. 202–15; Arnold Pfister, "Michael Furt(t)er," *Neue deutsche Biographie*, vol. V, p. 737; Karl Stehlin, *Regesten zur Geschichte des Buchdrucks bis zum Jahre 1520 aus den Büchern des basler Gerichtsarchivs* (3 vols., Leipzig, 1887–91), *passim*; and Charles William Heckethorn, *The Printers of Basle in the XV and XVI Centuries* (London, 1897), pp. 75–85. For information on the various editions of the *Margarita philosophica* see Ferguson, "The *Margarita philosophica* of Gregorius Reisch." See n. 29, p. 207 below.

21 The Swiss artist Urs Graf lived from *ca.* 1485 to 1527 or 1528. Trained first as a goldsmith, he soon turned to designing and executing woodcuts for the burgeoning book-publishing industry in Basel. He contributed numerous illustrations for printers in that city. For more on his life and works see Walther Lüthi, *Urs Graf und die Kunst der alten Schweizer* (Zurich, 1928); and Emil Major and Erwin Gradmann (with preface by Kenneth Clark), *Urs Graf* (London, 1942).

22 Facs. edn. and English trans. by Elizabeth Barber, Bibliotheca Organologica, CXIII (Buren, 1980); facs. edn. and modern German version by Paul Smets (Mainz, 1959); almost complete English trans. by Franklin S. Miller in *Organ Institute Quarterly*, 7/4 (Winter 1959), 13–23; 8/1 (Spring 1960), 11–17; 8/3 (Autumn 1960), 27–31; 10/1 (Spring 1962), 15–18; 10/4 (Winter 1963), 14–19 (based on the modern German version by Ernst Flade [Kassel, 1951]).

23 Sig. π4. Pi here stands for a lacking signature.

24 These are transcribed and analyzed by Lenneberg in "The Critic Criticized," pp. 1–6.

25 Among them Hans Joachim Moser, *Paul Hofhaimer*, 2nd enlarged edn. (Stuttgart, 1929; repr. Hildesheim, 1966), p. 44; and Meyer, *Sebastian Virdung*, p. 11.

26 This was also the conclusion of Bertha Wallner in "Sebastian Virdung von Amberg: Beiträge zu seiner Lebensgeschichte," *Kirchenmusikalisches Jahrbuch*, 24 (1911), 106.

27 This was the observation of Yvonne Rokseth in "Othmar Nachtgall, dit Luscinius," *L'Humanisme en Alsace: Congrès de Strasbourg, 1938* (Paris, 1939), p. 201.

28 Rudolf Hirsch, *Printing, Selling and Reading. 1450–1550*, 2nd edn. (Wiesbaden, 1974), p. 76, and illustration 4 (opp. p. 110, containing a photocopy of the original order, now in the Universitätsbibliothek

of Basel). Calvo requested a number of copies of twenty-three other books in Latin as well. All of these were "representative of the humanistic activities which by then had begun to flourish also in the Holy Roman Empire" (Hirsch, p. 77).

29 When the printer of *Musica getutscht*, Michael Furter, died in 1517, his equipment was dispersed. The woodcuts from *Musica getutscht* evidently were sold (or traded) to the Strassburg printer Johann Schott (before or after Furter's death) for this projected work by Luscinius. Furter and Schott had earlier collaborated to produce the 1508 edition of Gregor Reisch's *Margarita philosophica*. Since Furter used the woodcuts from their joint venture for a reprint of this same work in 1517 (his last finished production before his death), an exchange may have taken place between the two printers for the purposes of their individual projected works. Of the woodcuts of instruments from *Musica getutscht*, only the lutenist on sig. I2v (famous because it is the only one in the treatise signed by Urs Graf; p. 149 above) and the lute on sig. B2 (p. 103 above) did not appear in *Musurgia*. (See also n. 8, p. 217 below.) Furter may earlier have singled out these cuts as suitable for use on their own. Although no example of either woodcut has come down to us in another publication, a copy of one by another cutter (prepared for the 2nd edn. of *Musica getutscht*; see pp. 48–52 above) did appear independently as an embellishment for the title page of a print from *ca.* 1515. See Ripin, "A Reevaluation," p. 202 (text and nn. 37 and 38).

30 Ripin, "A Reevaluation," p. 208.

31 Peter Schöffer's *Liederbuch* (RISM 1513^2). Transcriptions of these songs are given by Meyer in *Sebastian Virdung*, pp. 134–45. The presence in this print of so many Lieder by members of the musical establishment of Duke Ulrich of Württemberg suggests that the compositions by Virdung were written by him during or prior to his employment at Stuttgart. Colleagues of his at the Württemberg court whose works are represented in this print include Georg Brack, Johannes Fuchswild, Johannes Siess, and possibly Jorg Schönfelder and Martin Wolff. (See articles on all of these men by Hans-Christian Müller in *New Grove*, vol. III, pp. 149–50; vol. VII, p. 5; vol. XVII, p. 304; vol. XVI, p. 730; and vol. XX, p. 506, respectively.) A man named Martin Wolf was associated with Heidelberg (Pietzsch, *Quellen*, p. 684), as was another of the composers, Heinrich Eitelwein (Pietzsch, *Quellen*, pp. 667–8).

32 The record of this transaction has been transcribed by Ripin in "A Reevaluation," p. 204. A facsimile of the original catalogue entry can be found in Archer M. Huntington, ed., *Catalogue of the Library of Ferdinand Columbus* (New York, 1905), no. 922.

33 This is the suggestion of Meyer, *Sebastian Virdung*, p. 17.

34 Only the longer documents – those of major importance to an understanding of Virdung and his situation – are translated here in full, namely, nos. 8–11, 22, and 23.

35 Quoted by Gerhard Pietzsch in *Quellen*, p. 668.

36 Ferdinand Geldner, "Das Rechnungsbuch des Speyrer Druckherren, Verlegers und Grossbuchhändlers Peter Drach," *Archiv für Geschichte des Buchwesens*, 5 (1962), 135. The Wild Man in Nuremberg was the same address as the one on the earliest known advertising broadsheet, a flyer from the shop of the printer Peter Schöffer. According to Albert Ehrman, "This suggests that the 'Wilde Mann' [*sic*] was a customary resort of booksellers and perhaps even a clearing house" ("The Fifteenth Century," in Graham Pollard and Albert Ehrman, *The Distribution of Books by Catalogue from the Invention of Printing to A.D. 1800* [Cambridge, 1965], p. 26).

37 Richard Lossen, "Pfälzische Patronatspfründen vor der Reformation aus dem geistlichen Lehenbuch des Kurfürsten Philipp von der Pfaltz," *Freiburger Diözesan-Archiv*, 38, n.s. 11 (1910), 198.

38 Quoted in Pietzsch, *Quellen*, p. 669. According to Pietzsch, Virdung would have to have been at least twenty-four years old to hold this position.

39 "Wednesday after Invocavit Sunday" (*Mittwoch nach Invocavit*). "Invocavit," the first Sunday after Ash Wednesday, occurred on 28 February in 1490; the following Wednesday was, therefore, 3 March. Information for arriving at this date comes from Grotefend, *Taschenbuch*, p. 184.

40 This must refer to Jorg Eberhart, the only member of the chapel with that given name (see Pietzsch, *Quellen*, pp. 666–7, 669). In the same year (on 23 July), Eberhart was named in a controversy with Johannes von Soest (reported by Stein, *Zur Geschichte der Musik*, pp. 22–3).

41 Quoted in Pietzsch, *Quellen*, p. 669, with an interpretation of the incident in the same author's article, "Sebastian Virdung," *MGG*, vol. XIII, col. 1801.

42 Pietzsch, *Quellen*, p. 669; Lossen, "Pfälzische Patronatspfründen," p. 234.

43 Pietzsch, *Quellen*, p. 669; Lossen, "Pfälzische Patronatspfründen," p. 243.

44 Pietzsch, *Quellen*, p. 669.

45 "Friday after St. James the Holy Apostle's Day" (*fritag nach Sant Jacobs des heyligen appostels tag*). St. James's Day being 25 July, the following Friday was 31 July in 1500 (see Grotefend, *Taschenbuch*, p. 201). This

corrects the date given by Wallner in "Sebastian Virdung von Amberg," p. 88. The mistake was repeated by Meyer in *Sebastian Virdung*, p. 12.

46 For the full German text of this contract, see Appendix, above pp. 182–3.

47 "Thursday after St. Dionysius's Day" (*Dornstag nach Dionisij*). Bertha Wallner ("Sebastian Virdung von Amberg," p. 90) gave this date incorrectly as 9 October 1503. That was St. Dionysius's Day, a Monday in that year. The Thursday after occurred on 12 October (Grotefend, *Taschenbuch*, p. 195). The mistake was repeated by Pietzsch (*Quellen*, p. 669) and Meyer (*Sebastian Virdung*, p. 12)

48 See n. 5, p. 204 above.

49 Johannes Karg. See Pietzsch, *Quellen*, pp. 661–2.

50 See Pietzsch, *Quellen*, p. 678.

51 Johannes Virdung von Hassfurt. See Pietzsch, *Quellen*, p. 623, n. 1; and Wallner, "Sebastian Virdung von Amberg," p. 94.

52 This man has not been identified.

53 For the original German text, see Appendix above, p. 183.

54 Transcribed in Wallner, "Sebastian Virdung von Amberg," p. 91.

55 Franchinus Gaffurius, *Practica musicae* (Milan, 1496), trans. Clement A. Miller, Musicological Studies and Documents, XX (American Institute of Musicology, 1968); and trans. Irwin Young, *The Practica Musicae of Franchinus Gafurius*. On the influence of this treatise on Virdung, see Bullard, "Musical Instruments," pp. 342–5.

56 Virdung must refer here to the *Compendium musicae practicae* (*ca.* 1322) of Jean de Muris. See Staehelin, "Bemerkungen," p. 432; and Bullard, "Musical Instruments," pp. 236–9. The German text (from Wallner, p. 91) reads: "Dy ander müsik ist nit gedrückt, Hatt tinctoris oder Okeghem gemacht vnt hebt also an wye der donat. Partes prolacionis qu(ae) sunt."

57 "Tuesday after All Saints' Day" (*dinstag nach allerheiligen dag*). All Saints' Day (1 November) was Wednesday in 1503; therefore, the following Tuesday was 7 November (see Grotefend, *Taschenbuch*, p. 195).

58 For the complete original German text of this document, see Appendix above, p. 184.

59 "Friday after New Year's Day" (*freytag nach den neuen Jahrs tag*). 1 January in 1504 was on Monday; therefore, the following Friday was 5 January (see Grotefend, *Taschenbuch*, p. 176).

60 Surviving records show that Michel Haberkorn acted in capacities similar to this one on behalf of the court at Heidelberg (Wallner, "Sebastian Virdung von Amberg," p. 98, n. 2).

61 From his description (pp. 38–9 above) of Ockeghem's canonic

motet as "a motet of six voices [of which] each . . . is a canon *a 6,* so that altogether [there are] 36 voices," it appears that Virdung here meant an eight-voice motet in the disposition 4 × 2 (i.e., four voices written out, with an additional voice to be derived canonically from each one).

62 Virdung was thus unaware that Ockeghem had died almost eight years before (6 February 1497).

63 This is a lost work by Ockeghem. Because of the disposition of voices, this motet cannot be the same as the "Deo gratias" attributed to Ockeghem (but now listed among his doubtful works), which had four notated voices – each of which made a nine-part canon. See Dragan Plamenac, "Johannes Ockeghem," *MGG,* vol. IX, col. 1834; and Leeman Perkins, "Johannes Ockeghem," *New Grove,* vol. XIII, p. 495. For an opposing view on this question, see Edward Lowinsky, "Ockeghem's Canon for Thirty-six Voices: An Essay in Musical Iconography," *Essays in Musicology in Honor of Dragan Plamenac on his Seventieth Birthday,* ed. Gustave Reese and Robert Snow (Pittsburgh, 1969; repr. New York, 1977), pp. 155–80, esp. pp. 174–8.

64 In *Johannes Ockeghem: Collected Works,* ed. Dragan Plamenac, 2 vols., vol. II (New York, 1947; repr. 1966), pp. 21–36.

65 *Ibid.,* vol. I (New York, 1959 = 2nd edn. of Publikationen älterer Musik, Jg. I, pt. 2 [Leipzig, 1927]), pp. 44–56.

66 Virdung undoubtedly refers to a decorative oven from the period that would have been the focal point of a social gathering, especially in winter, the season during which he wrote this letter. See for example the one dating from 1489 – a veritable objet d'art now in the Landesmuseum at Zurich – illustrated in Paul Ganz, *Geschichte der Kunst in der Schweiz von den Anfängen bis zur Mitte des 17. Jahrhunderts* (Basel and Stuttgart, 1960), Plate X.

67 For the original German text to this document, see Appendix above, pp. 184–5.

68 Manfred Schuler, "Der Personalstatus der konstanzer Dokmantorei um 1500," *AfMw,* 21 (1964), 265–6.

69 Pietzsch, *Quellen,* p. 669.

70 Schuler, "Personalstatus," p. 266.

71 *Ibid.*

72 Lossen, "Pfälzische Patronatspfründen," p. 217.

73 Schuler, "Personalstatus," p. 266.

74 *Ibid.*

75 *Ibid.*

76 *Ibid.*

77 *Ibid.*

78 Schlick here notes that the musical examples in *Musica getutscht*

were printed from woodcuts (an old-fashioned method) rather than being typeset (a modern innovation) as his were to be in the *Tabulaturen.*

79 See pp. 31–2 above.
80 Schlick apparently retaliates for his rival's having misquoted the title of *Spiegel* in *Mus. get.* by incorrectly naming Virdung's treatise here. In addition, Schlick may be making a facetious pun by using the German *engellischen,* which could mean "angelic" as well as "English."
81 30 November. For the complete German text of this document, see Appendix above, pp. 185–8.
82 For the original German text, see Appendix above, p. 188.
83 For aid with this translation I am indebted to Robert Sider. For a transcription of the original Latin text, see Appendix above, pp. 189–90.
84 Joseph Chmel, *Regista chronologico-diplomatica Friderici IV. Romanorum regis (Imperatoris III)* (Vienna, 1838; repr. Hildesheim, 1962), p. 562, no. 5668.
85 This is reported without a reference to its source by Pietzsch in "Sebastian Virdung," col. 1800.
86 Pietzsch, *Quellen,* p. 668.

3 The publication history of "Musica getutscht"

1 Ripin, "A Reevaluation," pp. 192–204.
2 Since the signatures of *Mus. get.* proceed directly from A to O without a separate gathering for preliminary matter, it may be assumed that printing of the treatise took place after delivery of the dedication and not before, as was sometimes the case.
3 Sig. π4v; see above, pp. 43–4.
4 On Furter, see n. 20, pp. 205–6 above.
5 Robert Eitner, *Quellen-Lexikon,* vol. IX, p. 104; Ripin, "A Reevaluation," p. 189.
6 RISM B₆; *Ecrits imprimés concernant la musique,* ed. François Lesure (2 vols., Munich and Duisburg, 1971), vol. II, p. 865; and Meyer, *Sebastian Virdung,* p. 18.
7 RISM B₈/₁: K. Ameln, M. Jenny, and W. Lipphardt, *Das deutsche Kirchenlied* (Kassel, 1975), vol. I, p. 2.
8 See Ronald B. McKerrow, *An Introduction to Bibliography* (Oxford, 1928), p. 169; and Daniel Heartz, "Typography and Format in Early Music Printing," *Notes,* 15 (1967), 702–3.
9 See Dragan Plamenac, "Excerpta Colombiniana: Items of Musical Interest in Fernando Colon's 'Registrum'," in *Miscellánea en*

homenaje a Monseñor Higinio Anglés (2 vols., Barcelona, 1958–61), vol. II, pp. 670–1.

10 See above, pp. 59–60.

11 Regarding Urs Graf, see n. 21, p. 206 above.

12 Ripin, "A Reevaluation," p. 190, n. 5.

13 "Some Remarks About Sixteenth-Century Music Illustration," unpubl. paper, delivered on 4 May 1979 at the Seventh International Conference of RIdIM, to which the author kindly gave me access. A summary by Barbara Renton was published in the *RIdIM/RCMI Newsletter*, 4/2 (June, 1979), pp. 2–3.

14 Dr. Hieronymus communicated to me his views on this subject in a private conversation at Basel in 1984. For more on this controversy, see Bullard, "Musical Instruments," pp. 388–97.

15 Regarding printings A1 and A2, see above, pp. 52–3.

16 For example, on sig. C2v the compositor of printing B added the missing tittle (diacritical mark of abbreviation) on the first *o* of the word *coponiert*, making it read as it should: *componiert*; on sig. D he unscrambled the letters of *hotlseligkeit* to the correct *holtsäligkait*; and on sig. M3v he filled in the contraction *gebraulich* to read *gebrauchlich*.

17 Most notably, *Psalter Spiel* instead of *Platerspiel* (sig. B4); *zu ainer zeit* instead of *zu aller zeit* (sig. A4v of printing B, sig. A3v of printing A); *genant* for *Gamaut* (sigs. F3v and Nv); *schwartzen* for *schwantz* (sig. H); *lauten* for *leitern* (*laitternen* in A2) (sig. I3); the number "3" for "2" (sig. L); and *aigne* for *aynige* (sig. O2v). In addition, the musical examples in mensural notation and in tablature – as well as the didactic diagrams – incorporated new errors in printing B.

18 For instance, *hymeln* instead of *zymeln* (sig. A4 of printing B, sig. A3 of printing A); *soluisiren* instead of *solmisiren* (sig. Ev); *clavis* for *clains* (sigs. Lv and O4); and *b fa b mi* for *b fa h mi* (sig. N2ɣ).

19 According to Fredson Bowers in his *Principles of Bibliographical Description* (Princeton, 1949), pp. 141–4, a compartment is a discrete enclosure into which one places a title or an illustration. A frame, on the other hand, consists of distinct separate pieces that could be used individually.

20 The two title pages can be seen juxtaposed in Ripin, "A Reevaluation," pp. 192–3.

21 I personally observed this style of embellishment in numerous printed books from that period displayed at the Exposition of Basel Book Illustration, 1500–45 (Ausstellung Basler Buchillustration 1500–1545), at the Basel Universitätsbibliothek, 31 March to 30 June 1984.

22 We do not know whether in this case these two functions were done by a single individual or by more than one person.

23 For the few clues regarding this unknown illustrator, see Georg Kaspar Nagler, *Die Monogrammisten* (5 vols., Munich, 1858–79), vol. II, p. 43 (no. 113).

24 Ripin shows these two cuts on p. 203 of "A Reevaluation."

25 See Ripin, "A Reevaluation," pp. 197, 201–2.

26 On the use of the double-line border specifically at Augsburg in that period see Arthur M. Hind, *An Introduction to a History of Woodcut* (2 vols., Boston and New York, 1935; repr. New York, 1963), vol. I, p. 287.

27 Ripin, "A Reevaluation," p. 202.

28 Alfred Götze, *Die hochdeutschen Drucker der Reformationszeit* (Strasbourg, 1905), pp. 8–9. Orthographic and linguistic idiosyncrasies characteristic of works acknowledged to have been printed by Schönsperger conform to those in *Musica getutscht*, printing B.

29 In addition to Ripin, "A Reevaluation," scholars taking this position include Stradner, *Spielpraxis*, vol. I, p. 22; and Meyer, *Sebastian Virdung*, p. 18. An alternative view, put forth without supporting evidence by Gerhard Schuhmacher (RISM $B_{8/1}$: *Kirchenlied*, p. 2), that Erhard Öglin printed *Mus. get.* B, has not generally been accepted.

30 See Ripin, "A Reevaluation," p. 204.

31 Stradner's estimate is 1513 (*Spielpraxis*, vol. I, p. 22). However, an informal survey that I have conducted of many title pages from this period shows that the title page of printing B has a kind of design (i.e., a non-architectural compartment executed with a unified iconographic theme – in this case, musical instruments) that came into general use later, around 1519–20.

32 *British Museum General Catalogue of Printed Books to 1955* (263 vols., London, 1964), vol. CCIL, col. 440.

33 Ripin, "A Reevaluation," p. 196.

34 The term "variant states" refers to the fact that individual copies of the same typesetting of an early printed work may have slight differences. These variations derive from corrections done to the sheets during the process of printing. Some of these involved important mistakes made by the author or by the typesetter that were caught as production progressed (proofreading was routinely done after printing began); other instances involved deterioration, displacement, or loss of a letter during printing of the sheets. For a discussion of this phenomenon see McKerrow, *An Introduction*, pp. 204–13. See above, pp. 20, 42; and n. 73, p. 233 below.

35 The watermarks confirm this: the one found on sheet N of the British Library's copy of A2 (Hirsch I. 594) is one of the marks found throughout their copy of A1 (M.K. 8. c. 9.), i.e., Ripin's mark *a* ("A Reevaluation," p. 196). Sheets I and K of A2 have a later watermark (Ripin's mark *d*). Sheets L, M, and O of A2 have Ripin's marks *a* and *c*, both belonging to A1 as well, indicating that the stockpile of paper used for A1 had not been used up at the time the run was completed by the printing of A2. Therefore, not much time may have elapsed between the two independent typesettings of the second half of the book.

36 Lucien Febvre and Henri-Jean Martin, *The Coming of the Book* [*L'apparition du livre* (Paris, 1958)], trans. David Gerard (London, 1976), pp. 34–5.

37 Transcribed in Ripin, "A Reevaluation," p. 204. *Virdvarg* would appear to be Columbus's incorrect solution of the tittle representing the letter *n* on the title page of printing B: "vir-/dūg". See the title page illustrated on p. 193 of Ripin, "A Reevaluation"; and the facs. of this entry in Huntington, ed., *Catalogue of the Library of Ferdinand Columbus*, No. 922.

38 Had Ferdinand Columbus not ceased his foreign travels for the purpose of collecting books in May of that very year, he would most probably have purchased a copy of this work as a companion to the earlier volume by Luscinius in his possession – *Musicae institutiones* (*ca.* 1515) – which Columbus had acquired in 1522. See Catherine Weeks Chapman, "Printed Collections of Polyphonic Music Owned by Ferdinand Columbus," *JAMS*, 21 (1968), pp. 34 and 42; and Plamenac, "Excerpta Colombiniana," p. 671.

39 The Biblioteca Colombina in Seville. Columbus listed this book in his catalogue as "Tablatures per manichordion lut et flutes in gallico." See Chapman, "Printed Collections," p. 84; and Howard Mayer Brown, *Instrumental Music Printed Before 1600: A Bibliography* (Cambridge, MA, 1965), pp. 27–8 (1529_2). A facs. edn. by John Henry van der Meer appears in Early Music Theory in the Low Countries, IX.

40 Facs. of the 1568 edn. by van der Meer, *ibid.* Not all scholars have acknowledged the 1554 exemplar, however, including Klaus Wolfgang Niemöller, who omitted it from his article "Sebastian Virdung" in *New Grove*, vol. XIX, p. 869. Brown cites both extant copies in *Instrumental Music*, pp. 162–3 (1554_9) and 237–8 (1568_8).

41 For example, Brown, *Instrumental Music*, pp. 28, 163, 237; Ripin, "A Reevaluation," pp. 207–8; and Stradner, *Spielpraxis*, vol. I, pp. 38–9.

42 The late Charles Warren Fox pointed this out to me in a personal conversation. He noted this view publicly in his review of the facs. edns. in *Notes*, 33 (1976), 79.

43 This popular little song was composed by Jacques Barbireau (*ca.* 1420–91), a native of Antwerp, the city where publication of *Dit* and *Livre* took place. See Charles Warren Fox, "Jacques Barbireau," *New Grove*, vol. II, pp. 140–1; and Richard Taruskin's preface to his edn. of "Een vrolic Wesen" (Ogni Sorte Editions, Miami, 1979), pp. 2–3.

44 See Taruskin, "Een vrolic wesen," p. 3.

45 For example, in 1525 Vorsterman brought out both *Den strijdt geschiet over tgheberchte voer de stadt van Pavye . . .* and *La bataille faicte par dela les mons devant la ville de Pavie . . .* (Eugène Polain, *Guillaume Vorsterman, imprimeur à Anvers* [Liège, 1892], pp. 21 and 31; and *Bibliotheca Belgica: Bibliographie générale des Pays-Bas*, ed. Marie-Thérèse Lenger [6 vols., Brussels, 1964–70], vol. V, pp. 281–2). In 1527 he printed *Die triumphlijke Incomst ende coronatie . . . Ferdinande* and *La triumphante entree et couronnement de Fernant . . .* (Polain, *Vorsterman*, p. 31, and *Bibliotheca Belgica*, vol. I, p. 263).

46 Vorsterman hired translators so that he could publish books in many languages. These included Danish as well as French and Netherlandic. See Maria Elizabeth Kronenberg, "De drukker van de deensche boeken te Antwerpen (1529–1531) is Wilhem Vorsterman," *Het Boek*, 8 (1919), 1–8.

47 Together they published *Fasciculus myrre*. See Anne Rouzet, *Dictionnaire des imprimeurs, libraires et éditeurs des XVe et XVIe siècles dans les limites géographiques de la Belgique actuelle*, Collection du Centre national de l'archéologie et de l'histoire du livre, III (Nieukoop, 1975), p. 71.

48 Ripin, "A Reevaluation," p. 205.

49 As was *Margarita philosophica* in 1503, for example (see Ferguson, "The *Margarita philosophica* of Gregorius Reich.").

50 For a discussion of this topic see Chapter 2, "Privileges and Regulations in Germany 1450–1698," in *Books and Their Makers During the Middle Ages*, by George Haven Putnam (2 vols., New York and London, 1897), vol. II, pp. 409–36.

51 See n. 34, pp. 196–7 above.

52 See n. 35, p. 197 above.

53 *Syntagma musicum*, vol. II, fol. 5v (preliminaries) and pp. 75–6.

54 "Zu wünschen wehre es wol, dass man was eigentlich für *Musica*liche *Instrumenta* und *Organa Ecclesiastica* vor und zu *Davidis, Salomonis* auch nach deren zeiten, und wie ein jedes nach seiner Art eigentlich gestalt, gestimmet und beschaffen gewesen, jetziger zeit

wissen und zum gebrauch haben könte. Es ist aber solches leider in keinen *Antiquiteten* hinderlassen, daher uns denn der Alten *Musica Instrumentalis* so wenig, ja gantz unnd gar unbekant blieben. Man findet in etzlichen *Bibliotecken* ein Buch *Anno Christi* 1511. zu Basel in 4to getruckt, darin etzliche der Alten, so wol auch etliche der jetzigen *Instrumenta* abgerissen: Aber es ist ein solches Werck so gar Alt nicht, und kan noch darzu der abgerissenen *Instrumenten* gebrauch und eigentschafft nicht sonderlich daraus vernommen werden" (*Syntagma musicum*, vol. II, fol. 5v).

Edwin Ripin quoted the last two sentences out of context, mistakenly concluding that Praetorius had condemned the book as utterly useless regarding its entire contents ("A Reevaluation," p. 214). In fact, Praetorius lists Virdung in his index as one of sixteen music historians (*historici*) whom he recognizes as sources of information in his work (see his table of authors in *Syntagma musicum*, vol. II, p. 205). For Praetorius quotes Virdung not only on the Jerome instruments but also on other instruments (see above, p. 60). He includes pictures copied from *Mus. get.* in his plates as well (Plates XXXII–XXXIV). While Virdung's treatise may have its shortcomings (especially from a modern point of view; see above, pp. 11ff.), Ripin erroneously attributed to Praetorius a harsh judgment about its overall usefulness – one that Praetorius never made.

55 *Syntagma musicum*, vol. II, p. 76: "Und dieweil ich. sonsten keinen Bericht oder Nachrichtung haben können, wie und welcher gestalt dieselbe uns jetziger zeit unbekante *Instrumenta* gebraucht worden; Habe ich der Notdurfft seyn erachtet, ihre Beschreibung aus demselben Buche von Wort zu Wort allhier mit einzubringen."

56 *Syntagma musicum*, vol. II, pp. 76–9; from *Mus. get.*, sigs. C3–D3v.

57 *Syntagma musicum*, vol. II, p. 78; from *Mus. get.*, sig. D3v. Praetorius adds the triangle to Virdung's list.

58 *Syntagma musicum*, vol. II, p. 60; from *Mus. get.*, sigs. E2–E3v.

59 Burney, *A General History of Music*, vol. II, pp. 203–4.

60 Hawkins, *A General History of the Science and Practice of Music*, vol. I, pp. 328–32.

61 For a discussion of scholarship on *Musica getutscht*, see Stradner, *Spielpraxis*, vol. I, pp. 5–7.

62 See above, pp. 196 and 202, nn. 32, 33, 34, 35, and 72. To date, the rev. edn. of *Mus. inst. deudsch* (1545) can only be found in a misleading diplomatic facs. There is also no facs. available of *Mus. get.* printing B.

4 The offspring of "Musica getutscht"

1 See above, pp. 32–3.

2 For the entire text of Luscinius's remarks concerning the inception of this work, see *Musurgia*, sigs. a2–a2v, translated as doc. no. 23, pp. 44–5 above.

3 *Ibid.*, sig. a2v.

4 *Ibid.*

5 *Ibid.*

6 *Ibid.* (This is a reference to the *Ars poetica* of Horace.)

7 Sig. a3. In his dedication to *Musurgia* (doc. no. 23 above), Luscinius describes Bartholomew Stoffler as a compatriot of his from Strassburg and "a man skilled in letters and in the subject of music." Comparing their relationship with that of Sebastian and Andreas in *Mus. get.*, Luscinius states that they too had "conversed most happily in stolen hours, [touching upon] many things concerning music – which [things] I shall never be ashamed to have written" (sig. a3). Stoffler contributed some verses to a publication by Luscinius dating from April 1517 (*Ex Luciano quaedam iam recent traducta* [Strassburg]). From 1528 to 1538 Stoffler served as canon at St. Thomas's church, where Luscinius had earlier been employed. (This biographical information comes from Martin Vogeleis, *Quellen und Bausteine zu einer Geschichte der Musik und des Theaters im Elsass 500–1800* [Strasbourg, 1911; repr. Geneva, 1979]), p. 190.)

8 The woodcuts Luscinius dropped are the following: the arms of the Bishop of Strassburg (sig. Av), the picture of the lute (sig. B2), the portrait of the lutenist (sig. I2v), the diagrams of keyboards without tablature symbols (sigs. E3v and E4v), the examples of mensural notation (sigs. G4–Hv), the drawing of the hands testing strings (sig. H4v), the simple diagram of the courses on a lute (sig. Kv), and the illustrations of a recorder with symbols drawn upon them (sigs. Nv and N2v).

9 Sigs. b2–b2v. Cultural chauvinism on the part of Italians of the time stemmed from a prevailing historical perspective, derived from Tacitus, which identified contemporary Germans as descendants of the barbarians who had overthrown classical civilization. Italians, on the other hand, had fallen heir to the revival of this golden age in the then modern times by virtue of their legitimate lineage from the Romans and, before that, the Trojans.

10 See above, p. 193, n. 10.

11 Characteristics of the two generations of humanists in Germany in the fifteenth and sixteenth centuries are discussed by Johannes Janssen in *History of the German People at the Close of the Middle Ages*,

trans. M. A. Mitchell and A. M. Christie (16 vols., London, 1907–28), vol. III, pp. 1–8 and ff.

12 In 1505. He learned this subject well enough to give lectures there; he had also taken organ lessons from Wolfgang Grefinger.

13 Klaus Wolfgang Niemöller, in his articles in *MGG* ("Othmar Luscinius," vol. VIII, col. 1327) and *New Grove* ("Othmar Luscinius," vol. XI, p. 340; and "Sebastian Virdung," vol. XIX, p. 868), states without documentation that they indeed had met at this time.

14 For information about the life of Luscinius, I am indebted to Klaus Wolfgang Niemöller, "Othmar Luscinius, Musiker und Humanist," *AfMw*, 15 (1958), 41–59; and Yvonne Rokseth, "Othmar Nachtgall, dit Luscinius," *L'Humanisme en Alsace* (Paris, 1939), pp. 192-204.

15 Rokseth, "Othmar Nachtgall," p. 200.

16 On Johann Schott, see Leona Rostenburg, "The Printers of Strassburg and Humanism," *Papers of the Bibliographic Society of America*, XXIV (1940), 76–7; and Joseph Benzing, *Die Buchdrucker des 16. und 17. Jahrhunderts im deutschen Sprachgebiet* (Wiesbaden, 1961), p. 412. In 1508 Schott collaborated with Michael Furter, printer of *Mus. get.* (see above, pp. 205–6, and nn. 20 and 29). He was one of the earliest printers in Strassburg to have a font of Greek type.

17 For a list of his publications, see Charles G. A. Schmidt, *Histoire littéraire de l'Alsace à la fin du XVe et au commencement du XVIe siècle* (2 vols., Paris, 1879; repr. Hildesheim, 1966), vol. II, pp. 412–18.

18 e.g., Curt Sachs in *The History of Musical Instruments* (New York, 1940), p. 299.

19 Examples of this phenomenon include Dante's *Divine Comedy* (first translated in 1392) and Boccaccio's *Decameron* (published in Latin at Cologne *ca.* 1470). Well-known German examples can be cited as well: among them were a medical work by Johann von Cube, *Hortus sanitatis* (with the alternate title in German of *Gart der Gesundheit*), published at Mainz in 1485, which appeared in a Latin reworking as *Ortus sanitatis* in the same city in 1491 (with numerous reprintings until 1536), and Sebastian Brant's famous *Narrenschiff* (Basel, 1494), which saw Latin edns. as *Stultifera navis* from 1497 into the ensuing decades. (Indeed it was the Latin version of Brant's work that formed the basis of the English translation [1509]).

For more on this topic, see W. Leonard Grant, "European Vernacular Works in Latin Translation," *Studies in the Renaissance*, 1 (1954), 120-56.

20 Roger Bauer *et al.*, "Les Problèmes de la traduction à l'époque de la renaissance et spécialement chez les humanistes rhénans," *Revue d'Allemagne*, 1 (1969), 93.

21 Virdung therefore only mentions and then rejects stringed instruments for which tablature would not apply, namely, unfretted bowed stringed instruments with but one to three strings (i.e., rebec and trumpet marine, sig. B3 – pp. 104–5 above).

22 "The following instrument is an ignoble one, on account of its great clashing of tones as they mutually obstruct one another" ("Sequens Instrumentum ignobile est, propter ingentum strepitum, sese praepedientium").

23 Given Virdung's translation of this phrase to mean trombones (see sig. A3, p. 98 and n. 24 below), Luscinius probably means this specific instrument here as well.

24 "Furthermore, certain drawn tubes [? trombones] are made . . . which, although they sound no more than a single tone at a time, nevertheless, they have mechanisms so that, if they were capable of producing many tones at once, each individual [fundamental] tone would suffice, rendering plainly up to four different tones. And, indeed, in this aspect of Music, [these instruments] abound in such a variety of tones that you do not know whether you will wonder more at the beneficence of nature or of art" ("Fiunt praeterea quaedam tubae ductiles . . . Quae quamvis monophona sint tantum, tamen habent systema; ut si polyphona essent, sufficerent plane ad quadrifarias voces reddendas singulae; adeoq[ue] in hac parte Musicae voces multiphariam exuberant, ut nescias, artis beneficia, an naturae mireris magis").

25 These purposes are stated in *Mus. inst. deudsch*, sigs. Av–A2; and *Mus. get.*, sig. Ev, p. 122 above. For passages in Agricola's work, see the translation by Hettrick.

26 These included *Ein kurtz deudsche Musica* (Wittenberg, 1528), which appeared in 1533 as *Musica choralis deudsch*; and *Musica-figuralis deudsch* (Wittenberg, 1532). See the facs. edns. of all three in one vol. (Hildesheim, 1969).

27 Because the pages of *Mus. inst. deudsch* are only half the size of *Mus. get.*, some of the borrowed drawings and diagrams were cut down in size (the bagpipe and brass instruments, for example; sigs. B2v and B8v). Others, however (e.g., harp and psaltery; sigs. G6 and G6v) were enlarged.

28 Apparently he did this in order to add tablature letters to the strings (*Mus. inst. deudsch*, sig. G6; *Mus. get.*, sig. B2v), as he did for the psaltery as well (sig. G6v).

29 See Peter Downey, "The Trumpet and its Role in Music of the Renaissance and Early Baroque," unpubl. Ph.D. diss., The Queen's University of Belfast (1983), p. 41.

30 See below, n. 36, pp. 225–7.

31 *N.B.*: Although four instruments are depicted, they came in three sizes. See above, p. 76.

32 This improvement is true of *Musurgia* as well (sig. d2).

33 E.g., Gerald Hayes, *The Viols and Other Bowed Instruments*, vol. II of *Musical Instruments and their Music 1500–1750* (London, 1930), p. 252.

34 See, for instance, the discussion of this phenomenon by Ian Woodfield in *The Early History of the Viol* (Cambridge, 1984, pp. 71, 77–8, 100–1.

35 Virdung had mentioned the xylophone in passing, citing it as an example of "tomfoolery." His name for it differed from that of Agricola: Virdung called it *hülzig gelechter* or "wooden laughter" (sig. D4, p. 119 above).

36 On this instrument, see n. 48, p. 230 below.

37 Agricola did not conflate the charts for three sizes of recorder as Virdung had done earlier. By keeping each instrumental range separate, Agricola could conflate *instruments* instead, e.g., discant recorder and discant crumhorn on one chart, etc.

38 An exception to this would appear to be the crumhorns, which Virdung shows in four different sizes (sig. B4). Perhaps crumhorns came in a larger number of sizes owing to this instrument's smaller range of pitches relative to the range of other wind instruments. But this may be an error of the illustrator; see n. 50, p. 231 below.

39 Agricola, like Virdung, presents tablatures only in imperfect mensuration.

40 The facs. edn. of *Livre* has several transposed pages within sig. E of the treatise: in the facs., sig. E incorrectly follows sig. E2v; sig. Ev precedes sig. E4; sig. E4 comes before sig. E3; and sig. E3v precedes sig. F.

41 One person would have to have been versed in musical matters (especially lute tablature), others in linguistic matters. The unevenness in both aspects of this work points to collaboration by several translators (having varying levels of understanding about the subjects at hand), all of whom the printer employed to work on *Dit.* Nevertheless, in this study these people will collectively be referred to in the singular for the sake of convenience.

42 The 1528 edn. of Attaingnant's volume of lute intabulations with this name survives only as an entry in the catalogue of the choir-school of St. Anne in Augsburg as "Frantzösische Musicbüehl Mense Julio 1528. Tres Familiare." See Daniel Heartz, *Pierre Attaingnant: Royal Printer of Music* (Berkeley and Los Angeles, 1969), p. 132; and Richard Schaal, *Das Inventar der Kantorei St. Anna in Augsburg,*

Catalogus musicus, III (Kassel, 1965), p. 63. The earliest extant edn. of this work, from 6 October 1529 (Heartz, *Attaingnant*, pp. 225–6), was published in transcription along with a diplomatic facs. of the tablature by Daniel Heartz, ed., *Preludes, Chansons, and Dances for Lute*, Publications de la Société d'autrefois, II (Neuilly-sur-Seine, 1964). Regarding earlier manuscript use of the French type of lute tablature – in an Italian source – see Walter Rubsamen, "The Earliest French Lute Tablature," *JAMS*, 21 (1968), 186–99.

43 In *Tabulatur auff die Laudten* (Nuremberg, 1533), Gerle spoke about the lute tablature used by Italians, which had numbers, and the tablature used by Netherlanders, which had letters (sig. A2). See facs. edn., ed. Hélène Charnasse and Robert Meylan, with French translations and notes by Robert Meylan (*Hans Gerle: Tablature pour les lutes. Nuremberg, Formschneider, 1533*), Publications de la Société française de musicologie, VI/1 (Paris, 1975), p. xviii.

44 See Taruskin, "Een vrolic wesen."

45 Charles Warren Fox, "An Early Duet for Recorder and Lute," *The Guitar Review*, 9 (1949), 24–5. The author supplies transcriptions of the two instrumental parts as they appear in *Livre*, putting them together in score for modern performance.

46 This is one of the few instances of corruption in *Dit* not found in *Livre*.

47 Transcriptions of the vocal, clavichord, and lute settings of "Een vrolijck wesen" from *Dit* and *Livre* can be found in the facs. edn. of both prints, ed. van der Meer, pp. xvi–xxi.

48 He omitted only one of them: the picture of hands testing gut strings (*Mus. get.*, sig. I4v). None of the diagrams pertaining to German lute tablature appear, owing to their irrelevance in this context.

49 All references to *Dit* given here are to the 1568 version found in facs. in Early Music Theory of the Low Countries, IX.

50 See p. 127 below and nn. 101–3, pp. 236–7.

51 "So wanneer dat ghi vint staende twee ofte drie letteren deen boven den anderen, dat beteekent dat die selve snaren te samen moeten ghegrepen ende ghespeelt sijn daer die lettren op staen."

52 "vanden ghelijcksten ende minsten datmen ghecrijgen mach, oft mogelijck is om vinden."

53 "een instrument daer men op leert, om in der kercken op die orghelen te spelen."

54 "elcken bant van twee snaerkens bi een."

55 "dat en wort oock niet ghesonghen oft gheaddeert. Maer die noten daer tusschen often by staet die wort ghedivideert."

56 "Maer die selve snaren die van dien anderen dermen oft substantien ghemaect worden clincken wel op ander instrumenten daerse men onderleyt met ijsere oft houte."

57 "ghelijck in ghelasen veynsteren staen . . ."

58 "alle simpele menschen die gheenen sanck oft discanten connen . . ."

59 "soudense die edel mate niet connen ghehouden op die andere snaren die hier na noch bescreven sullen worden."

60 "Want sonder dat en sout gheen proporcie van resonantien gheven, maer het soude staen clincken ende cresselen alle eenderhande thoon. Ende midts desen ghevlochten lakene so hetiet zijn volcomen resonancie van tertien tot tertien. Van quinten tot quinten. Van octaven tot octaven ende alsoo voorts na zijn behoorte."

61 "Clavicordium gheloof ick dat zijn die instrumenten die welcke Guido aretinus monocordium ghenoempt hetst. Iae vander eender siden weghen. Ende dat wordt afghedylt oft afghemeten, nae den diatonischen gheslechte alleen beschreven ende ghereguleert. Daer af vindt ick ghenoech beschreven in haerlieder boecken, dat sulck monocordium een langhe viercante laye is ghelijck eender kisten oft eenen coffere. In welcker layen deene side ghetrocken wordt die afghedeylt is met allen consonancen, door die proportien, die alle dinghen bringhen in zijn wesen ende statueren. Welcke divisien al gheteeckent worden met poinctkens. Op de binnensten grondt van desen monocordium staet noch ghefigureert eenen cirkel duer den welcken die thoonen luyden oft huere gheluyt gheven. Die divisen die op der achterster siden van den selven monocordium staen dat wort ghenoemt den steeck. Ende hier aen so ghaets vele weder dat monocordium goet is oft quaet. Want den steeck dats den thoon die sine proportien houden. Op die voorseide poinckens daer hier voor af geruert is salmen op elck seiten eenen sluetele. Door welcke ick dencken wille dat nu gheheeten wordt Clavicordium."

62 This particular blunder was noted above (p. 56) as a major factor in proving the anteriority of *Dit* over *Livre*.

63 "Want men steltse op harpen, op vedelen, op lieren, op scarmeyen, ende op meer andere dyer ghelijcke instrumenten."

64 *Musurgia* had two printings; *Musica instrumentalis deudsch* had four of the first edition and one of a revised edition; *Dit* had at least three printings; and *Livre* may have had more than the one printing from which the only extant copy survives.

1 In this sense, a treatise on music.

2 It is evident throughout the treatise that Virdung uses the term *gesang* as the German equivalent of the Latin *cantus*. Whereas in this case *gesang* denotes polyphonic compositions written in mensural notation, elsewhere in *Mus. get.* Virdung uses the word with different connotations. He applies it to the practice of singing (or playing) counterpoint, including diminution (sig. D4v, p. 120 above), and to mensural notation by itself (sig. E, p. 121 above). The English word "song," then, is an inadequate translation of an inadequate translation; therefore, the German *gesang* will be rendered here into English in subsequent passages by terms closer to the meanings implied by the individual contexts.

   On *cantus*, see Owen Jander's entry in *New Grove*, vol. III, p. 737; and Margaret Bent, "*Resfacta* and *Cantare Super Librum*," *JAMS*, 36 (1983), 371–91.

3 In *Mus. get.* (sigs. E2–H4, pp. 123–44 above), Virdung deals specifically with the clavichord. However, his references to the organ in this context show that for him the two instruments are closely related. See nn. 108 and 129 below.

4 Wilhelm Honstein. See n. 13, p. 193 above. (Regarding use here of the German form, "Strassburg," see n. 12, p. 193 above.)

5 Emperor Maximilian opened the Imperial Diet there in March of 1510. Honstein and his entourage remained in Augsburg until it ended in May of that year. See Wolf, *Reichspolitik*, pp. 45–6.

6 Later (sig. E), Virdung calls this work "A German *Musica*."

7 Honstein's chaplain has not been identified, owing to a lack of surviving records.

8 See above, p. 29.

9 The manuscript of this larger work has never come to light, and Virdung did not succeed in having it published (see above, pp. 11–12, 33).

10 See n. 19, p. 205 above.

11 v. 16 in the Vulgate (no. 89 in Jewish and Protestant Bibles).

12 The English translations of the psalm passages given here derive from the German wording of Virdung, not from any standard English translation of the Bible.

13 vv. 1–2 (Ps. 95 in Jewish and Protestant numbering).

14 Luke 10.38–41. Virdung's identification of this Mary with Mary Magdalen was traditional in his day. This Biblical passage, along with apocryphal legends connecting Mary Magdalen with asceticism, made her a symbol of the contemplative (versus the active) life

in the Renaissance. For more on this topic see Marina Warner, *Alone of All Her Sex: The Myth and the Cult of the Virgin Mary* (New York, 1976), pp. 228–9; and Colin Slim, "Mary Magdalene, Musician and Dancer," *EM*, 8 (1980), 460–73.

15 vv. 2–3.

16 vv. 1, 3–4.

17 Virdung here gives an anachronistic translation of the Latin *In ecclesia sanctorum.*

18 When English translation of the name of an instrument poses problems in interpretation, the original term will here be retained.

19 vv. 3–5.

20 *Trummeren* in the original print should read *trummeten*. Hereafter, only misprints causing substantive changes in the text will be noted.

21 See the illustration of *zymeln* on sig. C2 (p. 000 above).

22 *Hymeln = zymeln.*

23 vv. 5–6 (Ps. 98 in Jewish and Protestant Bibles).

24 Virdung uses this German phrase to translate the Latin *in tubis ductilibus.*

25 v. 4 (in Jewish numbering Ps. 92.4; in Protestant numbering Ps. 92.3).

26 Ps. 80.4 (to Jews and Protestants, Ps. 81.3).

27 Ps. 133.1–2 (by Jewish and Protestant numbering, Ps. 134.1–2).

28 v. 20. XXXIII in the original print should read XXXVIII.

29 i.e., Sebastian Virdung.

30 See above, p. 29.

31 See nn. 17 and 18, p. 205 above.

32 i.e., authors from classical antiquity.

33 For studies of individual instruments in *Mus. get.* as well as bibliographies pertaining to them, see the entries for each instrument in Stradner, *Spielpraxis*, vol. I, 60–428; and in *New Grove MI*. For information on professional music making with instruments that took place near the time and place of *Mus. get.*, see Keith Polk, "Instrumental Music in the Urban Centres of Renaissance Germany," *EMH*, 7 (1987), 159–86. For another perspective on some of the instruments included for consideration in *Mus. get.* (many of the winds and strings) see Johannes Tinctoris, *De inventione et usu musicae* (Naples, *ca.* 1487). The original Latin text appears in Karl Weinmann, *Johannes Tinctoris (1445–1511) und sein unbekannter Traktat "De inventione et usu musicae"* (Regensburg, 1917; repr. Tutzing, 1961), pp. 27–46. Sections of this treatise that deal with then contemporary instruments are trans. by Anthony Baines in "Fifteenth-Century Instruments in Johannes Tinctoris's *De inventione et usu musicae*," *GSJ*, 3 (1950), 19–26.

Many of the instruments that Virdung includes in his treatise also appear in a pictorial source from nearly the same time and region as *Mus. get.* – in the series of 137 woodcuts depicting a hypothetical grand triumphal entry of Emperor Maximilian I. The Emperor himself commissioned the work, engaging some of the greatest artists of the day, of whom Hans Burkmair (1473–1531) was the major contributor. The project was cut short with the death of Maximilian in 1519. The scenes of music making in this work are of high artistry. They show actual members of Maximilian's musical entourage (in various groupings) in the act of performing as they ride in the wagons that make up the lavish parade. Thus, instruments can be seen being played in a contemporary context. Most of the instruments (and several of the instrumentalists) are named in the descriptive text that served as the generative force behind this project. The woodcuts, along with an English trans. of the text, are provided in Stanley Appelbaum, trans. and ed., *The Triumph of Maximilian I* (New York, 1964). The original German texts for the musical sections are given by Rolf Dammann in "Die Musik im Triumphzug Kaiser Maximilians I," *AfMw*, 31 (1974), 245–89.

Pictorial concordances with instruments in *Mus. get.* that can be found in the Triumph – from the beginning of the train to the end – include fifes and drums (Appelbaum, ed., *Triumph*, Plates 3–4); lutes and viols (Plate 18); trombone, crumhorns, and shawms (Plate 20), positive and regal(?) (Plate 22); viol, harp, lute, quintern, wind-cap shawms (called here *rauschpfeiffen*), pipe and tabor (Plate 24); trombone, cornet (Plate 26); Jew's harp, schwegel (Plate 30); shawms, tenor shawms, wind-cap shawms (*rauschpfeiffen* [?]), trombones (Plates 77–9); kettledrums, military trumpets (Plates 115–17); pipe and tabor (Plate 135). In addition, bells (*passim*), and hunting horns (see n. 74 below) can also be seen in the procession. (Other instruments not in *Mus. get.* are found in Plates 1, 26, 129, and 133.)

Cf. Virdung's woodcuts with those in both edns. of Agricola's *Mus. Inst. deudsch*, trans. Hettrick (see nn. 34 and 35, pp. 196–7 above).

34 Virdung here clearly refers to tablature. He makes the important point that tablature has didactic potential beyond its practical value as a method of notation.

35 On Virdung's clavichord, see Ripin, "A Reevaluation," pp. 218–20.

36 From the illustrations given here, it is difficult to discern what Virdung meant as distinguishing the instrument he calls *clavicimbalum* from the one he calls *virginal*, for they appear in essence simply as mirror images of each other. (Woodcut makers in this era did not always bother to reverse pictures to make them conform to

technical reality; therefore the mirror image *per se* does not necessarily give us essential information.) Since the term *clavicimbalum* is historically associated with the wing-shaped instrument we call "harpsichord" today, the label *clavicimbalum* may have been wrongly applied in this print to the picture of another instrument. If so, the one pictured here could be some kind of *arpichordum*, an instrument that Virdung describes verbally in close proximity to this illustration but does not otherwise name (see n. 38 below). Perhaps this is the *harpfentive* that Virdung lists later (sig. I4v, p. 152 above). Presumably, the correct caption (had it appeared) would have taken care of this ambiguity. If this is the case, then the real *clavicimbalum* (wing-shaped?) remained for some reason unpictured – probably inadvertently. Later in the treatise (sig. E, p. 121 above), Virdung apparently refers to the *clavicimbalum* by its Germanized form, *clavizymell*.

We have evidence from at least two sources in the fifteenth and sixteenth centuries linking this term with an instrument having an alar form. In a manuscript dating from more than half a century earlier than *Mus. get.* (*ca.* 1440 [Paris, Ms. B.N. Lat. 7295]), Henri Arnaut de Zwolle pictures a *clavisimbalum* as a wing-shaped instrument having one of four possible mechanisms to enable the keys to strike or pluck the strings. According to Arnaut, then, in the mid fifteenth century, this term could be used in a generic sense as well as a specific one, implying several possible varieties of those keyed stringed instruments that had one string (or one choir of strings) for each key of the keyboard – at least as far as their means of sounding was concerned. (See the facs., transcr., and trans. of the musical parts of this ms. in *Les Traités d'Henri-Arnault de Zwolle et de divers anonymes*, ed. G. Le Cerf and E.-R. Labande [Paris, 1932; repr. Kassel, 1972, Documenta musicologica II/4, ed. François Lesure], Plate VI, and text pp. 3–10; and fig. 2 in Edwin Ripin and Howard Schott, *et al.*, "Harpsichord," *New Grove*, vol. VIII, p. 218.)

A second witness, Othmar Luscinius, in *Musurgia* (the treatise he wrote prior to 1518 to explicate in Latin the very woodcuts prepared for the original 1511 print of *Mus. get.*; see above, pp. 61–72), applied the term *clavicimbalum* to a bentside instrument, in this case to the upright harpsichord that Virdung had called *claviciterium* (*Musurgia*, sig. b4). (Confusingly, Luscinius applied the name *clavicitherium* to the picture of Virdung's *clavicimbalum* [*Musurgia*, sig. b3v].)

It may be significant as well in this regard that the artist of the Rughalm Codex (Erlangen, Ms. 1463), who drew and then hand-colored copies of many of the instruments as they appear in

Virdung's treatise, omitted the picture of the *clavicimbalum* (see Zirnbauer, *Musik in Nürnberg*, p. 16; and Lutze, *Die Bilderhandschriften*, pp. 69–70). The fact that this is the only one of Virdung's keyboard instruments to be overlooked in this course supports the impression that some ambiguity or confusion about either the name or the form of this instrument – or both of them – existed at the time.

Evidence supporting the other side of this question, however – namely, that Virdung's picture and label for the *clavicimbalum* might correctly and accurately reflect an actual instrument with that name and shape at the time – is provided by Agricola's cutter for *Mus. inst. deudsch*. Working in 1528 or 1529, he carefully copied the woodcuts of the virginal and the *clavicimbalum* so they would appear much the same as they had in *Mus. get.* (except for the angle from which these instruments are seen by the viewer, which in both cases in the reverse of Virdung's, and except for the keyboard on the virginal, which is the same as that on Virdung's *clavicimbalum*); and he retained Virdung's labels. As with Arnaut, however, in the minds of Virdung and his contemporaries, the term *clavicimbalum* may have had a flexibility of meaning – regarding the shape or the mechanism of the instrument, or both. (And the same may also be true of the name *claviciterium*.) In any case, as Virdung himself points out (sig. C4, p. 113 above), the functioning internal shape of an instrument is more important than any external outlines it might have. For more on this problematic use of nomenclature and the pictures to which the terms are applied, see Stradner, *Spielpraxis*, vol. I, pp. 118–21. See also n. 140 below.

37 See n. 36 above and n. 38 below.

38 This ambiguous passage vexes the modern organologist. Since both the *clavicimbalum* and the *claviciterium* are illustrated in close proximity to the pronoun "that" (*das*), Virdung (or the compositor) has not made clear which of these two – or what other instrument – he is describing. Most scholars have assumed that Virdung here meant the clavicytherium (e.g., Jacob Eisenberg, "Virdung's Keyboard Illustrations," *GSJ*, 15 [1962], 85; and Frank Hubbard, *Three Centuries of Harpsichord Making* [Cambridge, MA, 1965], p. 166); others argue that he alluded to the *clavicimbalum* (e.g., Curt Sachs in *The History of Musical Instruments* [New York, 1940], p. 339). Another opinion has is that *das* refers to an instrument that had been left out of the pictorial instrumentarium (Stradner, "Bemerkungen," pp. 80–1).

Virdung's description here does suggest some kind of keyed harp or "harp virginal," perhaps akin to or a predecessor of the *arpicordum* described by Praetorius a century later as a stop on a virginal or other plucked stringed keyboard instrument, which produced a harp-like effect because of little metal hooks under the strings (i.e., brays) (*Syntagma musicum*, vol. II, p. 67). See n. 26 above. For a discussion and description of an extant sixteenth-century keyboard instrument that at one time had brays provided for one of its choirs, see Wilson Barry, "The Lodewyk Theewes Claviorganum and its Position in the History of Keyboard Instruments," *JAMIS*, 16 (1990), 5–41 (esp. 8–15). Barry takes Virdung's description here to refer to the *clavicimbalum*, and he hypothesizes that the illustrator was meant to have shown the brays on its bridge as the main feature distinguishing it from the virginal. Thus, Virdung may here refer to a special stop provided on the *clavicimbalum*, not a separate instrument. But see n. 140 below. On this question see also Armand Nevin, "L'arpicordo," *Acta*, 42 (1970), 230–5; and Stradner, *Spielpraxis*, pp. 118–31.

39 By the term *bünde* Virdung evidently means frets made by tying gut around the neck of an instrument. He recognizes here (but does not describe) other methods of fretting. Later in the treatise (sig. Iv4, p. 152 above) he refers to wood or iron frets.

40 Two sizes of lute, besides the small one called *quintern*, are documented in iconographical sources. (See, for example, Appelbaum, ed., *Triumph*, Plates 18 and 24 [text, p. 5].) Like the term *Lauten* here, quite a number of Virdung's labels to his woodcuts appear with an *n* or *en* added to the stem of the word, making a form that – at the time – could signal a plural meaning as well as a singular one. That Virdung almost always depicts only one instrument to illustrate these terms (except in the case of recorders, chime bells, and kettle drums) argues for our interpreting these captions as singular in form. However, Keith Polk, in his article "Vedel and Geige – Fiddle and Viol," points out (p. 508) that the plural form here "implies the possibility of various sizes." Consideration of all of Virdung's captions in this light lends support to Polk's theory, for most of the instruments so labeled we know did come in several sizes at the time (although Virdung may not have maintained absolute consistency in this regard). Other instruments in *Mus. get.* besides lutes that Virdung labels with names which could be plural but pictures in only one size are the following: *Geigen* – both *Gross* and *clein* – i.e., viol and rebec (sigs. B2 and B3, pp. 103 and 105 above), harp (sig. B2v, p. 104), cornett (sig. B4, p. 107), and trombone (Sig. B4v, p. 108), as well as clapper bell and crotal-shaped sectioned bell (sig. C2, p. 110), drum (sig. D, p. 115), and several "foolish" instruments (sig. D3v, p. 119), viz., Jew's harp, bell, cowbell, and beating

stick on the pot. Recorders (sig. B3v, p. 106), crumhorns (sig. B4, p. 107), hammers (sig. C2, p. 110), chime bells (sig. C2, p. 110), and kettle drums (sig. D, p. 115) being pictured in multiple sizes, Virdung therefore gives their names in the plural.

Perhaps the plural names accorded some of the instruments imply several forms as well as sizes. An example of this phenomenon would be viols (*Gross Geigen*), for we know from other iconographical evidence (e.g., *The Triumph of Maximilian I* – see Polk, "Vedel and Geige – Fiddle and Viol," fig. 3, p. 512, or Appelbaum, ed., *Triumph*, Plate 24 [text, p. 5]), that some, if not most, German viols at the time had forms that differed from the one illustrated in *Mus. get.* This may also be true for cornetts (to include the curved and mute varieties otherwise not mentioned in *Mus. get.*) and for *clein Geigen* (to include various fiddles – see Appelbaum, ed., *Triumph*, Plates 24 and 26 [the latter in which Apollo and one of the muses are seen on the frieze of the wagon], and text, p. 5).

Owing to the greater inclusiveness of this approach, I have chosen here to translate Virdung's names for the instruments – whenever they end with an added *n* – as nouns in the plural. Since the other interpretation is also possible, however, I have placed the English plural ending within parentheses.

Luscinius omitted the picture of the lute in *Musurgia*, even though there is space for this important instrument on the appropriate page (sig. b4v). This woodcut, along with the cut of the lutenist by Urs Graf (from sig. I2v of *Mus. get.*), which Luscinius also left out of his treatise, probably had been sold or lost before *Musurgia* was put to press (see n. 29, p. 207 above).

41 See n. 40 above. Unlike the viol pictured here, which has nine strings and an ambiguous number of pegs, the copy of this illustration found in the Rughalm Codex shows a viol with seven pegs and approximately seven strings (unclear). See Zirnbauer, *Musik in Nürnberg*, p. 16. For another style of large viol with seven strings (six pegs visible), see Appelbaum, ed., *Triumph*, Plates 18 and 24 (text, pp. 4–5). A plucked variety of this instrument is seen in the hands of one of the muses on the wagon frieze in Plate 26. See also Howard Mayer Brown, "The Trecento Fiddle and its Bridges," *EM*, 17 (1989), pp. 308–29, in which a bowed string instrument with a lute bridge, like Virdung's, and with seven strings, like the copy of Virdung's instrument in the Rughalm Codex, is pictured in a fifteenth-century Italian source (Illustrations 1 and 1a., pp. 308–9). See also n. 34, p. 220 above. Cf. Agricola's treatment of viols in *Mus. inst. deudsch*, trans. Hettrick; and see above, pp. 75–6.

42 Luscinius, in *Musurgia*, labels this instrument *lutina* (sig. b4v).

Henceforth names of musical instruments in *Musurgia* will be noted here only if they differ substantially from those given by Virdung (excluding Latin cognates, such as *organum* for *orgel*, *positivum* for *positive*, etc.).

43 Luscinius labels this instrument *Cythara* (*Musurgia*, sig. cv).

44 See n. 2 above.

45 Luscinius omits the word *clein* (*Musurgia*, sig. c). On possible other meanings for the term *clein Geigen*, see n. 40 above.

46 On professional playing of wind instruments in German cities at the time, see Polk, "Instrumental Music."

47 See p. 114 above (sig. C4v) and n. 69, p. 232 below.

48 Note that the small fipple flute illustrated here by Virdung is an instrument very different from the one generally associated during the twentieth century with the word *Rauchspfeife*, which had a reed and a windcap (see above, n. 33). For more on this topic, see Barra R. Boydell's article "Rauschpfeife," *New Grove MI*, vol. III, pp. 197–8; and his book *The Crumhorn and Other Renaissance Windcap Instruments: A Contribution to Renaissance Organology* (Buren, 1982), pp. 353–70. Boydell contends that in the sixteenth century both terms (*russ pfeiff* [*sic*] and *rauschpfeife*) could stand for woodwind instruments in general, with a narrowing specificity to reed instruments in general, then, perhaps, to wind-cap reed instruments in particular.

Linguistic evidence can be brought to bear to bolster Boydell's argument: Both the verbs *rauschen* and *russen* at the time could mean "to make a noise" (= modern *lärmen*); thus, the terms *russpfeif* and *rauschpfeife* imply pipes used for music rather than for other purposes, such as conducting water, etc. But *rauschen* in Virdung's day also meant specifically "to make music" (= modern *musizieren*; see Alfred Götze, *Frühneuhochdeutsches Glossar* [Berlin, 1967], p. 174). If *russpfeif* and *rauschpfeife* had essentially the same meaning at the time, then Virdung may here be using a generic term that also applied to this specific instrument. If these terms had slightly different meanings, however, then *russpfeif* (a "noisy pipe" or "shrill pipe," as opposed to *rauschpfeife*, a "music-making pipe") may have connoted to him an especially high, shrill wind instrument, like the small four-holed fipple flute he illustrates. Cf. Agricola's depiction of the same instrument on sig. B3v or the 1529 edn. of his *Mus. inst. deudsch* (trans. Hettrick).

Agricola's *Klein Flötlein mit vier löchern* (illustrated on sig. B7v of the same edn. along with a fingering chart specifically for it) is clearly a separate instrument. On this point and for more on the *russpfeif*, see William E. Hettrick, "Identifying and Defining the

Ruszpfeif: Some Observations and Etymological Theories," *JAMIS*, 17 (1991), 53–68.

49 See n. 40 above.

50 The copy of this illustration found in the Rughalm Codex shows a consort of only three crumhorns in three sizes, like the recorders in Virdung's chapter on the recorder below (see Zirnbauer, *Musik in Nürnberg*, p. 16). Agricola has fingering charts for only three sizes of crumhorns in his *Mus. inst. deudsch* (sigs. B–B2 of the 1529 edn.; see Hettrick's trans.).

51 The bagpipe belongs to the first category of wind instruments, those with finger holes. It appears here with brass instruments only because it would not fit on the appropriate page.

52 On the trombone and trumpets in German lands, see Polk, "Instrumental Music," pp. 167–74.

53 See sig. C4v, p. 114 above.

54 *Incus* and *Mallei* to Luscinius (*Musurgia*, sig. d4).

55 Both types of bell are called *zÿmbl* in the Rughalm Codex (see Zirnbauer, *Musik in Nürnberg*, p. 16); to Luscinius they are *Cimbala* (*Musurgia*, sig. d4).

56 *Campana* to Luscinius (*Musurgia*, sig. d4v).

57 On the transference of the Pythagoras legend to the Biblical Tubal/ Jubal, see James McKinnon, "Jubal vel Pythagoras, quis sit inventor musicae?," *MQ*, 64 (1978), 1–28.

58 Anicius Manlius Severinus Boethius, *De institutione musica* (early sixth century) – found in Virdung's day in mss. and print (in *Opera* [Venice, 1491–92]); Latin text as *De musica* in J. P. Migne, *Pat. Lat.*, vol. LXIII, cols. 1167–300; trans. Calvin M. Bower as *Fundamentals of Music*, Music Theory Translation Series, ed. Claude Palisca (New Haven and London, 1989). Although Boethius discusses proportions in detail, he gives no specific information on organ pipes or percussion instruments *per sè*.

59 On these fictitious instruments, see Hammerstein, "Instrumenta Hieronymi"; and Page, "Biblical Instruments."

60 Johannes von Soest (Lat., Susato) (1448–1506), served as music director (*Sängermeister*) at the Heidelberg court from 1472 to 1495. Virdung had employment there as well from *ca.* 1483 (see above, pp. 25–6); thus the two men had a professional association that lasted some twelve years. Virdung's styling him *myn meister* may mean that he studied with Soest. For more on this erudite musician and physician, see Gerhard Pietzsch, "Johannes von Soest," *MGG*, vol. XII, cols. 824–5.

61 Virdung here may refer to Soest's lost treatise, "Musica subalterna." See Pietzsch, "Soest," col. 824.

62 Either Virdung or the compositor seems to have omitted a passage here.

63 Although Virdung's meaning is clear (each key on the virginal excites a separate string with its own length and pitch), this statement does not follow logically from the previous sentence. For each string to be raised in pitch, each string must be shorter than the next.

64 Virdung gives another *non sequitur*: the square psaltery depicted here has strings of equal length, like a clavichord.

65 From Exodus 15.20: "And Miriam the prophetess took a timbrel (*tympanum*) in her hand . . ."

66 That kettle drums were associated with trumpets is attested to in German archives of the period (see Polk, "Instrumental Music," p. 175) and in iconographic sources (see, for example, Appelbaum, ed., *Triumph*, Plates 115–17).

67 Virdung may mean here that players of trumpets and kettle drums provided music while members of the court were dining (most likely to announce each course and to provide a flourish for the entry of each delicacy) or before the meal (to announce the banquet and possibly to conduct the guests to the table). For a description of court ceremonies at Brussels in 1501 in which trumpets took part at the banquets, see W. F. Prizer, "Music and Ceremonial in the Low Countries: Philip the Fair and the Order of the Golden Fleece," *EMH*, 5 (1985), 122–5. (See esp. p. 124, where kettle drums ["nakers"] are described as being played at a banquet along with trumpets, shawms, and other drums – an ensemble that was compared by one contemporary listener to an earthquake.) The same events are recounted by Martin Picker in "The Hapsburg Courts in the Netherlands and Austria, 1477–1530," in *The Renaissance: From the 1490s to the End of the Sixteenth Century*, ed. Iain Fenlon (Englewood Cliffs, NJ, 1989), p. 223.

68 *Kumpelfesser* = *Rumpelfesser*.

69 See *Orchésographie* by Thoinot Arbeau (pseudonym for Jehan Tabourot) (Paris, 1588). The author describes and illustrates this drum, corroborating Virdung's evidence that in the first quarter of the sixteenth century a *tabourin à main*, in combination with a *longue flutte* (played with the left hand alone), was the most popular instrumentation for dancing in France. See the facs. edn., sigs. Fv–F3, F4 (fols. 21v–23, 24); and Sutton's edn. of Evans's trans., pp. 46–8, 51. For pictures of pipe and tabor in a German setting, see Appelbaum, ed., *Triumph*, Plates 24 and 136.

70 The term *hochzyt* had an older generic meaning of "festival," a wedding (modern *Hochzeit*) being but one type of "high time."

71 These typeset identifications appear in reverse order to the instruments pictured in the woodcut.

72 On the bell of Virdung's depiction of the *chorus* are found in mirror image the letters "A.B.M.C.L." Sixteenth-century brass instruments had such embossed garlands (see the simpler one on the military trumpet [sig. B4v, p. 108 above]) to reinforce and decorate the fragile bells. There the maker could inscribe some or all of the following elements: his name (or initials), his mark, the name of the town, the date of the instrument's construction. If "A.B." in this illustration was meant by the cutter to stand for an imaginary maker, then "M.C.L." must represent the date 1150, a time of origin that Virdung (or the real Andreas – see above, p. 29) could have rightly attributed to the manuscript depicting the Jerome instruments from which Andreas Silvanus derived his knowledge of them. Of the medieval manuscript sources for the Jerome instruments still extant today, however, only the latest of them (Cambridge, Peterhouse 198, from the fourteenth century) shows the *chorus* with a bell (see Hammerstein, "Instrumenta Hieronymi," Plate 4, p. 122).

73 This leaf was incorrectly signed D3 in some copies of printing A1 (Boston and Nuremberg) and in both extant copies of printing A2 (London[Hirsch] and Wolfenbüttel). See above, pp. 52–4; n. 34, p. 213.

74 Of the two types of horn illustrated here, the hunting horn seen in tapestries, woodcuts, and paintings of this period will be found on the right. See for example Appelbaum, ed., *Triumph*, Plates 7, 9, 11, 13, and 14.

75 According to Anthony Baines (in *Brass Instruments: Their History and Development* [London, 1976], pp. 138–9), it is possible that the term *acher* denoted an instrument made of clay, i.e., a pottery or ceramic horn.

76 The word *britschen* (sing., *britsche*) had a variety of meanings connected with striking. It applied to clappers as well as to sticks for drumming. Therefore, three interpretations are possible for *britschen* in this context: First, the term may refer to the clappers with attached pellet bell pictured on the lower right of the illustration (otherwise unnamed), in which case the instrument depicted on the far left must bear the unlikely designation *uff dem hafen*. Secondly, it may form part of an entire phrase describing the instrument on the left, in which case the pucntuation between *britschen* and *uff dem hafen* as a mark of division between separate entities must be discounted. Thirdly, it may apply to both instruments, the compositor having telescoped the two appellations for reasons of space. Several factors lend support to the second interpretation: (1) if the instrument on the left is called *britschen uff*

dem hafen, then (a) all identifying terms are consistently backwards with respect to the picture (excepting possibly the *schellen* and *küschellen*), a phenomenon noted earlier – see n. 71 above), and (b) the awakwardness of calling an instrument by a prepositional phrase rather than by a modified noun would thus be eliminated; (2) the compositor of the later second edition (printing B; see above, pp. 47–52) omitted the punctuation between *Britschen* and *auff* [*sic*] *dem Hafen.* Neither of these observations, however, disproves the third option, that the term *britschen* applied to both instruments. *Uff dem hafen* would then form a qualifier for only one of the two instruments included under this denomination. All things considered, this interpretation seems the most plausible: punctuation could thus be rationalized; all instruments depicted would be named and encompassed in the caption (albeit not in exact order); and both meanings of *britschen* would be represented.

77 See n. 76 above.

78 *Geplatet* ("stripped") most probably = *geplaset* ("blown").

79 See n. 2 above.

80 *Schlüssel* in this sense, a translation of the Latin *claves* (sing., *clavis*), carried neither modern meaning of the word "keys" as tonalities or as mechanisms on instruments. Rather, the term referred to the letter names of the notes of the scale (*a* through *g* applied to three and a half octaves, with a Greek *gamma* as the very lowest note and *e* as the highest). Virdung echoes here the understanding of Tinctoris as expressed in his *Terminorum musicae diffinitorium* (Treviso, 1495): *Clavis est signum loci linae vel spacii* ("A letter name is the indication of the degree on the staff of a line or space"; Engl. trans. by Carl Parrish as *Dictionary of Musical Terms* [London, 1964], pp. 14–15). See also Virdung's description of this invention by Guido, p. 128 above (Sig. Fv). Earlier theorists had considered *claves* to be the letter names conjoined with the syllables that placed the notes in the system of overlapping hexachords (e.g., *e la mi* and *e la*; see Virdung's diagram above, p. 129 – sig. F2v). On this point, see Margaret Bent, "Diatonic *Ficta*," *EMH*, 4 (1984), 7–10.

81 Virdung apparently claims in this passage that counterpoint and composition cannot be taught by means of tablature. The logic of his statement in this context seems to derive from the fact that he has limited the subject of the present treatise to tablature, whereas the other topics he mentions as important to an instrumentalist constitute matters he has reserved for discussion in the larger work.

82 It is difficult to discern whether Virdung here meant that music resulting from the practice of diminution (adding improvised figuration patterns to the given notes) could not be adequately

written out in notation or that description of the process in words would prove too lengthy for this little treatise. On diminution in this era, see Howard Mayer Brown, *Embellishing Sixteenth-Century Music*, Early Music Series, I (Oxford, 1976).

83 i.e., tablature.

84 The anonymous person (or persons) who adapted and translated *Mus. get.* into the Netherlandic language for publication at Antwerp in 1529 or earlier began the treatise, *Dit is een seer schoon Boecxken om te leeren maken alterhande tabulaturen wten Discante . . .*, at approximately this point. See above, pp. 78ff.

85 See nn. 36 and 38 above.

86 Sebastian never answers this question, suggesting that a passage has been omitted here.

87 For a discussion of distinctions between composition, counterpoint, and "singing on the book," as delineated in theoretical works by Tinctoris, see Bent, "*Resfacta.*"

88 A translation of the passage beginning here and ending on sig. E4v is included by Ruth Halle Rowen in *Music Through Sources and Documents* (Englewood Cliffs, NJ, 1979), pp. 98–101.

89 Guido mentioned use of the monochord (not the clavichord) in all of his extant writings: *Aliae regulae* (*GS*, II, 34–42; trans. Oliver Strunk in *Source Readings in Music History* [New York, 1950], pp. 117–20); *Epistola de ignoto cantu* (*GS*, II, 43–50; trans. Strunk, *Source Readings*, pp. 121–5; a passage he omitted can be found in *GS*, II, 46–50); *Micrologus* (*GS*, II, 2–24; trans. Warren Babb in *Hucbald, Guido, and John on Music*, ed. Claude Palisca, Music Theory in Translation, III [New Haven and London, 1978], pp. 57–83, with an introduction by Claude Palisca, pp. 49–56); and *Regulae rhythmicae* (*GS*, II, 25–34). He discussed the diatonic division of the string on the monochord in *Micrologus*, Chapter 3 (Babb, *Huchbald, Guido, and John*, pp. 60–1). Virdung's belief that Guido's monochord was an early form of clavichord is apparently based upon the etymological evidence that the term "monochord" often applied to the clavichord in the late fifteenth and early sixteenth centuries, and upon the important morphological similarity between the two instruments involving acoustic division of the string. See sig. E3 (p. 124 above).

90 Pseudo-Odo, *Enchiridion musices*, Chapter 3 (*GS*, II, 50; trans. Strunk in *Source Readings*, p. 105).

91 Some copies of *Mus. get.* have "thirty" (*dryssig*) here (Edinburgh, Munich, Nuremberg), including the facs. edn. by Eitner (PäptM, XI). This mistake shows an earlier, uncorrected state of the print. Guido actually named twenty-one pitches in his *Micrologus*. (See

Babb, *Hucbald, Guido, and John*, pp. 59–60.) Virdung's own diagram below (sig. E3v) shows twenty white keys and two black ones, making a total of twenty-two. (The added note is the highest *e* [*e la*].) Later in the treatise (sig. F2v, pp. 129–30 above) Virdung reserves the term "keys" for white keys, calling the black keys "semitones." With this line of reasoning his sum of twenty "keys" exactly matches his diagram. Another way of thinking (expressed on sig. E4, p. 125 above) has *B♮* and *B♭* counted as only one key (this time in the Guidonian sense), which also results in a total of twenty "keys."

92 See n. 58 above.

93 *De institutione musica, Pat. Lat.,* vol. LXIII, cols. 1188–91; trans. Bower, *Fundamentals,* pp. 39–41.

94 Virdung's description of the chromatic genus does not match that of Boethius. The ancient Greek chromatic genus consisted of four tones within the span of a tetrachord. The tones were derived by dividing the tetrachord into a minor third and two semitones (ex., in modern terminology, in descending order of the notes: E, C#, C♮, B). The wording of Boethius on this point in the chapter Virdung cites is somewhat ambiguous, however: "The chromatic [genus] . . . is sung through semitone, semitone, and three semitones" (trans. Bower, *Fundamentals,* p. 40). Boethius's calling the minor third "three semitones," gave rise, perhaps, to Virdung's misunderstanding.

95 *E la* itself had been added to the original Guidonian plan. See Babb, *Hucbald, Guido, and John,* pp. 59–60. The system of designating pitches in modern terminology adopted in the present study follows Helmholtz (see p. xiii).

96 Sebastian has never mentioned a third genus during this conversation.

97 See n. 3 above and nn. 108 and 129 below.

98 Virdung here refers to Arnolt Schlick's *Spiegel der Orgelmacher und Organisten* (Mainz, 1511), sig. B3v (facs. edn. and trans. by Elizabeth Barber, Bibliotheca Organologica, CXIII [Buren, 1980], p. 330). Schlick (*ca.* 1460 to *post* 1521) served as organist to the Heidelberg court from *ca.* 1482 to the end of his life. He and Virdung thus worked there as colleagues for some twenty or more years. On the precursors for and repercussions of Virdung's attack on Schlick in *Mus. get.,* see above, pp. 30–2, 40–4, and 126–7 above.

99 Virdung refers to this passage on sig. E3v, p. 125 above (*De institutione musica,* Book I, Chapter 21). See n. 93 above.

100 Virdung here alludes to Schlick's blindness. On the latter's response to this attack, see above, pp. 31–2.

101 Although Virdung uses the form *stehelin* for the white strings of a

keyboard instrument, this word at the time did not mean what we understand by "steel." According to Martha Goodway and Scott Odell (*The Metallurgy of Seventeenth- and Eighteenth-Century Music Wire*, The Historical Harpsichord, II [Stuyvesant, NY, 1987]), "steel" to Virdung's generation would have denoted a highly refined type of iron (see pp. 19–26 and 34–43). See also W. R. Thomas and J. J. K. Rhodes, "Harpsichords and the Art of Wire-Drawing," *Organ Yearbook*, 10 (1980), 126–39, esp. 130–1.

102 According to Goodway and Odell, *Metallurgy* (p. 29), yellow brass consisted of about 30 percent zinc, whereas red brass had only about 15 percent zinc. (See also pp. 27–34.)

103 Scott Odell suggests the words "rich" or "mellow" for brass and "bright" for iron (in a private conversation at the National Museum of American History at the Smithsonian Institution, Washington, DC, 1988). On the differing sound properties of brass and iron wire (including their harmonics) see Goodway and Odell, *Metallurgy*, pp. 85–103, 111.

104 That is, the sound produced if both sides of the string (which is simultaneously divided and struck by the tangent) were allowed to ring.

105 See n. 80 above.

106 In naming the notes in his text according to the Guidonian scale, Virdung begins by indicating the lowest ones by means of capital letters, as they appear in the illustration on sig. F2v. However, since he (or the typesetter) does not maintain consistency in this regard, lower-case letters will be used for all the names of notes in this translation.

107 Guido named this line *B* (see sig. F3, p. 130 above), but the traditional square shape of the letter representing B♮ ("hard B") led to the German practice of writing and referring to it as *H*. For the upper-case letter *H*, the type font used for *Mus. get.* has a letter in the shape of a large lower-case *h* (see facs. edn., ed. Eitner [1882, repr. 1966]). However, in the facs. edns. by Schrade (1931) and Niemöller (1970, repr. 1983), at some point in the history of the original print from which these facsimiles were made, the large *h* was filled in by hand at the bottom of the character to make a large lower-case *b*. Thus, the text here reads (incorrectly for this treatise): *b* and *b mi.*

108 Within this discussion of the clavichord, Virdung seems to use the term "organist" as a generic designation for a player of any keyboard instrument. A century later, Praetorius also uses the term in this way. See his *Syntagma musicum*, vol. II, p. 11 (trans. Blumenfeld, p. 11; and Crookes, p. 30). See n. 3 above and n. 129 below.

109 Here Virdung uses the term "claves" to denote actual keys of the keyboard.

110 Here the definition of the term *claves* is still narrower (see n. 91 above).

111 Guido's system, as set forth in his *Micrologus*, began on the *gamma* below the capitalized alphabet and did not extend beyond *dd*. See Babb, *Hucbald, Guido, and John*, p. 60.

112 According to the diagram of a keyboard on sig. Gv (p. 134 above), the octaves changed their symbols at the note F. In view of this discrepancy with Guidonian practice (in which the change came at the note A, as here), it appears that in this and his previous exposition of the alphabet as applied to music, Virdung was demonstrating the principles involved and relating present practice to the time-honored system attributed to Guido rather than discussing an actual tablature from *A* upwards used by Virdung and his contemporaries. The picture of the keyboard, on the other hand, would represent one practical application to tablature of these general principles – the one he himself used for his intabulation on sigs. Iv–I2 (pp. 147–8 above). Virdung cites yet another system, however, on sig. G3 (p. 136), with the change in signs for the octave occurring at the note G. For discussions of these discrepancies among Virdung's several didactic examples relating to German keyboard tablature, see Stradner, *Spielpraxis*, vol. I, pp. 83–91; Meyer, *Sebastian Virdung*, p. 101; and Jürgen Eppelsheim, "Buchstaben-Notation, Tablatur und Klaviatur," *AfMw*, 31 (1974), 57–72.

  The most usual point of change in German practice of the sixteenth century was the note H (B♮). In the written text for his *Musurgia* (but not in the accompanying diagram, since this is a reprint of Virdung's illustration on sig. Gv), Luscinius gives the H octave as the one used by his illustrious organ teacher, Paul Hofhaimer (sig. fv) (see above, pp. 70–1). Thus Luscinius underscores Virdung's main point here on this page, that intabulation for keyboard instruments could be accomplished in a variety of ways, each way being a specific manifestation of the basic principles.

113 The letters that Virdung and his contemporaries recognized included all but three of the modern alphabet of twenty-six letters, namely, *J*, *U*, and *W*. At that time, one did not differentiate between *I* and *J* or between *U* and *V*. *W*, though present in German, was considered as two *V*s.

114 Virdung may refer here to the survival in his day of an ancient instrumental notation using the letters *A* through *P* to represent two

diatonic octaves. More probably, his schooling in medieval theory may have led him to mention an archaic practice (see Boethius, *Fundamentals*, trans. Bowers, p. 199), which he then anachronistically adapted to contemporary conditions (i.e., the presence of twenty-three rather than fifteen keys or pitches). For discussions of such a notation in the middle ages, see Jos Smits van Waesberghe, "Les Origines de la notation alphabétique au moyen âge," *Annuario musicale*, 12 (1957), 3–16; and Christopher Page, "The Earliest English Keyboard," *EM*, 7 (1979), 309–14.

115 *Clavis = clains.*

116 In the explanatory diagram of the keyboard (sig. Gv, p. 134 below), this *f* is not underlined. See n. 112 above.

117 The cutter evidently failed to underline the second version of this symbol; but see nn. 112 and 116 above.

118 *Under = ander.*

119 On the cut of the keyboard below, this key (f#') is erroneously labeled as *f* with a line over it.

120 On the cut of a keyboard below, this key (b♭') is erroneously labeled as *h* with a line above it.

121 To Virdung, all notes outside the accepted Guidonian system (i.e., *gamma ut* up to *e la*) were considered "chromatic." See his discussion of the chromatic genus on sig. E4 (pp. 125–6 above).

122 See nn. 112, 119, and 120 above.

123 Virdung here links the shift from black to white notation with two then recent phenomena: (1) the shift from parchment to paper and (2) the concomitant rise in popularity of polyphonic music written in mensural notation. Further implications of this complex sentence seem to be that: (1) black notation required parchment (because the ink would not soak through this material), whereas white notation was suited to paper; and (2) had black notation still been used around the turn of the sixteenth century, the rising popularity of notated polyphonic music would have caused a shortage not only of parchment but of paper as well, since only one side of a sheet of paper could be used, owing to the fact that the ink soaked through it. Graeme M. Boone has argued that the origin of white notation can be traced instead to the gradual shift in scribal practice in the copying of texts – during the course of the fourteenth century and the beginning of the fifteenth – from formal book hands requiring a pen with a wide nib (used for black notation, as Virdung here makes clear) to cursive scripts accomplished with a narrow-nibbed pen (used for white notation). With white notation, then, scribes copying both text and music had no need to change pens ("The Origins of White Notation," unpubl.

paper given at the American Musicological Society convention in Philadelphia, Oct. 1984 [forthcoming]).

124 Juvenal, *Satires* IV, 223.

125 See n. 2 above.

126 On the definition of a continuous quantity, see Boethius, *Fundamentals*, trans. Bowers, p. 53.

127 *Selb = halb.*

128 That is, it adds length to the note to which it is appended, just as does a dot today. This feature distinguishes it from the *punctus divisionis*, which indicates groups of notes in perfect time ("perfections").

129 Tablature for clavichord was evidently called "organ tablature," as clavichord players were called "organists" (see nn. 3 and 108 above).

130 Transcriptions of this piece into modern notation can be found in Meyer, *Sebastian Virdung*, pp. 132–3; and in Stradner, *Spielpraxis*, vol. II, pp. 105–6.

131 *Processionale monasticum ad usum congregationis gallicae ordinis Sancti Benedicti* (Solesmes, 1893), p. 38.

132 *Ibid.*, pp. 245–6.

133 *Ibid.*, pp. 242–3.

134 A transcription of this keyboard intabulation in modern notation can be found in Stradner, *Spielpraxis*, vol. II, pp. 107–8.

135 With this sentence begins the second typesetting of the latter part of Virdung's text, printing A2. See above, pp. 52–3.

136 See above, p. 48.

137 A translation of Virdung's chapter on the lute is given by Uta Henning in "The Lute Made Easy: A Chapter From Virdung's *Musica getutscht* (1511)," *LSJ*, 15 (1973), pp. 20–36. Although some of the language has been misinterpreted (e.g., *gar schlect* [sig. M3] as the modern meaning of "so poor" [p. 32] rather than "so very simply," which this phrase meant to Virdung), the transcriptions of Virdung's diagrams (sigs. L4v and Mv) into modern typography are most helpful (Plates 6 and 7).

138 Virdung's mention of three types of lutes (those having five, six, or seven courses – with nine, eleven, and thirteen or even fourteen strings respectively), but four different types of tablatures for them, remains enigmatic. If by a fourteenth string Virdung meant a separate one added to extend the lower compass of a lute, then, since such a string would normally contribute only a few bass notes when needed on occasion, perhaps he could not on that account properly call this string an eighth "course"; nevertheless, its presence might necessitate a distinct type of tablature.

Several of Virdung's separate kinds of tablatures could, however, simply have involved an alternative system of symbols for the lowest course of a six-course lute. Hans Newsidler, for example, gave four such alternatives (see Newsidler's diagram reproduced in Marc Southard and Suzana Cooper, "A Translation of Hans Newsidler's Ein Newgoerdent Künstlich Lautenbuch . . . [1536]," *JLSA*, 11 (1978), p. 11; or the same diagram from 1544 reproduced in Zirnbauer, *Musik in Nürnberg*, p. 31). Similarly, Hans Gerle, in *Musica und Tabulatur auff die Instrument der kleinen und grossen Geygen, auch Lauten* (Nuremberg, 1546), taught three different sets of symbols for the sixth course (see the facs. edn. [Geneva, 1977], sig. L4). Thus, Virdung's four kinds of tablatures may have consisted of the following: one for a lute with five courses, two variants for a lute of six courses, and one for an instrument with seven courses. If, however, he chose not to treat tablature for the five-course lute separately – it could have been thought of as incorporated within the notational system for the six-course lute – then Virdung could have included three varieties for the six-course lute in his larger, unpublished treatise.

139 In view of the ambiguity that could result from translating the term *quintsaite* (or, as Virdung has it most often, *quintsait*) literally as "fifth string," when it means the "sixth course," the original German name will be retained here.

140 Virdung here mentions this unidentified instrument for the first time. If Stradner is correct (see n. 38 above), then the *harpfentive* could be the missing instrument to which Virdung referred in his puzzling description on sig. Bv (p. 103 above). Like that one, this instrument had gut strings; and the root "harp" implies that it too sounded like a harp. The suffix "-entive" suggests a keyboard instrument, as in "positive" and "portative."

141 See n. 101 above.

142 *Bezeichnen* ("to notate") = *beziehen* ('to string"). The correct verb appears in printing B (see above, pp. 49ff.).

143 Whereas this typeset numeral "two" – in the text of *Mus. get.* – resembles the modern *2*, the woodcut version of this character in the illustration below (sig. K3 – p. 000) looks more like a modern letter *z*.

144 Conrad Paumann, *ca.* 1410–73, gained fame as town organist of Nuremberg while a young man. He died in Munich after twenty-three years of service to three dukes of Bavaria. Virdung's hearsay knowledge of Paumann's invention of German lute tablature could have come from two reliable sources: First, Virdung's father lived in Nuremberg, at least while Virdung was a student at Heidelberg; thus, Virdung would well have absorbed local history on this subject.

Secondly, Paumann seems to have visited the Heidelberg court the very summer that Johannes von Soest (see n. 60 above) joined the musical establishment there; Soest could have learned about the system from Paumann himself and then communicated it to Virdung a decade later when Virdung sang under Soest at the Heidelberg court (see above, p. 29).

145 In other words, there arose a variety of solutions to the problem of adding a sixth course to a tablature that had originally been devised for five courses. See n. 138 above.

146 Boethius, *Fundamentals*, trans. Bowers, pp. 88–91. On placement of frets in the sixteenth century see J. Murray Barbour, *Tuning and Temperament: A Historical Survey* (East Lansing, MI, 1951), pp. 11–12, 185–8; Mark Lindley, *Lutes, Viols and Temperaments* (Cambridge, 1984); and Antonio Corona-Alcade, "'You will raise a little your 4th fret': An Equivocal Instruction by Luis Milan?", *GSJ*, 44 (1991), 2–45.

147 *Clavis = clains.*

148 See n. 147 above.

149 *Fünfften* in the original text is incorrect.

150 The text of the original print reads *x* incorrectly here.

151 Discussion of the seventh fret on the third course has been omitted in the text. The Innsbruck copy has this information handwirtten at the bottom of sig. L2 (in translation): "Finger and strike the third course on the seventh fret. That gives you *sol* [*sic*] of *d la sol ut*." (This should read "diatonic *d la sol re*" [d'].) The notational symbol *gg* is not given.

152 German type fonts of the time had two forms of the letter *r*. The *r* that could easily be mistaken for the number *2* appears on the title page (sig. A, p. 95 above) as the final letter of line 4, in the word *Or/geln*.

153 It was the lower-case *z* that could be confused with the number *3*. See the many zs on the title page (sig. A, p. 95 above), e.g., *kurtzlich* (line 6).

154 See n. 138 above.

155 Presumably, adding ornaments or making divisions.

156 See n. 42, pp. 197–8 above.

157 It is unclear whether Andreas means to begin another intabulation or another instrument.

158 A transcription of this intabulation in modern notation can be found in Stradner, *Spielpraxis*, vol. II, pp. 109–10; and Henning, "The Lute Made Easy," pp. 33–4. See above, pp. 14–15

159 For another translation of this final chapter of Virdung's treatise, see William E. Hettrick, "Sebastian Virdung's Method for Recorders

of 1511: A Translation With Commentary," *The American Recorder*, 20 (1979), 99–105 (and see n. 4, p. 113 of William E. Hettrick, "Martin Agricola's Poetic Discussion of the Recorder and Other Woodwind Instruments, Part I: 1529," *The American Recorder*, 21 [1980], 103–13).

160 Lit., "little ear finger" (*orfingerlin*).

161 Hereafter translated as "ring finger."

162 *Der* = *oder*.

163 Regarding coeval examples in manuscript of recorder tablatures for which note letters are used, see n. 2, pp. 191–2 above.

164 These notes actually sounded an octave higher than written. Furthermore, as was the case with the lute (and also the clavichord), all pitches given here by Virdung are relative. Within a given consort of recorders made specially to be played together, however, pitches would be compatible with each other, but not necessarily with other instruments.

165 See n. 80 above.

166 Virdung considered *fa* under *gamma ut* a chromatic note because it was not included in the accepted scale of Guido. See n. 121 above.

167 As noted above (n. 143), there is a confusing difference between two forms of the numeral "two." The woodcut version illustrated here resembles a modern *z*.

168 In the original print, the fourth hole is incorrectly listed as one that should be opened.

169 This symbol in the diagram of tablature below (sig. O3v, p. 180) is missing the intended sharp sign.

170 The symbols for the notes *b* and *bb* are reversed in the diagram of tablature (sig. O3v, p. 180 above).

171 See n. 170 above.

172 This symbol is placed incorrectly in the left column of the diagram of tablature below. To be consistent with the fingering chart, it should appear on the right.

173 This symbol is missing in the illustration of tablature below.

174 This symbol and the next are reversed in the illustration of tablature below.

175 i.e., *8 3 2 1*.

176 See n. 174 above.

177 For a transcription of this fingering chart into a modern one showing blackened circles for the holes to be closed, see Hettrick, "Sebastian Virdung's Method for Recorders," p. 104.

178 *Clavis* = *clains*.

179 From the illustration on sig. B3v (p. 106 above), it appears that a

chest of four recorders normally included one discant, two tenors, and one bass.
180 i.e., the usual disposition of four recorders (see n. 179 above) will suffice.

Bibliography

Agricola, Martin. *Musica instrumentalis deudsch.* Wittenberg: 1529. Facs. edn. (Published along with *Ein kurtz deudsche Musica* [Wittenberg: 1528] and *Musica figuralis deudsch,* [Wittenberg: 1532]), Hildesheim: 1969.

Musica instrumentalis deudsch. Trans. and ed. William E. Hettrick in *Musica instrumentalis deudsch: A Treatise on Musical Instruments (1529 and 1545) by Martin Agricola.* Cambridge: forthcoming.

Musica instrumentalis deudsch. Diplomatic facs. edn., ed. Robert Eitner. Publikation älterer praktischer und theoretischer Musikwerke, XX. Leipzig: 1896. Reprint, New York: 1966.

Musica instrumentalis deudsch. Revised and enlarged edn. Wittenberg: 1545. Diplomatic facs. edn., ed. Robert Eitner. Publikation älterer praktischer und theoretischer Musikwerke, XX. Leipzig: 1896. Reprint, New York: 1966.

Ameln, Konrad, Markus Jenny, and Walther Lipphardt, eds. *Das deutsche Kirchenlied.* Répertoire international des sources musicales, B₈. Kassel: 1975.

Anonymous. *Akhak Kwebŏm (Guide to the Study of Music),* ed. Sŏng Hyŏn. Seoul: 1493. Facs. edn. Seoul: 1968.

Anonymous. *Dit is een seer schoon Boecxken . . .* [= partial translation of Sebastian Virdung's *Musica getutscht*]. Antwerp: Jan van Ghelen, 1554. Facs. edn. of the 1568 edn., ed. John Henry van der Meer. Early Music Theory in the Low Countries, IX. Amsterdam: 1973.

Anonymous. *Livre plaisant et tres utile . . .* [= translation of *Dit is een seer schoon Boecxken*]. Antwerp: Willem Vorsterman, 1529. Facs. edn., ed. John Henry van der Meer. Early Music Theory in the Low Countries, IX. Amsterdam: 1973.

Apel, Willi. *The Notation of Polyphonic Music, 900–1600.* 5th edn. Cambridge, MA: 1953.

Appelbaum, Stanley, trans. and ed. *The Triumph of Maximilian I.* New York: 1964.

Arbeau, Thoinot (pseudonym for Jehan Tabourot). *Orchésographie.* Paris: 1588. Facs. edn. Hildesheim: 1980.

Orchgésographie. Trans. Mary Stewart Evans, ed. Julia Sutton. New York: 1967.

Orchésographie. Facs. of 1589 edn., ed. Laure Fonta. Paris: 1888. Reprint, Geneva: 1970.

Aristotle. *Physics.* Trans. and ed. Hippocrates G. Apostle (*Aristotle's Physics*). Bloomington and London: 1969.

Baier, Hermann. "Vorreformationsgeschichtliche Forschungen aus der Diözese Konstanz," *Freiburger Diözesan-Archiv*, 41 n.s. 14 (1913), 29–81.

Baines, Anthony. *Brass Instruments: Their History and Development.* London: 1976.

"Fifteenth-Century Instruments in Johannes Tinctoris's *De inventione et usu musicae*," *Galpin Society Journal*, 3 (1950), 19–26.

Barbour, J. Murray. *Tuning and Temperament: A Historical Survey.* East Lansing, MI: 1951.

Barry, Wilson. "The Lodewyk Theewes Claviorganum and its Position in the History of Keyboard Instruments," *Journal of the American Musical Instrument Society*, 16 (1990), 5–41.

Bauer, Roger, *et al.* "Les Problèmes de la traduction à l'époque de la renaissance et spécialement chez les humanistes rhénans," *Revue d'Allemagne*, 1 (1969), 92–105.

Bebel, Heinrich. Oration in Praise of Germany ("Heinrich Babel's Oration in Praise of Germany Given Before Maximilian I [1501]") in Gerald Strauss, comp., *Manifestations of Discontent on the Eve of the Reformation*, pp. 64–73. Bloomington and London: 1971.

Beier, Paul. "Right Hand Position in Renaissance Lute Technique," *Journal of the Lute Society of America*, 12 (1979), 5–24.

Benecke, Gerhard. *Society and Politics in Germany, 1500–1750.* Studies in Social History, ed. Harold Perkins. London and Toronto: 1974.

Bent, Margaret. "Diatonic *Ficta*," *Early Music History*, 4 (1984), 7–10.

"*Resfacta* and *Cantare Super Librum*," *Journal of the American Musicological Society*, 36 (1983), 371–91.

Benzing, Joseph. *Die Buchdrucker des 16. und 17. Jahrhunderts im deutschen Sprachgebiet.* Beiträge zum Buch- und Bibliothekwesen, XII. Wiesbaden: 1963.

Bergquist, Peter. "Conradus Protucius Celtis," *The New Grove Dictionary of Music and Musicians,* ed. Stanley Sadie, vol. IV, p. 54. London: 1980.

Bernstein, Lawrence F. "The Bibliography of Music in Conrad Gesner's Pandectae (1548)," *Acta Musicologica,* 45 (1973), 119–63.

Binnart, Martin, comp. *Biglotton sive dictionarium teuto-latinum novum.* Amsterdam: 1649.

Boethius, Anicius Manlius Severinus. *De institutione musica.* In Jacques Paul Migne, comp. *Patrologiae cursus completus . . . series latina.* vol. LXIII, cols. 1167–299. Paris: 1847. Reprint, Turnhout: 1980.

  De institutione musica. Trans. Calvin M. Bower as *Fundamentals of Music.* Music Theory Translation series, ed. Claude Palisca. New Haven and London: 1989.

Boone, Graeme. "The Origins of White Notation," unpubl. paper given at the American Musicological Society convention in Philadelphia, 1984, forthcoming.

Bourgeois, Louis. *Quand la cour de France vivait à Lyon, 1494–1551.* Paris: 1980.

Bower, Calvin M. "Boethius' *The Principles of Music:* An Introduction, Translation, and Commentary." Ph.D. dissertation, George Peabody College for Teachers: 1967.

Bower, Calvin M. trans. Boethius. *Fundamentals of Music* (= *De institutione musica*). Music Theory Translation Series, ed. Claude Palisca. New Haven and London: 1989.

Bowers, Fredson. *Principles of Bibliographical Description.* Princeton: 1949.

Boydell, Barra R. *The Crumhorn and Other Renaissance Windcap Instruments: A Contribution to Renaissance Organology.* Buren: 1982.

  "Rauschpfeife," *The New Grove Dictionary of Musical Instruments,* ed. Stanley Sadie, vol. III, pp. 197–8. London: 1980.

Brady, Thomas, A., Jr. *Turning Swiss: Cities and Empire, 1450–1550,* Cambridge Studies in Early Modern History, ed. J. H. Elliott, Olwen Hufton, and H. G. Koenigsberger. Cambridge: 1985.

British Museum General Catalogue of Printed Books to 1955. 263 vols. London: 1964.

Brooke, Kenneth. *An Introduction to Early New High German.* Oxford: 1955.

Brown, Howard Mayer, "Alta," *The New Grove Dictionary of Musical Instruments,* ed. Stanley Sadie, vol. I, pp. 49–50. London: 1984.

   Embellishing Sixteenth-Century Music, Early Music Series, I. Oxford: 1976.

   Instrumental Music Printed Before 1600: A Bibliography. Cambridge, MA: 1965.

   "The Trecento Fiddle and its Bridges," *Early music,* 18 (1989), 308–29.

Bullard, Beth. "Musical Instruments in the Early Sixteenth Century: A Translation and Historical Study of Sebastian Virdung's *Musica getutscht* (Basel, 1511)." Ph.D. dissertation, University of Pennsylvania, 1987.

Burney, Charles. *A General History of Music.* 4 vols. London: 1776. Reprint, London: 1789. Reprint (1789 edn.), ed. Frank Mercer. 2 vols. New York: 1935.

Caldwell, John. "Sources of Keyboard Music to 1600," *The New Grove Dictionary of Music and Musicians,* ed. Stanley Sadie, vol. XVII, pp. 717–33. London: 1980.

Carpenter, Nan Cooke. *Music in the Medieval and Renaissance Universities.* Norman, OK: 1958.

Chapman, Catherine Weeks. "Printed Collections of Polyphonic Music Owned by Ferdinand Columbus," *Journal of the American Musicological Society,* 21 (1968), 34–84.

Chaytor, Henry John. *From Script to Print: An Introduction to Medieval Vernacular Literature.* Cambridge: 1945. 2nd edn. London: 1966. Reprint, Folcroft, PA: 1974.

Chiesa, Ruggero. "Storia della Letteratura del Liuto e della Chitarra: Il Cinquecento," *Il Fronimo,* 2 (1974), 23–8.

Chmel, Joseph. *Regista chronologico-diplomatica Friderici IV. Romanorum regis (Imperatoris III).* Vienna: 1838. Reprint, Hildesheim: 1962.

Chrisman, Miriam Usher. *Lay Culture, Learned Culture: Books and Social Change in Strasbourg, 1480–1599.* New Haven and London: 1982.

Corona-Alcade, Antonio. "'You will raise a little your 4th fret': An

Equivocal Instruction by Luis Milan?," *Galpin Society Journal*, 44 (1991), 2–45.

Cotgrave, Randle, comp. *A Dictionarie of the French and English Tongues*. London: 1611. Facs. edn., with intro. by William S. Woods. Columbia, SC: 1950.

Dammann, Rolf. "Die Musik im Triumphzug Kaiser Maximilians I," *Archiv für Musikwissenschaft*, 31 (1974), 245–89.

Danner, Peter. "Before Petrucci: The Lute in the Fifteenth Century," *Journal of the Lute Society of America*, 5 (1972), 4–17.

Dart, Thurston, and John Morehen. "Tablature," *The New Grove Dictionary of Music and Musicians*, ed. Stanley Sadie, vol. XVIII, pp. 506-15.

Derwa, Marcelle. "Le Dialogue pédagogique avant Erasme," *De Gulden Passer*, 47 (1969), 52–60.

Doucet, Roger. "Le XVIᵉ siècle," in Arthur Kleinclausz *et al.*, *Histoire de Lyon*. Publication de la Société lyonnaise des études locales. 3 vols. Vol. I. Lyons: 1939. Reprint, Marseilles: 1978.

Downey, Peter. "The Trumpet and its Role in Music of the Renaissance and Early Baroque," Ph.D. dissertation, The Queen's University of Belfast, 1983.

Du Cange, Charles du Fresne. *Glossarium ad scriptores mediae et infimae latinitatis . . .* Paris: 1678.

Ehrman, Albert. "The Fifteenth Century," in Graham Pollard and Albert Ehrman, *The Distribution of Books by Catalogue from the Invention of Printing to A.D. 1800*, pp. 1–46. Cambridge: 1965.

Eisenberg, Jacob. "Virdung's Keyboard Illustrations," *Galpin Society Journal*, 15 (1962), 82–8.

Eisenstein, Elizabeth. *The Printing Press as an Agent of Change: Communications and Cultural Transformation in Early-Modern Europe*. 2 vols. Cambridge: 1979.

Eitner, Robert, "Das alte mehrstimmige Lied und seine Meister," *Monatshefte für Musikgeschichte*, 26 (1894), 17–18.

Biographisch-bibliographisches Quellen-Lexikon der Musiker und Musikgelehrten der christlichen Zeitrechnung bis zur Mitte des neunzehnten Jahrhunderts. 10 vols. Leipzig: 1900–04.

Elyot, Thomas. *Bibliotheca Eliotae*. Augmented by Thomas Cooper. London: 1548. Facs. edn., ed. Lillian Gottesman. Delmar, NY: 1975.

Eppelsheim, Jürgen. "Buchstaben-Notation, Tabulatur und Klaviatur," *Archiv für Musikwissenschaft*, 31 (1974), 57–72.

Exposition of Basel Book Illustration, 1500–1545 (Ausstellung Basler Buchillustration 1500–1545), Universitätsbibliothek Basel. 31 March to 30 June 1984. Prepared by Frank Hieronymus.

Fallows, David. "Fifteenth-Century Tablatures for Plucked Instruments: A Summary, a Revision and a Suggestion," *Lute Society Journal*, 19 (1977), 7–33.

Febvre, Lucien and Henri-Jean Martin. *The Coming of the Book.* Trans. David Gerard. London: 1976. (Originally *L'apparition du livre.* Paris: 1958).

Fenlon, Iain. "Music and Society" in *The Renaissance: From the 1470s to the End of the Sixteenth Century,* ed. Iain Fenlon, pp. 1–62. Englewood Cliffs, NJ: 1989.

Ferguson, John. "The *Margarita philosophica* of Gregorius Reisch," *The Library*, 4th series, 10 (1929), 194–216.

Fox, Charles Warren. "An Early Duet for Recorder and Lute," *The Guitar Review*, 9 (1949), 24–5.

"Jacques Barbireau," *The New Grove Dictionary of Music and Musicians*, ed. Stanley Sadie, vol. II, pp. 140–1. London: 1980.

"A Pleasant and Very Useful Book (1529)," *Bulletin of the American Musicological Society*, 2 (1937), 22–4.

Review of facs. edns. of *Livre plaisant* and *Dit is een seer schoon Boecxken* (ed. John Henry van der Meer), *Notes of the Music Library Association*, 33 (1976), 79.

Franck, Johannes. *Franck's etymologisch woordenboek der Nederlandsche taal.* 2nd edn., ed. N. van Wijk. The Hague: 1912.

Gaffurius, Franchinus. *Practica musicae.* Milan: 1496. Trans. Clement A. Miller. Musicological Studies and Documents, XX. American Institute of Musicology: 1968.

Practica musicae. Trans. Irwin Young (*The Practica Musicae of Franchinus Gafurius*). Madison, Milwaukee, and London: 1969.

Ganassi, Silvestro. *Opera Intitulata Fontegara.* Venice: 1535. German edn., ed. Hildemarie Peter. Berlin-Lichterfelde, 1956. English trans. by Dorothy Swainson (from the German edn.). Berlin-Lichterfelde: 1959.

Regola rubertina. 2 vols. (vol. II = *Lettione seconda*). Venice: 1542–43. Facs. edn. (*Regola rubertina, Teil 1 und 2: Lehrbuch des*

Speils auf der Viola da Gamba und der Laute, Venedig 1542 und 1543), ed. Hildemarie Peter. Berlin-Lichterfelde: 1972.

Regola rubertina. Trans. Richard D. Bodig, "Ganassi's Regola Rubertina," Pt. 1: *Journal of the Viola da Gamba Society of America*, 18 (1981), 13–66. Pt. 2: 19 (1982), 98–163.

Ganz, Paul. *Geschichte der Kunst in der Schweiz von den Anfangen bis zur Mitte des 17. Jahrhunderts.* Basel and Stuttgart: 1960.

Geering, Arnold, ed. *Ein tütsche Musica, 1491: Festgabe der literarischen Gesellschaft zur Feier ihrer 500. Sitzung.* Schriften der literarischen Gesellschaft Bern, IX. 2 vols. Bern: 1964.

"Ein tütsche Musica des figurirten Gsangs 1491" in *Festschrift Karl Gustav Fellerer zum sechzigsten Geburtstag*, ed. Heinrich Hüschen, pp. 178–81. Regensburg: 1962.

Geldner, Ferdinand, "Das Rechnungsbuch des Speyrer Druckherren, Verlegers und Grossbuchhandlers Peter Drach," *Archiv für Geschichte des Buchwesens*, 5 (1962), 132.

Gerbert, Martin, comp. *Scriptores ecclesiastici de musica sacra potissimum.* 3 vols. St. Blasien: 1784. Reprint, Hildesheim: 1963.

Gerle, Hans. *Musica teusch, auf die Instrument der grossen und kleinen Geygen, auch Lautten.* Nuremberg: 1532.

Musica und Tabulatur auff die Instrument der kleinen und grossen Geygen, auch Lauten. (Revised and enlarged edn. of *Musica teusch.*) Nuremberg: 1546. Facs. edn. Geneva: 1977.

Tabulatur auff die Laudten. Nuremberg: 1533. Facs. edn., ed. Hélène Charnasse and Robert Meylan. French trans. and notes by Robert Meylan (*Hans Gerle: Tablature pour les luths. Nuremberg, Formschneider, 1533*). Publications de la Société française de musicologie, V/1. Paris: 1975.

Glareanus, Heinrich. *Dodecachordon.* Trans. Clement A. Miller. Musicological Studies and Documents, VI. 2 vols. American Institute of Musicology: 1965.

Gloeckler, Ludwig Gabriel. *Geschichte des Bisthmus Strassburg.* 2 vols. Strasbourg: 1879–80.

Götze, Alfred. *Frühneuhochdeutsches Glossar.* Kleine Texte für Vorlesungen und Übungen, ed. Kurt Aland, CI. Bonn: 1912. Reprint, Berlin: 1967.

Die hochdeutschen Drucker der Reformationszeit. Strasbourg: 1905.

Goff, Frederick R. "The Dates in Certain German Incunabula,"

The Papers of the American Bibliographical Society, 24 (1940), 17–97.

Gombrich, Ernst Hans. *Art and Illusion: A Study in the Psychology of Pictorial Representation.* 2nd rev. edn. Bollingen Series, XXXV. The A. W. Mellon Lectures in the Fine Arts, V (1956). New York: 1961.

The Image and the Eye: Further Studies in the Psychology of Pictorial Representation. Ithaca, NY: 1982.

Goodman, Nelson. *Languages of Art: An Approach to a Theory of Symbols.* Indianapolis and New York: 1968.

Goodway, Martha and Scott Odell. *The Metallurgy of Seventeenth- and Eighteenth-Century Music Wire.* The Historical Harpsichord, II. Stuyvesant, NY: 1987.

Grant, Edward, ed. *A Source Book in Medieval Science.* Source Books in the History of the Sciences. Cambridge, MA: 1974.

Grant, W. Leonard. "European Vernacular Works in Latin Translation," *Studies in the Renaissance,* 1 (1954), 120–56.

Grimm, Jacob and Wilhelm. *Deutsches Wörterbuch,* 16 vols. in 32. Leipzig: 1854–1959.

Grotefend, Hermann. *Taschenbuch der Zeitrechnung des deutschen Mittelalters und der Neuzeit.* 10th edn., ed. T. Ulrich. Hannover: 1960.

Guido d'Arezzo. *Aliae regulae.* Trans. William Oliver Strunk in *Source Readings in Music History,* pp. 117–20. New York: 1950. Original Latin text in Martin Gerbert, comp. *Scriptores ecclesiastici de musica sacra potissimum.* 3 vols. Vol. II, pp. 34–42. St. Blasien: 1784. Reprint, Hildesheim: 1963.

Epistola de ignoto cantu. In Gerbert, *Scriptores,* vol. II, 43–50; and Strunk, *Source Readings,* pp. 121-5.

Micrologus. Trans Warren Babb in *Hucbald, Guido, and John on Music,* ed. Claude Palisca, pp. 57–83. Music Theory in Translation, ed. Claude Palisca, III. New Haven: 1978.

Regulae rhythmicae. In Gerbert, *Scriptores,* II, 25–34.

Haeringen, Coenraad Bernardus van. *Netherlandic Language Research: Men and Works in the Study of Dutch.* Leiden: 1954.

Hammerstein, Reinhold. *Diabolus in musica: Studien zur Ikonographie der Musik im Mittelalter.* Bern and Munich: 1974.

"Instrumenta Hieronymi," *Archiv für Musikwissenschaft,* 16 (1959), 117–34.

Hamoed, Dirk Jacob. "The Arpicordo Problem: Armand Neven's Solution Reconsidered," *Acta Musicologica*, 48 (1976), 181–4.

Hawkins, Sir John. *A General History of the Science and Practice of Music.* 2 vols. London: 1776. Reprint, London: 1853. Reprint, 1853. Reprint, 1853 edn., ed. Charles Cudworth. New York: 1963.

Hayes, Gerald. *The Viols and Other Bowed Instruments* (= vol. II of *Musical Instruments and Their Music: 1500–1750*). London: 1930.

Heartz, Daniel. *Pierre Attaingnant: Royal Printer of Music.* Berkeley and Los Angeles: 1969.

"Typography and Format in Early Music Printing," *Notes of the Music Library Association*, 2nd ser., 23 (1967), 702–6.

Heartz, Daniel, ed. *Preludes, Chansons, and Dances for Lute.* Publications de la Société de musique d'autrefois, II. Neuilly-sur-Seine: 1964.

Heath, Terrence. "Logical Grammar, Grammatical Logic, and Humanism in Three German Universities," *Studies in the Renaissance*, 18 (1971), 9–64.

Heckethorn, Charles William. *The Printers of Basle in the XV and XVI Centuries.* London: 1897.

Heimpel, Hermann. "Characteristics of the Late Middle Ages in Germany," in *Pre-Reformation Germany*, ed. Gerald Strauss, pp. 43–72. New York, Evanston, San Francisco, and London: 1972.

Henning, Rudolf. "German Lute Tablature and Conrad Paumann," trans. Uta Henning, *Lute Society Journal*, 15 (1973), 7–10.

Henning, Uta. "The Lute Made Easy: A Chapter from Virdung's *Musica getutscht* (1911)," *Lute Society Journal*, 15 (1973), 20–34.

Hermelink, Siegfried. "Heidelberg," *Die Musik in Geschichte und Gegenwart*, ed. Friedrich Blume, vol. VI, cols. 24-33. Kassel: 1957.

Hettrick, William E. "Identifying and Defining the *Ruszpfeif*: Some Observations and Etymological Theories," *Journal of the American Musical Instrument Society*, 17 (1991), 53–68.

"Martin Agricola's Poetic Discussion of the Recorder and Other Woodwind Instruments," *The American Recorder*, 21 (1980), 103–13.

"Sebastian Virdung's Method for Recorders of 1511: A

Translation with Commentary," *The American Recorder*, 20 (1979), 99–105.

Hettrick, William E., trans. and ed. *Musica instrumentalis deudsch: A Treatise on Musical Instruments (1529 and 1545) by Martin Agricola*. Cambridge: in press.

Heyd, Ludwig Freidrich. *Ulrich, Herzog zu Württemberg*. 3 vols. Tübingen: 1841–44.

Hickman, Ellen. *Musica instrumentalis: Studien zur Klassification des Musikinstrumentariums im Mittelalter*. Sammlung musikwissenschaftlicher Abhandlungen, LV. Baden-Baden: 1971.

Hieronymus, Frank. *Oberrheinische Buchillustration*. 2 vols. Vol. II (= Catalogue of the Exposition of Basel Book Illustration, 1500–1545 [Ausstellung der Basler Buchillustration, 1500–1545], Universitätsbibliothek Basel. 31 March to 30 June 1984). Publikationen der Universitätsbibliothek Basel, V. Basel: 1984.

Hind, Arthur M. *An Introduction to a History of Woodcut*. 2 vols. Boston and New York: 1935. Reprint, New York: 1963.

Hirsch, Rudolf. *Printing, Selling, and Reading. 1450–1550*. 2nd edn. Wiesbaden: 1974.

Hirzel, Rudolf. *Der Dialog: Ein literature-historischer Versuch*. 2 vols. in one. Leipzig: 1895.

Hubbard, Frank. *Three Centuries of Harpsichord Making*. Cambridge, MA: 1965.

Huglo, Michael. "L'Auteur du 'Dialogue sur la musique' attribué à Odon," *Revue de Musicologie*, 55 (1969), 119–71. Reprint, *The Garland Library of the History of Music*, ed. Ellen Rosand. 14 vols. Vol. I, pp. 95–147. New York and London: 1985.

"Odo," *The New Grove Dictionary of Music and Musicians*, ed. Stanley Sadie, vol. XIII, pp. 503–4. London: 1980.

Huntington, Archer M., ed. *Catalogue of the Library of Ferdinand Columbus*. New York: 1905.

Ivins, William. *Prints and Visual Communication*. Cambridge, MA: 1953.

Jahn, Fritz. "Die Nürnberger Trompeten- und Posaunenmacher im 16. Jahrhundert," *Archiv für Musikwissenschaft*, 7 (1925), 23–52.

Jander, Owen. "Cantus," *The New Grove Dictionary of Music and Musicians*, ed. Stanley Sadie, vol. III, p. 737. London: 1980.

Janssen, Johannes. *History of the German People at the Close of the Middle Ages.* Trans. M. A. Mitchell and A. M. Christie. 16 vols. London: 1907–1928. (Originally *Geschichte des deutschen Volkes seit dem Ausgang des Mittelalters.* 8 vols. Freiburg im Breisgau: 1876.)

Joachimsen, Paul. "Humanism and the Development of the German Mind," in *Pre-Reformation Germany,* ed. Gerald Strauss, pp. 162–224. New York, Evanston, San Francisco, and London: 1972.

Johnson, Alfred Forbes. *German Renaissance Title Borders.* Bibliographical Society of London, Facsimiles and Illustrations, I. Oxford: 1929.

Kartomi, Margaret J. *On Concepts and Classifications of Musical Instruments.* Chicago Studies in Ethnomusicology, ed., Philip V. Bohlman and Bruno Nettl. Chicago and London: 1990.

Korrick, Leslie. "Instrumental Music in the Early Sixteenth-Century Mass: New Evidence, *Early Music,* 18 (1990), 359–70.

Krautwurst, Franz. "Bemerkungen zu Sebastian Virdungs 'Musica getutscht' (1511)," in *Festschrift Bruno Stäblein zum 70. Geburtstag,* ed. Martin Ruhnke, pp. 143–56. Kassel: 1967.

Kronenberg, Maria Elizabeth. "De drukker van de deensche boeken te Antwerpen (1529–1531) is Wilhem Vorsterman," *Het Boek,* 8 (1919), 1–8.

Lambrecht, Joos. *Naembouck.* Ghent: 1562. Facs, edn. (*Het naembouck van 1562, tweede druck van het Nederlands-Frans woordenboek van Joos Lambrecht*), ed. R. Verdeyen. Bibliothèque de la Faculté de philosophie et lettres de l'Université de Liège, XCVIII. Liège: 1945.

A Latin Dictionary Founded on Andrews's Edition of Freund's Latin Dictionary, revised, enlarged, and ed. by Charlton Lewis and Charles Short. Oxford: 1966.

Le Cerf, G. and E.-R. Labande, eds. *Les Traités d'Henri-Arnault de Zwolle et de divers anonymes.* Paris: 1932. Reprint, Documenta musicologica, III/4, ed. François Lesure. Kassel: 1972.

Lenger, Marie-Thérèse, ed. *Bibliotheca Belgica: Bibliographie générale des Pays-Bas.* 6 vols. Brussels: 1964–70.

Lenneberg, Hans. "The Critic Criticized: Sebastian Virdung and his Controversy with Arnold Schlick," *Journal of the American Musicological Society,* 10 (1957), 1–6.

Lesure, François, ed. *Ecrits imprimés concernant la musique.* 2 vols.

Répertoire international des sources musicales, B/$_6$. Munich and Duisburg: 1971.

Lindley, Mark. *Lutes, Viols and Temperaments.* Cambridge: 1984.

Lloyd, Llewelyn S. "Pitch Notation," *The New Grove Dictionary of Music and Musicians,* ed. Stanley Sadie, vol. XIV, pp. 786–9. London: 1980.

Lockwood, Lewis. "Rudolph Agricola," *The New Grove Dictionary of Music and Musicians,* ed. Stanley Sadie, vol. I, p. 167. London: 1980.

Lockwood, William Burley. *Historical German Syntax.* Oxford History of the German Language, L. Oxford: 1968.

Lossen, Richard. "Pfälzische Patronatspfründen vor der Reformation aus dem geistlichen Lehenbuch des Kurfürsten Philipp von der Pfaltz," *Freiburger Diözesan-Archiv,* 38, n.s. 11 (1910), 176–258.

Lowinsky, Edward. "Ockeghem's Canon for Thirty-six Voices: An Essay in Musical Iconography," in *Essays in Musicology in Honor of Dragan Plamenac,* ed. Gustave Reese and Robert Snow, pp. 155–80. Pittsburgh: 1969. Reprint, Da Capo Press Music Reprint Series. New York: 1977.

Lüthi, Walther. *Urs Graf und die Kunst der alten Schweizer.* Monographien zur Schweizer Kunst, IV. Zurich: 1928.

Luscinius, Othmar. *Musurgia seu praxis musicae.* Strassburg: 1536. Reprint, Strassburg: 1542.

Lutze, Eberhard. *Die Bilderhandschriften der Universitätsbibliothek Erlangen.* Katalog der Handschriften der Universitätsbibliothek Erlangen, VI. Erlangen: 1936.

Maaler, Josua. *Die Teutsch spraach . . . Dictionarium Germanicolatinum novum.* Zurich: 1561. Facs. edn., ed. Gilbert de Smet. Documenta linguistica: Quellen zur Geschichte der deutschen Sprache des 15. bis 20. Jahrhunderts, ed. Ludwig Erich Schmitt. Ser. I: Wörterbücher des 15. und 16. Jahrhunderts, ed. Gilbert de Smet. Hildesheim: 1971.

McKerrow, Ronald B. *An Introduction to Bibliography.* Oxford: 1928.

McKinnon, James. "Jubal vel Pythagoras, quis sit inventor musicae?," *The Musical Quarterly,* 64 (1978), 1–28.

"The Meaning of the Patristic Polemic against Musical Instruments," *Current Musicology,* 1 (1965), 69–82.

"Musical Instruments in Medieval Psalm Commentaries and

Psalters," *Journal of the American Musicological Society,* 21 (1968), 4–20.

"Representations of the Mass in Medieval and Renaissance Art," *Journal of the American Musicological Society,* 31 (1978), 21–52.

Major, Emil and Erwin Gradmann; preface by Kenneth Clark. *Urs Graf.* London: 1942.

Marx, Hans Joachim. "Arnolt Schlick," *The New Grove Dictionary of Music and Musicians,* ed. Stanley Sadie, vol. XVI, pp. 661–3. London: 1980.

Mendel, Arthur. "Pitch in the Sixteenth and Early Seventeenth Centuries," in *Studies in the History of Musical Pitch,* ed. Arthur Mendel, pp. 88–169. Amsterdam: 1966.

"Pitch in Western Music Since 1500 – A Reexamination," *Acta Musicologica,* 50 (1978), 1–93. Published separately. Kassel: 1979.

Meyer, Christian. *Sebastian Virdung. Musica getutscht: Les Instruments et la pratique en Allemagne au début du XVIe siècle.* Paris: 1980.

Michaels, Ulrich, ed. *Johannes de Muris: Notitia artis musicae et Compendium musicae practicae.* Corpus scriptorum de musica, XVII. American Institute of Musicology: 1972.

Die Musiktraktate des Johannes de Muris. Beihefte zum Archiv für Musikwissenschaft, VIII. Wiesbaden: 1970.

Miller, Clement A. "Gaffurius's *Practica musicae:* Origin and Contents," *Musica Disciplina,* 22 (1968), 105–28.

Miller, Clement A., trans. Franchinus Gaffurius. *Practica musicae.* Milan: 1496. Musicological Studies and Documents, XX. American Institute of Musicology: 1968.

Moeller, Bernd. "Religious Life in Germany on the Eve of the Reformation," in *Pre-Reformation Germany,* ed. Gerald Strauss, pp. 13–43. New York, Evanston, San Francisco, and London: 1977.

Morley, Thomas. *A Plaine and Easie Introduction to Practicall Musicke.* London: 1597. Modern edn., ed. R. Alec Harman. New York: 1973.

Moser, Hans Joachim. *Paul Hofhaimer: Ein Lied- und Orgelmeister des deutschen Humanismus.* 2nd enlarged edn. Stuttgart: 1929. Reprint, Hildesheim: 1966.

Müller, Hans-Christian. "Georg Brack," *The New Grove Dictionary of Music and Musicians,* ed. Stanley Sadie, vol. III, pp. 149–50. London: 1980.

"Johannes Fuchswild." *New Grove*, vol. VII, p. 5.

"Jorg Schönfelder." *New Grove*, vol. XVI, p. 730.

"Johannes Siess." *New Grove*, vol. XVII, p. 304.

"Martin Wolff." *New Grove*, vol. XX, p. 506.

Münzel, Gustav. *Der Kartäuserprior Gregor Reisch und die Margarita philosophica*. Freiburg im Breisgau: 1937.

Munrow, David. *Instruments of the Middle Ages and Renaissance*. London: 1976.

Nagler, Georg Kaspar. *Die Monogrammisten*. 5 vols. Munich: 1858–79.

Nedden, Otto zur. "Zur Musikgeschichte von Konstanz um 1500," *Zeitschrift für Musikwissenschaft*, 12 (1930), 449–58.

Nef, Karl. "Sebastian Virdungs Musica getutscht," in *Kongress Bericht, Basel, 1924*, pp. 7–21. Leipzig: 1925.

Nevin, Armand, "L'arpicordo," *Acta Musicologica*, 42 (1970), 230–5.

Nickel, Ekkehart. *Der Holzblasinstrumentenbau in der freien Reichstadt Nürnberg*. Schriften zur Musik, VIII. Munich: 1971.

Niemöller, Klaus Wolfgang. "Othmar Luscinius," *Die Musik in Geschichte und Gegenwart*, ed. Friedrich Blume, vol. VIII, vols. 1327–8. Kassel: 1960.

"Othmar Luscinius," *The New Grove Dictionary of Music and Musicians*, ed. Stanley Sadie, vol. XI, p. 340. London: 1980.

"Othmar Luscinius, Musiker und Humanist," *Archiv für Musikwissenschaft*, 15 (1958), 41–59.

"Sebastian Virdung," *The New Grove Dictionary of Music and Musicians*, ed. Stanley Sadie, vol. XIX, pp. 868–9. London: 1980.

Niemöller, Klaus Wolfgang, ed. "Nachwort" to his facs. edn. of Virdung's *Musica getutscht*. Kassel and Basel: 1970.

Ockeghem, Johannes. *Collected Works*, ed. Dragan Plamenac. 2 vols. Vol. I. New York: 1959 (= 2nd rev. edn. of Publikationen älterer Musik, Jg. I, pt. 2 [Leipzig, 1927]). Vol. II. New York: 1947. Reprint, New York: 1966.

Odo. See Pseudo-Odo, below.

Ong, Walter. *Interfaces of the Word: Studies in the Evolution of Consciousness and Culture*. Ithaca and London: 1977.

Ramus, Method and the Decay of Dialogue: From the Art of Discourse to the Art of Reason. Cambridge, MA: 1958. Reprint, New York: 1974.

Page, Christopher. "Biblical Instruments in Medieval Manuscript Illustration," *Early Music*, 5 (1977), 299–309.

"The Earliest English Keyboard," *Early Music*, 7 (1979), 309–14.

"The Fifteenth-Century Lute: New and Neglected Sources," *Early Music*, 9 (1981), 11–21.

Perkins, Leeman. "Johannes Ockeghem," *The New Grove Dictionary of Music and Musicians*, ed. Stanley Sadie, vol. XIII, pp. 489–96.

Pfister, Arnold. "Michael Furt(t)er," *Neue deutsche Biographie*, vol. V, p. 737. Berlin: 1961.

Pflugk-Harttung, Julius von, ed. *Kunstgewerbe der Renaissance*. Vol. 1: *Rahmen deutscher Buchtitel im 16. Jahrhundert*. Stuttgart: 1909.

Picker, Martin. "The Hapsburg Courts in the Netherlands and Austria, 1477–1530," in *The Renaissance: From the 1470s to the End of the Sixteenth Century*, ed. Iain Fenlon, pp. 216–42. Englewood Cliffs, NJ: 1989.

Pietzsch, Gerhard. "Johannes von Soest," *Die Musik in Geschichte und Gegenwart*, ed. Friedrich Blume, vol. XII, cols. 824–5. Kassel: 1965.

Quellen und Forschungen zur Geschichte der Musik am kurpfälzischen Hof zu Heidelberg bis 1622. [Mainz], Akademie der Wissenschaften und der Literatur, Abhandlungen der geistes- und sozialwissenschaftlichen Klasse, Jahrgang 1963, no. 6, pp. 585–763. Wiesbaden: 1963.

"Sebastian Virdung," *Die Musik in Geschichte und Gegenwart*, ed. Friedrich Blume, vol. XIII, cols. 1800–02. Kassel: 1966.

Zur Pflege der Musik an den deutschen Universitäten bis zur Mitte des 16. Jahrhunderts. Hildesheim: 1971.

Plamenac, Dragan. "Excerpta Colombiniana: Items of Musical Interest in Fernando Colon's 'Registrum'," in *Miscellánea en homenaje a Monseñor Higinio Anglés*. 2 vols. Vol. II, pp. 663–87. Barcelona: 1958–61.

"Johannes Ockeghem," *Die Musik in Geschichte und Gegenwart*, ed. Friedrich Blume, vol. IX, cols. 1825–38. Kassel: 1961.

Polain, Eugène. *Guillaume Vorsterman, imprimeur à Anvers*. Liège: 1892.

Polk, Keith. "Instrumental Music in the Urban Centres of Renaissance Germany," *Early Music History*, 7 (1987), 159–86.

"Vedel und Geige – Fiddle and Viol: German String Traditions in the Fifteenth Century," *Journal of the American Musicological Society*, 42 (1989), 504–46.

"Voices and Instruments: Soloists and Ensembles in the Fifteenth Century," *Early Music*, 18 (1990), 179–98.

Pollard, Alfred William. "The Transference of Woodcuts in the Fifteenth and Sixteenth Centuries," in *Old Picture Books*, pp. 73–98. London: 1902. Reprint, New York: 1970.

Practorius, Michael. *Syntagma musicum*. 3 vols. Wolfenbüttel: 1615–19. Facs. edn., ed. Wilibald Gurlitt. Documenta musicologica, 1st ser., XIV. Kassel: 1958.

Syntagma musicum: De organographia [vol. II of *Syntagma musicum*]. Trans. Harold Blumenfeld. Kassel: 1962. Reprint, Da Capo Press Reprint Series. New York: 1980.

Syntagma musicum: De organographia. Trans. David Z. Crookes. Early Music Series, VII. Oxford: 1986.

Prizer, William F. "Music and Ceremonial in the Low Countries: Philip the Fair and the Order of the Golden Fleece," *Early Music History*, 5 (1985), 113–53.

Processionale monasticum ad usum congregationis gallicae ordinis Sancti Benedicti. Solesmes: 1893.

Provine, Robert. *Essays on Sino-Korean Musicology: Early Sources for Korean Ritual Music*, Traditional Korean Music, II, ed. Korean National Commission for UNESCO. Seoul: 1988.

Pseudo-Odo. *Enchiridion musices*. Trans. William Oliver Strunk in *Source Readings in Music History*, pp. 103–16. New York: 1950.

Putnam, George Haven. *Books and their Makers During the Middle Ages*. 2 vols. New York and London: 1897.

Rapp, Francis. *Réformes et Réformation à Strasbourg: Eglise et Société dans le diocèse de Strasbourg (1450–1525)*. Collection de l'Institut des hautes études alsaciennes, XXIII. Paris: 1974.

Renton, Barbara. Summary of Tilman Seebass's unpubl. paper, "Some Remarks about Sixteenth-Century Music Illustration," *RIdIM/RCMI Newsletter*, 2 (June, 1979), 2–3.

Riemer, Erich. "Musicus und Cantor: Zur Sozialgeschichte eines musikalischen Lehrstücks," *Archiv für Musikwissenschaft*, 35 (1978), 1–32.

Ripin, Edwin. "A Reevaluation of Virdung's *Musica getutscht*," *Journal of the American Musicological Society*, 29 (1976), 189–223.

Ripin, Edwin and Howard Schott *et al.* "Harpsichord," *The New*

Grove Dictionary of Music and Musicians, ed. Stanley Sadie, vol. VIII, pp. 216–46. London: 1980.

Ritter, François. *Histoire de l'imprimerie alsacienne aux XVe et XVIe siècles*. Publications de l'Institut des hautes études alsaciennes, XIV. Strasbourg: 1955.

Ritter, Gerhard. *Die Heidelberger Universität*. Vol. I: *Das Mittelalter (1386–1508)*. Heidelberg: 1936.

Rokseth, Yvonne. "Othmar Nachtgall, dit Luscinius," in *L'Humanisme en Alsace: Congrès de Strasbourg, 1938*, pp. 192–204. Paris: 1939.

Rostenburg, Leona. "The Printers of Strassburg and Humanism, from 1501 until the Advent of the Reformation," *Papers of the Bibliographic Society of America*, 34 (1940), 68–77.

Rouzet, Anne, ed. *Dictionnaire des imprimeurs, libraires et éditeurs des XVe et XVIe siècles dans les limites géographiques de la Belgique actuelle*. Collection du Centre national de l'archéologie et de l'histoire du livre, III. Nieuwkoop: 1975.

Rowen, Ruth Hall. *Music Through Sources and Documents*. Englewood Cliffs, NJ: 1979.

Rubsamen, Walter. "The Earliest French Lute Tablature," *Journal of the American Musicological Society*, 21 (1968), 286–99.

Rücker, Ingeborg. *Die deutsche Orgel am Oberrhein um 1500*. Freiburg im Breisgau: 1940.

Ruhnke, Martin. *Beiträge zu einer Geschichte der deutschen Hofmusik-kollegien im 16. Jahrhundert*. Berlin: 1963.

Sachs, Curt. *The History of Musical Instruments*. New York: 1940.

Salman, Phillips. "Instruction and Delight in Medieval and Renaissance Criticism," *Renaissance Quarterly*, 32 (1979), 303–32.

Samuel, Harold E. "Nuremberg," *The New Grove Dictionary of Music and Musicians*, ed. Stanley Sadie, vol. XIII, pp. 451–5. London: 1980.

Sarton, George. *The Appreciation of Ancient and Medieval Science During the Renaissance (1450–1600)*. Philadelphia: 1955.

Introduction to the History of Science. 3 vols. in 5. Carnegie Institute of Washington, CCCLXXVI. Baltimore: 1927–31. Reprint vols. I and II, Baltimore: 1950.

Sartori, Claudio. *Bibliographia delle opere musicali stampato da Ottaviano Petrucci*. Biblioteca di bibliographia italiana, XVIII. Florence: 1948.

"A Little Known Petrucci Publication: The Second Book of Lute Tablature by Francesco Bossinensis," *The Musical Quarterly*, 34 (1948), 238–9.

Schaal, Richard. *Das Inventar der Kantorei St. Anna in Augsburg.* Catalogus musicus, III. Kassel: 1965.

Schedel, Hartmann. *Weltchronik* ["The Nuremberg Chronicle"]. Nuremberg: 1493.

Schlick, Arnolt. *Spiegel der Orgelmacher und Organisten.* Mainz[?]: 1511. Facs. edn. and English translation by Elizabeth Barber. Bibliotheca Organologica, CXIII. Buren: 1980.

Spiegel der Orgelmacher und Organisten. Facs. edn. and modern German version by Paul Smets. Mainz: 1959.

Spiegel der Orgelmacher und Organisten. Modern German version by Ernst Flade. Mainz: 1931. 2nd edn. Kassel: 1951.

Spiegel der Orgelmacher und Organisten. Incomplete English translation based on Flade's modern German version (1951) by Franklin S. Miller. *Organ Institute Quarterly*, 7/4 (Winter 1959), 12–23; 8/1 (Spring 1960), 11–17; 8/3 (Autumn 1960), 27–31; 10/1 (Spring 1962), 15–18; 10/4 (Winter 1963), 14–19.

Tabulaturen etlicher Lobgesang und Lidlein uff die Orgeln und Lauten. Mainz, 1512. Facs. edn. Kassel: 1977. Transcription of preliminaries into modern typography by Robert Eitner. "Tabulaturen etlicher lobgesang und lidlein uff die orgeln und lauten von Arnolt Schlick dem Jüngern [*sic*]." *Monatshefte für Musikgeschichte*, 1 (1869), 115–25.

Schmidt, Charles G. A. *Histoire littéraire de l'Alsace à la fin du XVe et au commencement du XVIe siècle.* 2 vols. Paris: 1879. Reprint, Hildesheim: 1966.

Schrade, Leo. "Renaissance: The Historical Conception of an Epoch," in *International Musicological Society Congress Report, Fifth Congress, Utrecht 1952*, pp. 19-32. Amsterdam: 1953. Reprint, Leo Schrade. *De Scientia Musicae Studia atque Orationes*, pp. 311-25. Stuttgart: 1967.

Schrade, Leo, ed. "Nachwort" to his facs. edn. of Virdung's *Musica getutscht*. Kassel and Basel: 1931.

Schuler, Manfred. "Die konstanzer Domkantorei um 1500," *Archiv für Musikwissenschaft*, 21 (1964), 23–44.

"Der Personalstatus der konstanzer Domkantorei um 1500," *Archiv für Musikwissenschaft*, 21 (1964), 255–86.

Scribner, R. W. *For the Sake of Simple Folk.* Cambridge Studies in Oral and Literate Culture, II, ed. Peter Burke and Ruth Finnegan. Cambridge: 1981.

Seebass, Tilman. "Some Remarks about Sixteenth-Century Music Illustration," unpubl. paper delivered 4 May 1979 at the Seventh International Conference of RIdIM, New York City. Summary by Barbara Renton in *RIdIM/RCMI Newsletter,* 4/2 (June 1979), pp. 2–3.

Silbiger, Alexander. "The First Viol Tutor: Hans Gerle's *Musica Teutsch* [*sic*]," *Journal of the Viola de Gamba Society of America,* 6 (1969), 34–48.

Sitzmann, Edouard. *Dictionnaire de biographie des hommes célèbres de l'Alsace.* 2 vols. Paris: 1909–10. Reprint, Paris: 1973.

Slim, Colin. "Mary Magdalen, Musician and Dancer," *Early Music,* 8 (1980), 460–73.

Smits van Waseberghe, Jos. "Les Origines de la notation alpha-bétique au moyen âge," *Annuario Musical,* 12 (1957), 3–16.

Southard, Marc and Suzana Cooper. "A New Translation of Hans Newsidler's Ein Newgeordent Künstlich Lautenbuch . . . (1536)," *Journal of the Lute Society of America,* 11 (1978), 5–25.

Staehelin, Martin. "Bemerkungen zum geistigen Umkreis und zu den Quellen des Sebastian Virdung," in *Ars Musica, Musica Scientia: Festschrift Heinrich Hüschen zum fünfundsechzigsten Geburtstag,* ed. Detlef Altenburg, pp. 425–34. Cologne: 1980.

"Neue Quellen zur mehrstimmigen Musik des 15. und 16. Jahrhunderts in der Schweiz," in *Schweizer Beiträge zur Musikwissenschaft,* Publikationen der Schweizerischen Musikforschenden Gesellschaft, ser. III, vol. III, pp. 62–4 and Plates 4 and 5. Bern and Stuttgart: 1978.

Stälin, Christoph Friedrich. *Wirtembergische Geschichte.* 4 vols. Stuttgart: 1841–73.

Stehlin, Karl. *Regesten zur Geschichte des Buchdrucks bis zum Jahre 1520 . . .* 3 pts. in one: I. *Regesten . . . aus den Büchern des basler Gerichtsarchivs;* II. *Regesten . . . aus den Büchern des Staatsarchivs, der Zunftarchive und des Universitätsarchivs in Basel;* III. *Regesten . . . aus den Basler Archiven.* Leipzig: 1887–88.

Stein, Fritz. *Zur Geschichte der Musik in Heidelberg.* Heidelberg: 1912.

Stockmeyer, Immanuel and Balthasar Reber. *Beiträge zur basler Buchdruckergeschichte.* Basel: 1840.

Stradner, Gerhard. "Bemerkungen zu den besaiteten Tasten-instrumenten in Sebastian Virdungs 'Musica getutscht . . . ','" in *Der klangliche Aspect beim Restaurieren von Zaitenklavieren*, ed. Vera Schwarz, pp. 79–85. Beiträge zur Aufführungspraxis, II. Graz: 1973.

"Neue Erkenntnisse zu Sebastian Virdung's 'Musica getutscht' (Basel, 1511)," *Die Musikforschung*, 29 (1976), 169.

Spielpraxis und Instrumenterium um 1500 dargestellt an Sebastian Virdung's "Musica getutscht" (Basel 1511). Forschungen zur älteren Musikgeschichte, IV. 2 vols. Vienna: 1983.

Strauss, Gerald. *Nuremberg in the Sixteenth Century: City Politics and Life Between Middle Ages and Modern Times*. Rev. edn. Bloomington: 1976.

"Topographical-Historical Method in Sixteenth-Century German Scholarship," *Studies in the Renaissance*, 5 (1958), 86–101.

Strauss, Gerald, comp. *Manifestations of Discontent on the Eve of the Reformation*. Bloomington and London: 1971.

Strauss, Gerald, ed. *Pre-Reformation Germany*. New York, Evanston, San Francisco, and London: 1972.

Strobel, Adam Walter and Louis Schneegans. *Code historique et diplomatique de la ville de Strasbourg*. 2 vols. Strasbourg: 1843.

Strunk, William Oliver. *Source Readings in Music History*. New York: 1950.

Tabourot, Jehan. See Arbeau, above.

Taruskin, Richard. "Een vrolic wesen." Ogni Sorte Editions, RS 2. Miami: 1979.

Thomas, W. R. and J. J. K. Rhodes. "Harpsichords and the Art of Wire-Drawing," *Organ Yearbook*, 10 (1980), 126–39.

Tinctoris, Johannes. *De Inventione et usu musicae*. Naples: *ca.* 1487. Text in Karl Weinmann, *Johannes Tinctoris (1445–1511) und sein unbekannter Traktat "De inventione et usu musicae."* Regensburg and Rome: 1917. Reprint, Tutzing: 1961. Parts of text in Anthony Baines, "Fifteenth-Century Instruments in Johannes Tinctoris's *De inventione et usu musicae*," *Galpin Society Journal*, 3 (1950), 19–26.

Terminorum musicae diffinitorium. Treviso: 1495. Trans. Carl Parrish as *Dictionary of Musical Terms*. London: 1964.

Tischler, Hans. "The Earliest Lute Tablature?", *Journal of the American Musicological Society*, 27 (1974), 100–3.

Toepke, Gustav, ed. *Die Matrikel der Universität Heidelberg von 1386 bis 1662*. Heidelberg: 1884. Reprint, Nendeln: 1976.

Trout, Shirley. "On Playing the Lute: Documentary Material. Translation of the Section on Playing the Lute from Sebastian Virdung's *Musica getutscht* (Basel, 1511)," *Bach: The Quarterly Journal of the Riemenschneider Bach Institute*, Pt. I: vol. 6/3 (1975), 36–40, Pt. II: vol. 6/4 (1975), 30–5.

Tschudin, Peter. "Des basler Papierhandwerk. Grundung und Entwicklung bis 1530," *Stultifera Navis*, 13 (1956), 116–24.

Vincent, John Martin. "Switzerland at the Beginning of the Sixteenth Century," *Johns Hopkins Studies in Historical and Political Science*, ser. 22, no. 5 (1904), 7–61.

Virdung, Sebastian. *Musica getutscht*. Basel: 1511. Facs. edn., ed. Robert Eitner. Publication älterer praktischer und theoretischer Musikwerke, XI. Berlin: 1882. Reprint, New York, 1966.

Musica getutscht. Facs. edn., ed. Leo Schrade. Kassel and Basel: 1931.

Musica getutscht. Facs. edn., ed. Klaus Wolfgang Niemöller. Documenta musicologica, 1st ser., XXXI. Kassel: 1970. Reprint, Kassel, Basel, and London: 1983.

Vocabularius Teutonico-Latinus. Nuremberg: 1482. Facs. edn., ed. Klaus Grubmüller. Documenta Linguistica: Quellen zur Geschichte der deutschen Sprache des 15. bis 20. Jahrhunderts, 1st ser.: Wörterbücher des 15. und 16. Jahrhunderts, ed. Gilbert de Smet. Hildesheim: 1976.

Voët, Leon. *The Golden Compasses: A History and Evaluation of the Printing and Publishing Activities of the Officina Plantiniana at Antwerp*. 2 vols. Amsterdam: 1969.

Vogeleis, Martin. *Quellen und Bausteine zu einer Geschichte der Musik und des Theaters im Elsass, 500–1800*. Strasbourg: 1911. Reprint, Geneva: 1979.

Wackernagel, Rudolf. *Geschichte der Stadt Basel*. Basel: 1924.

Wallner, Barbara. "Sebastian Virdung von Amberg: Beiträge zur seiner Lebensgeschichte," *Kirchenmusikalisches Jahrbuch*, 24 (1911), 85–106.

Warner, Marina. *Alone of All Her Sex: The Myth and the Cult of the Virgin Mary*. New York: 1976.

Weinmann, Karl. *Johannes Tinctoris (1445–1511) und sein*

unbekannter Traktat "De inventione et usu musicae." Regensburg and Rome: 1917. Reprint, Tutzing: 1961.

Winternitz, Emmanuel. *Musical Instruments and Their Symbolism in Western Art: Studies in Musical Iconology.* 2nd edn. New Haven and London: 1979.

Wolf, Christian. "Conrad Paumann," *The New Grove Dictionary of Music and Musicians,* ed. Stanley Sadie, vol. XIV, pp. 308–9. London: 1980.

Wolf, Richard. *Die Reichspolitik Bischof Wilhelms III. von Strassburg, Grafen von Honstein. 1506–1541.* Historische Studien, LXXIV. Berlin: 1909. Reprint, Vaduz: 1965.

Woodfield, Ian. *The Early History of the Viol.* Cambridge: 1984.

Young, Irwin, trans. *The Practica Musica of Franchinus Gafurius.* Madison, Milwaukee, and London: 1969.

Zirnbauer, Heinz. *Musik in der alten Reichsstadt Nürnberg: Ikonographie zur nürnberger Musikgeschichte.* Beiträge zur Geschichte und Kultur der Stadt Nürnberg, IX. Nuremberg: 1966.

Zülch, Walther Karl. *Johannes von Soest, der Sänger und Arzt.* Frankfurt am Main: 1920.

Index

Index

Index

Index

musical instruments (*cont.*)
external shape of, 113
order of study, 121
qualifications for consideration in
Musica getutscht, 9, 104, 115, 118–20
foolish ones, 119
classification, *see* instrumental
categories
Musurgia seu praxis musicae, see
Luscinius, Othmar
mutation, 122

Nachtgall, Othmar, *see* Luscininus,
Othmar
nobility, 31, 32
notation
mensural, *see* mensural notation
instrumental, *see* tablature
note values, *see* mensural notation
numerals, *see* Hindu-Arabic numerals
Nuremberg, 25, 34, 46, 52, 54, 156

Ockeghem, Johannes, 26, 37, 38
Missa cuivis toni, 39
Missa prolationem, 39
motet of 36 voices, 38–9
octave strings (lute), 150–1
Odo (= pseudo Odo), 123
organ (*Orgel*) (*see also* positive, *also*
portative, *also* regal; *see also*
tablature), 31, 40, 41, 42, 85, 109,
110, 126, 127, 144,
organ of Jerome, *see* Jerome, Saint,
instruments of
organ pipes, 110
organ tablature, *see* tablature
organists, 31, 43, 126, 127, 129, 130,
131, 132
Hofhaimer, Paul, 63
Luscinius, Othmar, 65–6, 71
Schlick, Arnolt, 30, 31, 47, 71
Orgel, see organ
Orpheus, 119

Padua
University of, 65, 66
Palatinate, the, 25, 26, 27, 34
Pan (god), 119
Paris, 65, 80
paücklin, clein (small drum used with
schwegel), see drums, tabor

Paumann, Conrad
invention of lute tablature, 6, 156
peasant, 4, 9, 22, 73, 119
pedals, *see* clavichord
percussion, *see* instrumental categories;
see also drums
perfect time, 71, 144
performance practice, 3, 5, 12, 14, 15,
78
Philip, Count (Elector of the
Palatinate), 25, 26, 34
pipes, organ, 110
pitch, relationships among the three
sizes of recorder, 13, 170–2
Platerspil, see bladder pipe
portative (organ), 110
positive (organ), 109
pot, beater on the, *see* drums
pot drum, *see* drums, beater on the pot
Praetorius, Michael, 17, 23, 48, 59, 60
De organographia, 23
Prolation Mass, *see* Ockeghem, Missa
prolationem
proportions, 37, 70, 77, 86, 87, 110, 111,
122, 123, 144, 158
Psalms, *see* Bible
psaltery, 6, 8, 16, 69, 76, 98, 104, 113,
121
psaltery of Jerome, *see* Jerome, Saint
Pseudo Odo, *see* Odo

quintern, 71, 75, 76, 103

rebec (*clein Geigen*), 69, 76, 104, 105, 152
recorder (*Flöten*), 4, 69, 76, 80, 81, 106
sizes (three), 5
chest of four (three sizes), 180;
choosing a fourth, 5, 180–1
"coppel" of six (two each of the three
sizes), 180
choice of in polyphonic music, 5
fingering 168–80; rule for semitones,
173–4
tonguing, 12, 168
hand positions, 168–70
various tablatures, 170–1
pitch relationship among the three
sizes of recorder, 13, 171–2
tablature symbols, 172–9
fingering chart, 3, 13, 172–80
upper register, 177–9; thumb half-

Index